Book of Value

BOOK of VALUE

The FINE ART *of* INVESTING WISELY

ANURAG SHARMA

HARPER BUSINESS

An Imprint of HarperCollins *Publishers*

First published in 2016 by Columbia University Press, New York

This edition published in India in 2018 by Harper Business
An imprint of HarperCollins *Publishers*

HarperCollins Publishers India, Cyber City, Building 10-A, Gurugram,
Haryana-122002, India
www.harpercollins.co.in

2 4 6 8 10 9 7 5 3 1

P-ISBN: 978-93-5302-341-6
E-ISBN: 978-93-5302-342-3

Printed and bound at
MicroPrints India, New Delhi

MIX
Paper
FSC FSC® C218906

This product is made of FSC®-certified and other controlled material.

HarperCollins Publishers, Macken House, 39/40 Mayor Street
Upper, Dublin 1, D01 C9W8, Ireland

For Mary, Helen, and Monika.

In memory of my father, Mahendra Bhushan

Contents

PART FIVE
Policy

Preface to the Indian Edition

GROWING UP IN INDIA in the 1970s and 1980s, I had never heard of Warren Buffett, let alone Benjamin Graham. Instead, the names that stood out during my teenage years were Ambani, Birla, Mahindra, Singhania, Tata, and other business families that controlled sprawling collections of companies across sectors. Through these companies, they dominated the economic landscape of the country.

The business houses of India were built around strong family ties and culture that inspired financial discipline in every aspect of running a company. In hindsight, it is no surprise that these leading business enterprises had the reputation of being so very careful with costs and expenses; they had emerged in a land that had endured scarcity for centuries. To be careful with one's money was deeply ingrained not only in the society at large but especially in the families that had built business empires.

I recall these thoughts because value investing made sense to me the moment I began reading about it, so much so that I had to start teaching it and eventually write this book to formally ground key precepts in western philosophy. I found value investing appealing for the same reasons that I think it will appeal to many among the middle class India. It makes sense to be careful with your money. It makes sense to pay as little as possible to get as much as possible. It is alright to bargain. It is okay to ask probing questions about implicit worth: how much is it? This basic defensive orientation toward money is widely shared in many different cultures, but it is especially resonant among those people who have faced and understood scarcity. In countries like India, obsession with getting a good deal is both widespread and deep. Bargaining is the lubricant that facilitates commerce. Without people haggling about this or that, daily business just doesn't happen. For investors here, value investing is a natural fit.

I wrote this book for an audience in the United States, especially for my students in the business school. I had intended to formalize an approach to investing that persists in practice but is virtually absent from business school curriculum. So, my intention was to show students what I saw in value investing and why they needed to think about it. But this does not mean that this content is not useful for a broader audience. I expect that the spirit and the content of this book will resonate with readers in many other parts of the world. Especially in India, I suspect that most aspiring investors will easily relate to the common thrust of value investing, viz. to know how much something is worth *before* paying for it.

Those who already know Graham and Buffett will find the arguments familiar. They understand that, because investing is a psychologically complex endeavor, I devoted a major portion of the book to the mental aspects of seeking, investigating, and acquiring financial assets. In fact, the entire first half of the book systematically develops a mental orientation that breeds caution and inspires diligence when investing in capital markets. The second half of the book is more analytical. Even though I have used famous American companies as examples, the same principals and techniques can be profitably applied to Indian companies with minor modifications to account for the reporting differences.

India is much different than what it was when I left for my graduation in 1986. Its economy is about nine times larger(in USD terms) than it was just over thirty years ago, and a key stock market index (S&P BSE Sensex) is more than sixty-four times dearer in local currency. The strong demographic tailwind of a young population continues to propel the country forward, with the future looking ever brighter given the immense amount of technical and managerial talent resident there. So, clearly, India is a country on its path to an ever greater prosperity, which the current stock market valuations anticipate very soon (BSE Sensex > 35,000; PE > 23).

The capital gains of the past two decades inevitably beckon the tons of millions of talented and aspiring young people who make up the growing and increasingly sophisticated middle class population in India. Many of these potential value investors have the discretionary incomes and savings which they want to carefully invest in truly promising assets; they'd rather not engage in the free-wheeling speculation that has been powering the red hot real estate sector in big cities. Over time, the emergent financial services sector will endeavor to help the middle class securely invest their hard-earned savings; but the skills requisite for successfully deploying capital need to be more widely available. In a country with a large and growing middle class that now dares to aspire to build generational wealth, average investors must feel empowered to take control of their own financial future. In such endeavors, access to rigorous methods of investing is critical. Value investing is a necessary part of the mix of methods that investors can use.

Of course, India has its share of successful stock market investors, embedded in there is cultural knowledge about how local markets work and how best to invest in Indian securities. Those with special talents will succeed at investing by the dint of their salary and hard-work, and perhaps a good amount of luck as well. Many others lacking skills or experience will make common mistakes, however, just as investors in other parts of the world have made repeatedly through time, viz. pay too much for a security and then sell on fear of loss, only to lose part or whole of the invested capital. I dedicate this special India edition of the Book of Value to this latter category of people, especially those among them who want to invest wisely and are open to learning from the experiences of others in a far-away world.

Anurag Sharma

Amherst, MA
June 2018

Preface

BY THE TIME I started teaching value investing more than a dozen years ago, I had already been reading Warren Buffett's letters to shareholders, Graham and Dodd's *Security Analysis*, and Phil Fisher's *Common Stocks and Uncommon Profits.* To these and many other successful financial minds, investing was largely about understanding people and analyzing businesses. As a professor of strategy, I had long studied how businesses were led, how they were organized, how they functioned, and how they created wealth. I felt these writers were attributing their personal success as investors to carefully evaluating the same things that I understood were important for building good businesses.

It was also clear that the successful investors I had come to admire did not pay much heed to theoretical finance, which was (and is) widely taught in business schools. In fact, they mostly ignored finance theory. Buffett once boldly declared something to the effect that academic finance was wrong-headed.[1] Many in academia retorted that Buffett and those like him were statistical anomalies, three-sigma events in a game of chance.[2] There was, in fact, great skepticism in academic finance that analysis of business fundamentals was even useful when investing. There is just too much randomness in the markets, academics argued, for investors to improve their investment performance by doing business analysis.

To me, these conflicting views raised an obvious question: Why is there such a large disconnect between academic finance and finance as practiced by so many successful investors?

I decided that I had to understand both sides. I was already immersed in the academic literature but began reading more of it broadly across disciplines and with a purpose. I needed to understand why and how the star performers did what they did. I wondered whether the stellar investment performance of successful investors was a long streak of good luck, or whether their success was grounded in some teachable set of skills. I wanted to understand how they made their choices and to see what the world of investing looked like through their eyes.

To accomplish such understanding, I took the obvious route that any dyed-in-the-wool academic would take: I hit the stacks in the library and began combing through the vast body of writings about the inner life of our species. Perhaps if I understood how people think and reason, and what psychological and emotional obstacles we have to overcome to live rationally in a rather perplexing world around us, I would be able to understand the mental machinery of the people I wanted to decode. I had my work cut out for me.

From my days as a graduate student and from years of reading across the disciplines, I was well aware that the individual (*homo economicus*) is at the center of economic and finance theories. I was also aware that academic finance almost willfully avoids treating investors as real people. Instead, finance researchers have long made (and continue to make) strong but naïve assumptions about economic actors in order to support conceptual arguments and ease mathematical modeling of investment behavior—and force, in effect, the methods of natural science on what is essentially a deeply human experience. There was (and continues to be) great consternation about these assumptions among researchers in disciplines such as psychology, sociology, anthropology, organizational behavior, and strategy. Within the economics profession as well, there is a long history of dissent against simplifying assumptions.[3] To so many thinkers past and present, in fact, human beings are deeply complex; to them, theories that ignore our psychological and social complexities are unhelpful at best and misleading at their worst. Yet, the caricature of individuals as atomized and homogenized, asocial and calculating utility maximizers persists in theories developed in finance journals and lessons delivered in classrooms. This disconnect between real people and those imagined in theories of finance is both surprising and puzzling.

I began to realize that finance as a discipline offered virtually no penetrating insights into the inner lives of investors as real people. Modern investment theory mostly ignores the fact that investors are severely constrained in their ability to comprehend the complexities inherent in the world in which they operate, that businesses are complex human systems, and that the financial markets are fundamentally human constructions that defy purely mathematical explanations. Yet, the orientation to make simplifying assumptions persists, perhaps because they enable the use of mathematical procedures that have been so successful in the natural sciences.[4]

It turns out that the dominant analytical frameworks for teaching investments in business schools are rooted in work started in the early 1950s, by then graduate student Harry Markowitz. Spurred by those at first obscure beginnings, academic finance has taken a strong turn toward the statistical analysis of prices, and, increasingly, toward the advanced mathematical techniques common in the hard sciences, such as physics and astronomy.

Such a sharp turn toward the complex mathematics of prices and returns has had three significant consequences. First, as I will discuss in this book, mathematicians have shaped investing in the image of their own long-standing fascination with the problem of *gamble*. Increasingly, investing is no longer conceived as being about carefully deploying capital in sound, well-run businesses; it's mostly about finding the best gamble with the quickest payoff.[5] The key analytical device for finding the best gamble is the seemingly objective but deeply flawed measure of risk as the standard deviation of returns (also expanded to other statistics such as skewness and kurtosis). Largely because of operationalizing risk as a statistic, the portfolio logic of diversification has been taken to the extreme to justify owning a very large number of poorly understood securities. Over time, as this view has taken root, investments courses in the curriculum no longer emphasize judgments about economic worth; they virtually ignore the business particulars of securities in a portfolio and encourage, instead, computing simple statistics so as to be able to solve the problem of optimizing a set of random variables.

The second consequence of this strong turn toward mathematics is that the study of investments has become increasingly insulated from advances in other spheres of intellectual activity. The breakthrough thinking of behavioral economists, for instance, is grudgingly accepted and then relegated to a small corner outside mainstream finance. Advances in Bayesian statistics have also remained mostly in the shadows, even as the old ways of frequentist statistics continue to dominate the methods of analysis. Perhaps most importantly, revolutionary insights about personality and identity, perception and attention, imitation and influence—factors that play immensely crucial roles in the framing of investment choices—all go largely missing from investment research and analysis.

Finally, hidden assumptions in sometimes unnecessarily complex mathematical models have fixed the attention of investors on prices and price movements; they have undermined the need to understand the real economic activity that produces those numbers. Such a focus on prices has decontextualized investment analysis, removing the act of investing from the direct experiences and meaning making of those doing the investing. Instead, the constant search for mathematical laws virtually removes from consideration the many important particulars of business-related factors that differentiate the few good investment opportunities from the many bad ones. Subjective judgments, company-specific analysis, and intuitions about qualitative factors, such as leadership, are cast aside as unscientific, leaving hapless investors with dry, lifeless statistics with which to make meaningful choices. Lost, as a result, is the ability of people to be discerning consumers of financial information.

Certainly, the mathematization of finance has brought some benefits to the study of investments in equity markets. We now know a great deal more about mathematical risk than we did 60 years ago. From normal distributions with fat tails to ubiquitous power laws, a better understanding of quantitative risk informs investment models in applications such as insurance and indexing. More importantly, the normative goal of efficient markets has encouraged an unrelenting demand for policies that make the financial markets deeper, more transparent and liquid, and, therefore, fairer.

In a way, the two staples of investment education—modern portfolio theory (MPT) and the efficient market hypothesis (EMH)—are powerful frameworks precisely because of their seductive, if misguided, simplicity and the normative implications of fairness. The strength of finance theory as we now know it lies in the fact that the elegance of mathematical models and the practicality of statistical analyses are impossible to defeat with vague protests that they are built on unrealistic assumptions about human rationality and unnecessarily reduce complex human endeavors. Even so, for all the reasons stated here, limiting investment education to mathematical modeling and the statistical analysis of prices is the wrong thing to do. We need a better approach.

Clearly, in our search for an alternative, we cannot just replace one simple, if elegant, model with another. Instead, we must integrate psychological insights that acknowledge our humanity with robust approaches for institutional analysis. Fuller models of investment analysis, although more complex, will be more in tune with the real world of real people; they will be more productive for investors.

In this book, I set about to outline such an approach. I argue that investing must be cast not as a mathematical problem of gamble but foremost as a very human problem of choice. Of course, there is choice in every gamble and gamble in every choice; but it matters a great deal which of the two is dominant in investing endeavors. While chance does influence investment performance, emotional and broadly analytical skills exert a much greater influence on the experiences that investors have when investing. Such a shift in emphasis from chance to choice puts the focus, and the onus, back on understanding how to use reason correctly and how to incorporate rich quantitative *and* qualitative data into a well-rounded investment analysis.

Sound analysis helps manage and leverage the powerful emotions that surround and cloud the judgments people make when doing anything related with money. Wise investing, I submit, flows from carefully made choices; investors *must* learn and habituate to making good choices.

Developing this way of thinking, of casting investing as a problem of choice and then drawing upon a broad range of disciplines to improve the quality of choice is, in essence, what I would like to accomplish in this book.

Acknowledgments

A LONG TIME in the making, this book could not have been written without the help of my students, colleagues, friends, and family.

Foremost, I thank the many students with whom I have had the privilege to work over the years. Their excellent questions helped refine and strengthen the reasons that we need to recast investing as a problem of choice, and especially as an issue that requires business judgment. Their enthusiasm for the subject matter propelled my own desire to gather these thoughts systematically and in writing. As every teacher knows, teaching is really about learning, and what a great experience it is to learn value investing with my students!

I have been fortunate to be part of a rich, scholarly environment, which my colleagues have built and sustained all the years I have been at the Isenberg School and the university campus at large. The intellectual diversity and openness of those around me were the keys that enabled me to pursue ideas wherever they led me—to a wide range of disciplines outside the area of scholarship that I call my intellectual home. Such intellectual wanderings have been rewarding in themselves, and I have been lucky to have friends who are similarly inclined.

Larry Zacharias and Bob Nakosteen, in particular, have deeply influenced my thinking through endless and enjoyable conversations over many years. Larry read the whole manuscript and several revised chapters; he was instrumental in helping me clarify the role of disconfirmation in investing choices. Bob was especially helpful in attuning me to the role that subjective probability plays in investing choices; he was and is my go-to colleague for anything related to statistics or macroeconomics, among other subject matter. Both have been and continue to be incredibly fun to talk with, to test my half-baked and untested ideas, in offices, at Newman Center, at Rao's, and at Amherst Coffee. Another such friend outside of the academy but deeply intellectual is Mike Rossen, with whom I occasionally travel far and wide in the world of ideas, especially to those worlds that have almost nothing to do with investing but which nonetheless greatly speak to it.

I thank Ben Branch for his comments on my approach to diversification, Pam Trafford for reading the sections on off-balance-sheet liabilities, and Tom O'Brien for being enthusiastic and encouraging about the book when he first read it. I want to thank the participants in the yearlong (2014–2015) interdisciplinary seminar on the theme of "value" at the University of Massachusetts Amherst. I benefited greatly from wide-ranging conversations about value, some of which became part of chapter 11 of this book. Also, Chuck McQuaid, James Palermo, Ben Happ, and Michael Brown read the first book draft and provided helpful feedback.

I would like to thank Ali de Groot for her guidance and excellent professional support as I developed the first complete draft of this book. Without her sharp eye and frequent words of encouragement, this book would have stayed incomplete. I am grateful to Dana Johnson for her expertise on the Serbian conflict and I thank Brian Charette for catching another set of errors after the first draft was printed. I thank my friend Suro Ghatak for helping think through sundry ideas in the book.

I was fortunate to meet Myles Thompson at a conference in Philadelphia and am thrilled that our conversation there led to this much-improved book. I want to thank both him and Stephen Wesley for their support through the publication process, and Stephen especially for extensive edits and excellent suggestions for improvement. Their deft guidance made it seem like publication was the easiest thing in the world, when I know that they worked tirelessly to make this happen. I also thank Ben Kolstad for coordinating the production of this book and Kara Stahl for copyediting.

Last but not least, this project was propelled in large part by the immense love and support of my family, far and near. I could not have pulled it off without the good-humored prodding of those dearest to me. Mary, Helen, and Monika have been part of this process every step of the way, tolerating my ill-timed references to crowd psychology and wondering why I was so interested in, of all things, investing; they are, without doubt, coproducers of this book. The moral support of my mother (Savita), brother (Alok), and sister (Anshu) were crucial for me to continue working on this project and seeing it to completion. To my family, I owe much more than this book.

Capital follows knowledge.
Get knowledge.

Prologue

A Short History of Investing

THOSE WHO HAVE taken it upon themselves to lay down the theories of investing, whether they have done so from the bully pulpit of the ivory tower or from the editorials of widely watched media outlets, have left the average investor confused between the conflicting urges of caution and aggression. Through a vast edifice of knowledge built over the last 60 years or so, the high priests of modern finance appear to have declared that investing is more mathematics than business, that Greek symbols are more important than common business sense, and that, in essence, investing is no different from speculation or gambling.

Increasingly, as a result, when people think about investing, they think not about carefully and defensively deploying their precious capital in sound businesses; instead, they appear to be preoccupied mostly with buying ticker symbols on the screen, hoping to sell out as soon as prices go up a little. The businesses underlying the ticker symbols figure very little, or in many cases nowhere, in much of the buying and selling. Far too often, it seems, parties to a market exchange neither fully comprehend nor much care about the rights and risks being exchanged. Such, unfortunately, is the unintended legacy of the many brilliant minds that built the foundations of modern finance.

In this book, I'd like to further develop the ideas of a different breed of people, those who subscribe to a commonsense view that investing must be approached with caution and remain firmly grounded in the principles of business analysis. To understand why this is so important, I will briefly review what the state of investment theory was before it became overly mathematized. I will show how the reasonable approach of applying mathematical thinking to operationalize and measure the risk of diversified portfolios morphed into symbol shunting and justification of unrealistic assumptions. Then, by degrees, symbol shunting became a goal unto itself, and subjective experiences requiring nuanced judgments were reduced to quantities that had little if any connection to underlying economic realities.

The Classics

About a decade or more before Harry Markowitz developed the tools of modern portfolio theory in the early 1950s,[1] two investment masterpieces had instructed investors on how to avoid getting caught up in the casino-like atmosphere that had led into the stock market crash of 1929. The first was *Security Analysis* (1934, 1940, and 1951) by Benjamin Graham and David Dodd, and the second was *The Theory of Investment Value* (1938) by John Burr Williams.[2] Both these books were upended by Markowitz and quickly became obscure, overshadowed by the rapid rise of investment theory as we know it today.

Security Analysis laid out a systematic approach to analyzing bonds and stocks, instructing investors in the art of evaluating securities for reasonableness of the prices at which they traded. Among the key lessons of the book was that price and value are distinct concepts, and investors need to learn to recognize when the two become separated. Graham and Dodd offered several criteria for evaluating bonds and stocks, developing along the way not just an analytical approach but also an outline of the psychological apparatus necessary for investing rationally.

The Theory of Investment Value picked up on the idea of intrinsic value; Williams agreed with Graham and Dodd that the real worth of a business was distinct from its market price. He argued that market prices of a stock were driven not just by expectations and counterexpectations of capital appreciation but also by the fundamental economic worth of that stock. He went a step further by formalizing the idea that the worth, or investment value, of a stock was the present value of future dividends (broadly conceived) and its eventual selling price. In doing so, Williams put the emphasis on future earnings and dividends and, therefore, on the ability of the underlying business to continue delivering profits and growth.

Williams's forward-looking approach was in contrast to Graham and Dodd, who were suspicious of projections and advised investors to scrutinize the present in terms of past performance. Investment professionals credit him fairly with the dividend discount model; he defined dividends in the model in broad terms, including cash dividends and all future earnings owed to shareholders. To this day, the discount model remains a helpful way to think about business worth.

The Graduate Student

Security Analysis and *The Theory of Investment Value* drew the attention of a graduate student Harry Markowitz, who was in search of a dissertation topic for his doctorate in economics. Intrigued by Williams's formulation of value, Markowitz noted that given the uncertainties about the future, the rate at which to discount expected dividends depended on the degree to which they were deemed risky, or the chance that the company may cut or stop paying the dividends. The conventional wisdom at the time was that investors should spread their bets; as Edgar Lawrence Smith had already shown in a well-received book, the usual practice was to control risk through broad diversification.[3] Markowitz agreed but noted that risk was a portfolio-level issue; the goal of investors, he argued, is to mitigate the risk not of a single purchased security but of the entire portfolio.

As he pondered the problem, Markowitz realized that no quantifiable measures of portfolio risk existed. Being mathematically oriented, he made the momentous decision to seek out basic statistics texts,[4] hoping to uncover potentially useful tools with which to quantify and objectively measure portfolio-level risk.

As a graduate student in economics, Markowitz was perhaps not fully versed in the debates that had been raging among the objectivist and subjectivist statisticians ever since Thomas Bayes's paper on chance was published posthumously in 1763.[5] The prevailing viewpoint was that the probability of any event was based on frequency count, that it was an objective measure of odds derived from previously recorded observations.

But a vocal minority of statisticians resisted this dominant view. They held that probability was a mode of judgment and that it did not inhere in the object or event but in the expectations of the person making the judgments. They strongly contested the orthodox view that probability was objective. Even so, statistics departments around the country shunned this alternative view of probability as subjective assessment.

Ironically, in his dissertation, "Portfolio Selection" (1955), Markowitz acknowledged Leonard (Jimmie) Savage,[6] who was perhaps the strongest and most vocal proponent of subjective probability at the time. Savage had been at the University of Chicago since 1947 and had founded the new statistics department in 1949, of which he was head from 1956 to 1960. In fact, in 1954, he had published an influential text[7] in which he challenged the frequentist approach to probability and argued that the whole of statistics ought to be validly seen and profitably recast in personal and subjective terms. He rejected objective probability.

Had Markowitz followed Savage, he probably would have continued in the tradition of Graham and Williams, perhaps even embellishing their work by formalizing the role of subjectivity and judgment in investment decisions.[8] But, perhaps urged on by his other teachers, such as Milton Friedman,[9] and not wanting to get mired in the debates of another discipline,[10] Markowitz chose to bow to the prevailing dogma and pursued the objective probability angle instead.[11]

Intent on bringing mathematics and statistics to investing, Markowitz applied the standard tools of objectivist probability to develop the idea that the effect of diversification on risk ought to be reflected in the variability of portfolio returns. As such, he developed the idea of portfolio risk as deriving from the variance of the returns of each individual stock and the covariances between each pair of stocks in the portfolio.

Since variances and covariances of past returns were easy to calculate as long as historical data were available, Markowitz declared that the problem of investing was really the problem of managing portfolio risk—by properly allocating stocks to build a portfolio that had the highest expected return for a given level of risk or the lowest risk for a desired expected return. He defined risk as the standard deviation of expected portfolio returns and operationalized it simply as a mathematical number computed using the historical returns of individual stocks in the portfolio.

By using standard deviation as a proxy for risk, Markowitz revealed the benefits of grouping uncorrelated stocks. Even more importantly, he showed that the benefits of systematic grouping were substantial even among partially correlated stocks. Complete independence of returns was not necessary for diversification to reduce risk.

A corollary to these ideas was the assertion that, in portfolios with a large number of stocks, the risk of an individual stock did not matter as much as the average pairwise covariance among stocks in the portfolio. That is, using standard statistical concepts, he shifted attention away from the risk of each stock to the weighted effect of any one stock on the overall portfolio risk. This insight was about all he needed; statistics took it from there. There was no longer the need to analyze each individual stock in detail; it was enough to simply assemble lightly correlated stocks with desired means and variances of returns and mix them up to engineer portfolios with the best expected risk–reward ratios. This was the birth of modern portfolio theory.

In essence, then, Markowitz developed this theory by quantifying risk using a simple, albeit computationally intense, mathematical formula. His notion of portfolio risk made diversification a mathematically solvable problem; others such as William Sharpe and John Lintner quickly followed and built on his work. Attracted by the successes of the pioneers, and arguably by the rewards of well-paid opportunities in business schools and on Wall Street, more mathematicians came pouring into the field. By the late 1970s, mathematical finance was well entrenched in business schools all over the country.[12]

Ever since Markowitz, the definition of risk as incorporating the variance and standard deviations of past returns has remained at the heart of mathematical finance. Measuring risk in this way meant that, as the size of the portfolio increased, the computational power needed to calculate portfolio risk increased exponentially. But that problem would soon be solved with computers and is even less of a limitation today.

Defining risk mathematically in a world where computational power was rapidly increasing solved an emerging problem, as it allowed investment theory to be delivered at an industrial scale. Billions of dollars were already coming into the capital markets from the savings and retirement accounts of a growing middle class after World War II; investing these funds successfully would have been difficult if investors had had to handpick one company at a time, based only on subjective assessments of risk.

Investing on a large scale was deemed especially challenging, as there were no sure-shot formulae to solve the problem of selecting stocks and bonds from a fast-expanding list. Mathematically computing the risk–return trade-off and dishing out advice backed by seemingly infallible mathematical formulae was an attractive alternative. The financial services industry eagerly adopted the formulaic approach made possible by math and the rise of computers.

At the same time, a strong theoretical framework (efficient markets) along with the availability of massive amounts of historical data allowed researchers to publish papers and teach computational techniques to the large numbers of students pouring into universities. Soon, multitudes of students were learning the new financial math in universities across the country and going on to apply them in the practical world of finance.

As a result of these developments, the revolution started by Markowitz quickly became deeply institutionalized both on Wall Street and in the ivory tower, with institutions in one sphere feeding those in the other to build a crescendo of approval for the mathematization of finance. What had started as the simple insight of a graduate student toiling in a university library had, in a few short decades, become a dominant model in the world of investments.

Over time, the computational tools have become increasingly more sophisticated,[13] with world-class universities offering graduate degrees in financial mathematics and financial engineering. Ph.D. programs in business schools now almost exclusively admit students with math and other quant-oriented training; articles in academic journals have become virtually incomprehensible to anyone not steeped in higher-order mathematics; financial institutions are populated with doctorates in physics or applied mathematics. Both the teaching and practice of investments are now inseparable from the maddeningly complex math of analyzing risk and the probabilistic movement of prices.

Markowitz and his followers used the mathematical logic of portfolio theory to reduce stocks to two simple quantities: mean and variance.[14] The focus on portfolio and risk defined simply as the standard deviation of past returns meant, in effect, that the details of the underlying businesses were no longer worthy of analysis. Risk was reduced to a measurable quantity and investing to a problem of optimization. Poof! In came portfolio engineering and out went business analysis and judgment. Investing became an exercise in mathematics.

Whereas practitioners such as Benjamin Graham and academics such as Arthur Stone Dewing[15] had long defined investing as being about investor psychology and institutional analysis, the mathematicians turned attention toward the analysis of financial markets and the processes underlying them.[16] It is not surprising, therefore, that the mathematical tools and techniques that they brought to finance made underlying processes visible, but they did so at the expense of making important particulars about securities and the institutions that issued them invisibile.

Ironically, such a focus on market processes meant that individual choice mattered only in an abstract, theoretical way. Even though the individual (*homo economicus*) was at the center of their economic theorizing, the mathematicians felt justified in caricaturing investors as undifferentiated, asocial utility maximizers. They built models using simplified assumptions on the argument that doing so was necessary to build theory; but they ignored the particulars of the securities and institutions necessary for making informed investment choices. To them, markets were where all the action was. How people actually made investment decisions and how wealth-building institutions actually operated did not seem to be the concerns.

Yet, because the mathematicians not only assumed but also insisted that real people behaved as those in their models, their view of the world did not sit well with many. To old-school practitioners, the models were unhelpful; to other theorists, the models were built on faulty assumptions and therefore suspect.

The Dissent

Even as modern portfolio theory was gathering steam, some remained skeptical about what they thought was an elaborate ruse. These were small dissenting voices at first, protesting the foundational assumptions that made the math possible.[17] These individuals were concerned that the models were faulty because they required the investor to be hyperrational, when much of the research in other disciplines was revealing that such an extreme form of rationality did not exist in the real world. Rejected and ignored at first, their small voices slowly gained traction and, ultimately, their objections to the unrealistic assumptions baked into the mathematical models were formalized.[18]

The first cracks began to appear in the early 1970s, barely 20 years after the first Markowitz paper, through the works of two psychologists,

Amos Tversky and Daniel Kahneman. Starting with a paper in 1971 and continuing for more than two decades, the pair began compiling impressive evidence about the systematic biases that plague people as they make choices. They argued, for example, that both lay people and professionals have markedly erroneous intuitions about the laws of chance. Over time, their experiments shredded the assumption that people maximize utility in all situations or that decision makers are even rational. In particular, they are credited with developing prospect theory, which highlights the difficulty people have in handling risk. Irrationality, they declared, was endemic in economic choices.

Prospect theory was picked up by economists and soon became a basis for what has come to be called behavioral economics. Over time, this line of thinking exposed not only cognitive biases but also social and emotional factors that influence how people make economic and investment decisions.

Much of what we now know about how people actually make decisions is at odds with the caricature of hyper-rational decision makers that modern portfolio theory relies on. Of particular help have been the insights into how people incorporate risk in decision making.

It turns out that risk is a much more complex issue than its simple conception as the standard deviation of past returns. Most situations encountered by investors involve not simply objective facts but subjective personal assessments of uncertainties about the future. Most investors have trouble grasping such uncertainties and make errors when making judgments about where and when to invest.

Even mathematically, the idea of standard deviation as risk is indefensible, as it incorrectly assumes that the underlying distributions are known in advance. Historical returns are typically assumed to be normally distributed, even though they may be skewed and have much larger spreads than those assumed by the usual models of risk;[19] unanticipated events happen a lot more frequently than assumed.[20] As such, even after decades of thinking on the subject, investment risk is still misunderstood and poorly captured by mathematical models.

So, a key contribution of prospect theory and behavioral finance has been an honest appraisal of how we humans make decisions. Such appraisal is missing from modern portfolio theory, which is underpinned instead by a caricature of decision makers as all knowing. Behavioral researchers have made great strides in highlighting common, systemic errors in judgment.

Yet, in spite of all the insights into the widespread biases and ineptitude of individuals as decision makers, behavioral finance ignores the large errors in judgment people are liable to make as social beings. Crowd psychology and social influence hardly figure in formal theorizing about investor behavior. Moreover, analyzing businesses for their investment potential is also not on the agenda of behavioral finance. Focusing on human frailties, theorists in behavioral finance are concerned with analyzing the investors, not the investment. They are as far removed from investments as portfolio theory is from analyzing the businesses that issue the securities.

Graham and Dodd had, in fact, intuited the commonsense findings of behavioral finance. Having observed the mania of the late 1920s, the collapse of 1929, and the subsequent Great Depression, Graham understood quite well that people get carried away and make foolish decisions in the financial markets. In fact, in *Security Analysis*, Graham and Dodd state that one of their motivations for writing the book was to offer a mental apparatus that would help investors be rational when investing.

Interestingly, the intellectual and empirical debates between behavioral and portfolio theorists revolve around investor behavior and its consequences for how the markets function. To the former, it is puzzling why the latter cannot see how irrational people can really be, especially when it comes to money and investing. To the latter, investor behavior is beside the point, as the invisible hand of the markets somehow solves the problem of individual irrationality. But to the befuddled investor watching these debates, neither of the two traditions seems concerned with the specifics of companies to understand how they create value.

Anomaly as Opportunity

Anchored in Markowitz's work and further embellished by other mathematicians who followed, modern investment theory now operates under a well-established paradigm of efficient markets—but one that is increasingly under stress. The search for objective measures of risk and "efficient frontiers" has produced increasingly complicated symbol shunting; but most of us remain woefully short of grasping what risk really means.

It may be that modern portfolio theory and the mathematical finance it spawned are stuck in what Thomas Kuhn once called normal science, which "attempt[s] to force nature into the performed and relatively inflexible box that the paradigm supplies . . . [but does not] call forth new sorts of phenomenon; indeed those that will not fit the box are often not seen at all."[21] Perhaps institutional and social pressures continue to limit the intellectual content of finance to mathematics at the expense of all other disciplines.[22] Perhaps we need to fundamentally redefine the problem of investing and seek new methodological tools that will create fresh insights into the world of investing.[23] As Fischer Black once noted, not symmetry and efficiency but asymmetries and inefficiencies are at the very root of how markets work.[24] Perhaps market efficiency simply assumed as constant in financial models is really a variable that changes with context[25]—markets need deep liquidity and unhindered bidding processes, for example, to facilitate exchanges as imagined in theory, but, in practice, these vary considerably with context. Perhaps it's time to widen the aperture and consider alternative ways of thinking about markets in general and investing in particular.[26]

As Kuhn once observed, a scientific discipline reaches a crisis point when it systematically ignores anomalies. New paradigms often evolve when seeming anomalies turn out not to be exceptions but persistent examples of alternative intellectual structures. It so happens that outsiders, not insiders, are the ones to resist attempts to explain away the anomalies; with little at stake in the status quo, they are often the ones to persistently question observations that don't fit the patterns of discovery or the normal problem-solving enterprise of the discipline.

One obvious anomaly that academic finance has systematically ignored or tried to explain away is the long-term performance of some well-known investors who openly question modern portfolio theory and its precepts. While there are many examples, perhaps the best one would be Warren Buffett. In his famous speech, "The Superinvestors of Graham-and-Doddsville," later published as an article in 1984, Buffett sharply questioned the assumption of market efficiency and outlined his objections to academic finance. It is, of course, easy to criticize a theory for being imperfect, but Buffett spoke from personal insight and practical experience. His words carry weight because he has accomplished noteworthy success while ignoring and even openly contesting the efficient market hypothesis and modern portfolio theory.

As shown in figure P.1, an investment of $100 in 1965 in Buffett's Berkshire Hathaway would by the beginning of 1985 have turned into just over $10,000 and then into more than $1.8 million by the beginning of 2015—compared with $449 and just over $11,000, respectively, if invested in the market index (S&P500) for the corresponding years. Even after 1984, when Buffett gave his now famous speech, an investment of $100 in Berkshire Hathaway at the beginning of 1985 would have grown to just under $17,700 by the beginning of 2015, compared with little over $2,600 if invested in the market index.

Certainly, we can argue that Buffett is exceptional or that his performance is not replicable. But he is only one of many phenomenally successful professionals who subscribe to a method of investing very different from the theories that dominate investment education. Many of Buffett's peers and a current generation of investors draw their inspiration from Benjamin Graham, who outlined a distinct approach more than 80 years ago. Therefore, we must at least consider the possibility of other intellectual frameworks for investing and investment education, those that emphasize psychology and institutional analysis against unquestioning deference to the efficient market hypothesis. If such a framework does exist, then it is a worthwhile project to try to flesh it out...or to at least start the process.

Back to Investing

More than 60 years ago, Markowitz opened the doors for many brilliant mathematicians to enter the world of investing. The age-old problems of chance, with which mathematicians had been fascinated for many centuries, now suddenly became incredibly interesting. Markowitz had led them to a rich bounty of data that seemed to suggest that prices move randomly and, therefore, that chance plays a mighty role for those investing in the stock market. This was a unique stage on which to apply and sharpen the long tradition of thinking about games of chance. Stock price was no longer about economic worth; it was a random variable in complex interactions with other random variables. In this way, Markowitz and those who followed him put in motion a movement that made investing less about business judgment and almost entirely about mathematical rules for gambling.

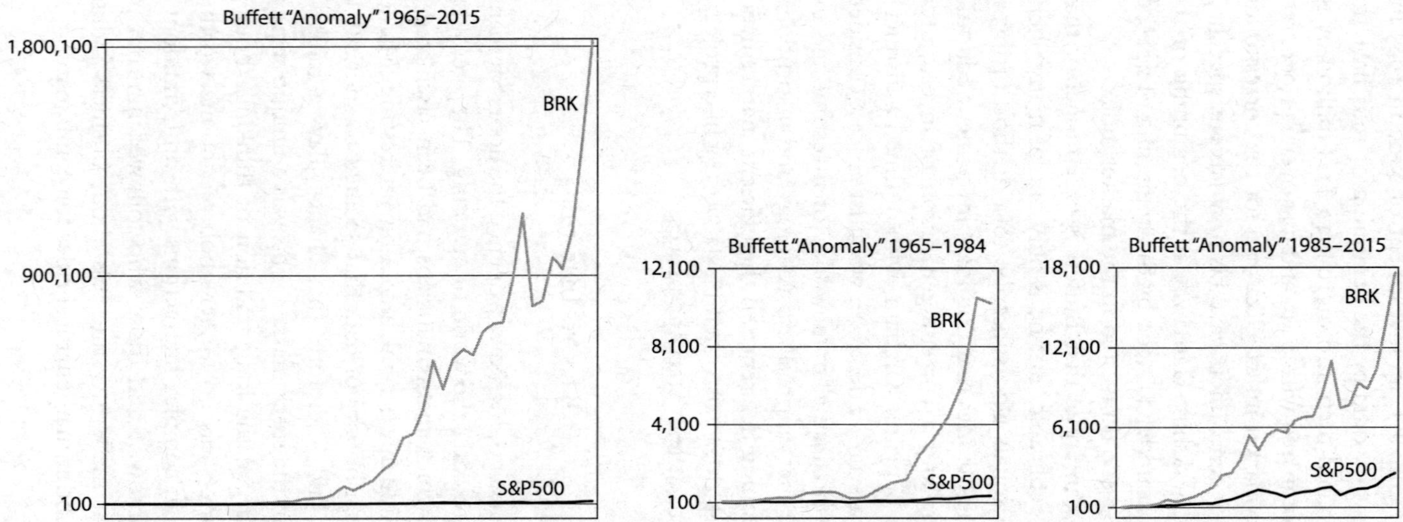

Figure P.1 Berkshire Hathaway versus S&P 500 average

Risk was no longer a subjective judgment about odds; it was an objective, quantifiable measure based on frequencies in historical data. It became a narrowly defined technical term measured solely from fluctuations in price data—to enable the mathematics of portfolio optimization. Accused of vagueness, business judgment started to look shabby next to the sharp and elegant models of mathematically trained financial economists.

It is important to understand that mathematical thinking is indispensable to investing. The mental discipline inspired by mathematical concepts is necessary for structuring thought, correctly framing investment problems, and synthesizing the influences of forces bearing down on an investment thesis. Properly used, simple mathematics helps identify salient issues, reveals relationships between constructs, and generally helps the mind grasp slippery concepts to focus attention on what is important.

Clearly, Graham was a strong proponent of seeking and organizing information, and, as evident in *Security Analysis*, he was among the first to insist on mathematical logic in investment analysis. To him, collating financial statistics and evaluating relationships between key variables were very much a part of making good judgments.[27]

But the mathematics we see in modern finance is often overly abstract and far removed from the real world of organizations and the people who inhabit them. The abstract mathematical models of investment theory seek, in fact, to remove subjective judgment by obscuring inconvenient complications, such as organization, leadership, strategy, products, relationships, and, above all, the many frailties of human decision makers.

Of course, I am not the first, nor will I be the last, to question the extreme mathematization of finance[28] in general and modern portfolio theory in particular.[29] As Donald MacKenzie has noted,[30] skepticism about the mathematical approaches to investing has been around ever since these approaches first began taking root in the middle of the last century. Criticisms have continued unabated but mostly to no avail, as academic journals and investment textbooks have largely ignored those criticisms.

While there are many institutional reasons for such a state of affairs, perhaps the strongest is a deep faith among academics in the math-heavy analytical approaches common in the hard sciences such as physics. This faith is based partly in the stunning advances such approaches have made possible in solving incredibly complex problems in a range of disciplines. From landing humans on the moon to putting computers in people's pockets, mathematical approaches have pushed the frontiers of science to the extent that few would have imagined only a few generations ago. Yet, investing is not a natural science, and the data that physicists and their kin work with are not characterized by the deep endogeneity that pervades the behavioral data implicit in financial models; we know that prices are recursively related to investor behavior. Financial models are much more unstable and vulnerable to error, as a result, and relying on simple proxies for key concepts such as risk makes those errors that much more grave.[31]

The dominance of complex mathematics in modern finance education has had real consequences for how we learn, teach, and practice investing. Not only has the heavy use of mathematical abstractions encouraged the framing of investing solely as a problem of gamble (given the randomness in "efficient" markets), it has also for the most part hindered the development of alternative approaches to investment analysis. Over time, the presumption of symmetries in the markets and corresponding affinity for abstractions has drawn substantial resources away from other lines of inquiry that would have put realism back into investing and once again located business judgment squarely at the center of investment education.

In fact, the overreliance on mathematical abstractions has insulated investment theory and education from other disciplines that more realistically assess the many constraints on our ability to comprehend the world around us. Consequently, even as investment researchers search for ever more abstract mathematical explanations for investment behavior, we continue to be starved for alternative approaches to making sound judgments about the many hazards of investing.

Behavioral economists do much to correct the gallant—and glaringly wrong—assumptions about how people think about risk and make judgments under uncertainty. But they do little to help investors evaluate the merits of the companies in which they may choose to invest. Behavioral insights are helpful in making us aware of the common and systematic biases we all have, but behavioral theorists have little to say about how to evaluate investment opportunities for their economic worth.

Understandably, both portfolio theory and behavioral finance have attracted many smart people who are mathematicians and psychologists but who do not necessarily have the affinity for or interest in making business judgments. High math is now the indispensable means with which to publish in intensely competitive academic journals; many in academic finance deem subjectivity and judgment as too vague to qualify as honest scholarly work. Graham and Williams are long forgotten in academia, their emphasis on business judgment a distant memory carried by the few stragglers who remain skeptical of the mathematical finance that now dominates business school curricula.

In this book, I strive to bring investors back to investing and to revive the study of investments in the spirit of Graham and Williams, with a nod to Buffett and the many other brilliant investors who pay no heed to the abstract mathematics found in academic journals. I go beyond the classics, however, by drawing on the many insights into human reasoning and business institutions that researchers have uncovered during the last several decades.

With investor psychology and institution analysis in focus, I build an investor-centric decision framework that leverages a subjective understanding of the world and show how to apply that framework in commonsense, nontechnical terms. As a check on the strong biases that potentially corrupt subjective assessments, I follow the work of a long line of thinkers to color the entire endeavor of investing with the principle of negation, the goal of which is to discover economic worth through a systematic process of disconfirmation.

In all, I show how to understand investing with the focus back on psychology and institutions—to build portfolios one stock at a time—with tools that are grounded in a current state-of-the-art understanding about how we really think and reason and how companies create wealth and value.

Introduction

Noise

THERE ARE ALMOST 20 trillion dollars sloshing around in the U.S. stock market alone, not to mention the tens of trillions more in stock exchanges around the world. Countless more dollars whiplash the system in bonds, commodities, options, and futures. In spite of so much money around us, research shows that many individual investors lose money because, perhaps disoriented by churn and noise in the markets, they trade too much.[1]

Successful investing is elusive because it requires putting up current real dollars for an uncertain future gain. Doing so means making connections between actions now and consequences later, in venues (the markets) that are incredibly complex and volatile. It's easy to make mistakes in investing, in other words, and those mistakes can be costly.

Some mistakes in investing are self-inflicted, whereas others are induced from the outside. They arise from the secret workings of formidable enemies both internal and external. Internal enemies are our own emotions, needs, and desires, those deep-rooted primal urges that tug at the psyche and cloud the mind. Fear, hope, and greed are as much part of the human psyche as anything else, always present, always lurking beneath the surface. When activated, they encourage behavior that is as foolish as it is harmful to our own economic interests.

As investors, we also have to contend with the push and pull of external influences, those that insist in whispers and shouts, from screen, print, and radio, to buy this and sell that. Tricks, cons, and outright lies are inextricably mixed with hints, allusions, and possible truths. The noise out there is deafening, an information din, as an unending array of thoughts, opinions, and hallucinations make it to the airwaves and onto our screens to invade the consciousness. They fray nerves, fragment imagination, and dissipate the most important resource that any investor has: his or her attention span. As a result, it is hard to distinguish signal from noise and good advice from deceit; the hapless investor is often buried in all this, prone to premature action, paralyzing confusion, or worse.

Contrary to daily hype and urgings dished out in the media, investing is a bewilderingly difficult game. Many are seduced into believing that they can make an easy buck with a quick buy here and a hasty sell there. Gripped by dreams of riches but unprepared for what awaits them, they go by the millions to the market, like cannon fodder to the front lines, to an arena where the odds are stacked against them.

The challenge for most lay investors, and some professionals too, is that they may not fully appreciate the complexity of the endeavor until they experience a few costly setbacks. Forays into the financial markets are often guided by the hopes of easy money, rather than by skilled efforts to solve the fundamental problem of choice that investing presents. Investors face the problem of picking from among a very large number of targets that are in constant motion on an incredibly noisy stage, and they do so under the unrelenting pull of internal urges and external inducements.

Successful investing is more involved than meets the eye; more than anything, it requires adequate defenses against some very powerful internal and external obstacles to making good choices. These defenses do not come naturally to us. They must be carefully built, concept by concept, to help overcome deep flaws in how we think and to help ward off the external influences that induce us to do foolish things with our money. Without such defenses, investors remain extremely vulnerable.

Method to the Rescue

Given the deep hazards inherent in investing, a systematic approach is essential for investors to be able to avoid steep losses and hold steady amidst the churn of the markets. Investing wisely requires a cautious mental orientation, a defensive approach, so as to minimize costly unforced errors. As the football aphorism goes, offense wins games, but defense wins championships.[2]

Over time and through trial and error, investors need to develop their own system of thinking to help sort information, focus attention, and provide consistency to decision making. If one's internal psyche and external enticements are formidable enemies, then the method, a systematic but guarded approach to investing, is the armor with which investors can join the battle and prevail.

There are more ways than one to approach the markets, however, and no single method can work equally well for everyone. Those who have the need for speed and quick gratification may gravitate toward high-speed trading systems, whereas those who are inclined to be cautious may be partial to slower analytical approaches. Fitting your method to your personality is particularly important—the last thing you want to do is fight yourself and your own natural inclinations in the thick of battle.

Examples are many, but consider just a few of the most famous names in investing from the last hundred years. Jesse Livermore became notorious for shorting stocks, in part because he was skeptical of and impatient with unjustified optimism among investors.[3] Benjamin Graham, having learned caution from early setbacks, developed an intellectual approach and numerical benchmarks to carefully uncover undervalued stocks and bonds.[4] Patient and thoroughly analytical, Philip Fisher used a systematic qualitative approach to evaluate future prospects of technology companies.[5] Philosophically oriented George Soros relied mostly on insights into interactions between economic stresses and mass psychology to develop what he called the *theory of reflexivity.*[6] Still countless others, such as Warren Buffett,[7] tactfully developed analytical approaches consistent with a mental orientation of extreme patience and steadfastness.

The markets are so large and complex that they offer an almost infinite variety of problems for investors to solve. Successful investors essentially reap rewards for properly defining and solving the problem of investing in ways that are consistent with their own temperaments and the analytical skills they bring to the task.

The Investment Problem

Not all problems are created equal, however. Some are highly complex and defy any solution, whereas others are more solvable with modicum of effort. Knowing where the prices are going to go next, for instance, is perhaps the most difficult of all problems. Considerable research and thinking suggest that market prices move randomly and are essentially unpredictable in the short to medium term.[8] Still, unwittingly perhaps, many in the market try to solve just this problem, and predicting whether prices will go up or down is a big preoccupation in the financial media. From thence come all varieties of chart readers, pattern seekers, market timers, and momentum traders—all speculating, swinging wildly and hoping that something hits.

At least part of the reason for such price-driven behaviors is that, ever since the early 1950s when modern portfolio theory came into being, investing has been cast as gambling. Naturally interested in the age-old problem of gamble, or chance, mathematically trained investment researchers have, over time, cast investing in their own image. Understandably, they look at the financial markets as a gold mine of data and problems that can be defined with the concepts of probability that mathematicians have been developing for several centuries. Defined this way, investing attracts those who are inclined to speculate and gamble and, in so doing, focus on prices and their probabilistic movements.

Although sensible speculation is sometimes a worthwhile endeavor, in this book I sidestep altogether the problem of trying to predict prices and focus instead on the relatively simpler, although not simple, problem of comparing prevailing prices with careful estimates of economic worth. That is, instead of focusing on the problem of chance, I recast investing as a problem of choice that requires judgments about the key uncertainties that may surround an investment prospect.

Learning to make judgments about economic worth keeps the spotlight on behaviors and actions that create economic value. Instead of passive indexing or frenzied buying and selling, I look to the fundamental drivers of economic worth. Such a shift in orientation expands the investment horizon and encourages thoughtful commitments of capital to economically attractive opportunities.

Make no mistake: both gambling and investing are about making decisions now for outcomes in the unknown future. As such, they both require making assessments about the odds; understanding the underlying math is essential in either case.[9] The difference is that where gamblers usually seek low odds with a high payoff (say, 1–9 odds for doubling their money or more), investors are inclined to seek out much more favorable odds for reasonably good returns (say, 9–1 odds for a 15 percent return with much upside potential). Marginally favorable odds (say, 51–49) would induce eager action from gamblers but none from investors.

Typically, gamblers depend a great deal on luck. The math of marginal odds is such that they require a very large volume of transactions for the endeavor to be profitable. As a result, gamblers are prone to trade a great deal and are not inclined to hold positions for long. This short time horizon, in turn, necessitates an unending search for new opportunities with marginally favorable odds. The math for such endeavors quickly becomes complex, and that is perhaps why mathematical finance has been so ascendant ever since the mathematicians, fascinated by the problem of chance, turned their attention to the financial markets.

In contrast, investors do not need high transaction volumes, as they prefer high odds of success that can deliver performance with just a few well-researched positions. As such, they seek near certainty by thinking strategically about the underlying factors that may be shaping the odds.[10] To the extent possible, investors work diligently to try to reduce reliance on luck and focus instead on the skills necessary for understanding the important drivers of economic performance and worth. It is this affinity for highly favorable odds that makes investors fundamentally different from gamblers: they focus on different problems. Gamblers want to take chances; investors want to make good choices. Gamblers want to trade; investors want to invest.

Clearly, analytical ability and technique are necessary for investing well. Knowing how to compute weighted probabilities or assess mathematical expectations is an important skill for investing wisely. But what is even more important is the ability to regulate emotions, think independently, and see clearly when making investment choices. Yet, controlling emotions and seeing clearly is not easy, as the financial markets are incredibly noisy and ripe with half-baked opinions, innuendos, and cons; they overwhelm the senses, confuse and disorient, and invite all varieties of deceptions and self-deceptions.

No lesson on investing is complete, therefore, without showing how our perceptions are easily distorted and how to correct those distortions. The problem of choice, or the problem of being able to see the true potential of investment opportunities, is harder than may seem at first glance; seeing clearly requires that we not only learn the particulars and apply moderately complex analytical techniques but also that we understand the powerful roles that emotion and desire, deception and self-deception play in our investment choices.

Overview of the Book

Unlike most other books on investing, I discuss at length why our perceptions are so prone to be distorted and how we can try to correct them when making investment choices. To this end, I ask you to take with me an intellectual journey, a short detour away from finance and into the world of philosophers who have long wrestled with the problem of how we humans think and how we find our way through the perplexing world in which we live. Although this material may seem strange at first, I hope you will realize that the key lessons from the works of many great philosophers have a direct bearing on how to make good investment choices.

I devote the first part of the book, therefore, to broadly discussing the problems of perception and then outline a decision framework to help correct the perceptual distortions that inevitably creep into our thinking. Making good investment choices requires, I argue, setting up a clear and credible investment thesis and then evaluating that thesis using a formal process of refutation and disconfirmation. Once I have developed and fleshed out the choice framework, I dive into the analytical techniques that are directly applicable to evaluating stocks and building investment portfolios.

PART ONE

Illusion

CHAPTER ONE

Opinions and Beliefs

CONSIDER THIS SIMPLE experiment. Each of four cards on a table has a letter on one side and a number on the other, but you can only see what is on the side facing up. What you see are two letters and two numbers:

A 4 D 7

Suppose the rule governing these cards is that if a card has a vowel on one side, it has an even number on the other side. Which two cards would you turn over to find out whether the rule is true?

If you're like most people, you'll turn over cards A and 4; in doing so, also like most people, you will have made the incorrect choice. And the error you made is one of the most common as revealed from hundreds of years of thinking about human reasoning, now known as *confirmation bias.*[1]

What you did was to try to confirm the rule that the cards with a vowel on one side will have an even number on the other side. Turning over A is an obvious choice, as being a vowel it can clearly falsify the rule if an odd number turns up on the other side. An even number on the other side of A would validate the rule, but you would not know whether the rule holds in all cases. But what is on the other side of 4 is not actually relevant. If you find a vowel behind 4, you will have confirmed the rule but would still not be able to declare that the rule is true; if there is a consonant behind 4, you have not violated the rule (the rule doesn't say that a consonant can't have an even number on the other side). So, turning over 4 gives you no useful information.

The correct response to the task is to turn over card A and card 7, both of which can show the rule to be false. The difference between cards 4 and 7 is that only the latter can provide disconfirming evidence. People turn over card 4 because our natural inclination is to want to confirm the rule.

This experiment was first devised by psychologist Peter Cathcart Wason in 1966, and over the years it has been repeated innumerable times by experimental psychologists trying to understand how people reason. Although the many variations of the experiment have yielded a range of results, one of the key insights gained is that confirmation bias is pervasive in human reasoning. People have a tenacious inclination to confirm seemingly correct rules, and whatever they already believe, no matter why they hold those beliefs or where their beliefs come from.

Beliefs and Their Persistence

Since beliefs play such an important role in how we choose, it is useful to consider that beliefs are propositional attitudes in the sense that people appear always to be tending toward some views on how the world works or ought to work, on what is or is not or ought to be or ought not to be.

History books are filled with examples of highly intelligent people holding beliefs that in hindsight appear to be patently ridiculous. For a millennium, those practicing medicine persisted in bleeding and purging patients even though the curative effects were few and painful death a more likely outcome. As Nickerson notes in a review, even when presented with evidence to the contrary, Galileo believed that tides were created not by the pull of the moon but by the "irregular" motion of the earth.[2] In fact, whole fields of scientists, presumably some of the most educated in society, have often clung to a theory despite the existence of rapidly developing evidence to the contrary. Nickerson notes that, in spite of numerous observations that contradicted it, Ptolemy's earth-centric view of the cosmos persisted among the keenest minds for more than a thousand years. Scientists of the day strongly opposed the heliocentric model that sought to replace it, discarding evidence that was not consistent with their idea that the earth was the center of the universe.

Beliefs have a tenacious hold on people, who often stubbornly resist even the most compelling counterevidence. It is now well understood that people with well-formed beliefs distort the selection, evaluation, and interpretation of data so as to justify their views. Especially when information is ambiguous, people with strong beliefs selectively co-opt the evidence for support. Such co-optation is not necessarily irrational, as people have been shown to use facile logic and complex reasoning to contort evidence to reinforce their preferential positions.

Belief persistence is not simply a malady of a bygone era. The modern world offers plenty of examples of how simple ideas take hold of the mind. In studies about how doctors make diagnoses, researchers have noted that the thesis about a patient's illness is often made early in the process. This initial thesis then guides the acquisition and interpretation of subsequent information and often constrains the range of options or alternative hypotheses considered. Faulty diagnoses, in other words, are usually the result of a persistence of belief that is formed early in the process of evaluation.[3]

The same phenomenon has been observed in studies of jurors.[4] Researchers have found that jurors often form initial impressions during or even before a trial begins, based on superficial cues such as the defendant's demeanor. They then selectively seek evidence to support that impression. In modern policy circles, many in the European Union believe that austerity is indispensable for economic recovery in troubled countries such as Greece and Spain. Their beliefs, perhaps based on a misreading of historical experiences, are such that they continue to ignore contrary evidence and arguments that rather than helping, severe austerity depresses the economies of affected countries even further, making them unable to meet the demands of creditors.

Whatever their source and content, a particularly interesting feature of beliefs is that they can form quickly, and often on the most tenuous grounds. Modern psychological studies have shown that even when presented with data with which to make decisions, people usually rely on information that already exists in their minds, is easily recalled, or is readily obtained from sources nearby. In general, people also give more weight to information that is obtained first. This tendency to quickly form opinions based on only readily available information, and then to selectively seek and creatively use subsequent information to support initial opinions, is called the *primacy effect.* Francis Bacon made this observation centuries ago, noting that the first conclusion colors everything that follows and pulls all later information toward it. In other words, we see what we believe.

Belief Persistence Among Investors

The primacy effect, belief persistence, and confirmation bias strongly influence what choices we make and how we make them. These deeply psychological dispositions interfere with both the acquisition and interpretation of information, and they do so without our even knowing it, subtly but powerfully shaping our thoughts and choices.

For investors whose success depends on making good choices about where to invest their money and where not to do so, such psychological hindrances can be costly. Taken to the extreme, mistakes induced by poor thinking can be disastrous; pulled into an investment on a hunch, a belief-enhancing cycle can induce an increasing commitment of resources until all is lost.

Another problem is that these interferences occur irrespective of whether the beliefs are true. Even though the examples above emphasize errors in judgment, confirmation bias operates equally strongly even when beliefs are based upon well-conceived standards or objective criteria. When caught in a confirmation cycle, lightly held beliefs and opinions that are legitimately grounded in some verifiable facts may become much stronger than is warranted. Strong beliefs can be built on hints of truth as easily as beliefs that have absolutely no basis in fact. We can easily stretch a little truth to absurd levels, out of all proportion to available evidence.

During the tech bubbles of the 1990s, the emergence of the Internet created legitimate opportunities for new business models and profit possibilities. Data traffic online started growing rapidly, at one point at the rate of 100 percent in only 90 days. This rate of growth then became a mantra that was repeated for the next several years, even though such a high level of growth was discernible for only a short time. As is now widely known, the little truth about the web, extrapolated to the extreme, contributed to one of the most rapid rises in asset prices ever seen.

Researchers have argued that self-deception is all too common among investors and makes them vulnerable to predatory exploitation by shrewd firms and institutions.[5] Research also shows that, perhaps because of confirmation bias, individual investors are overconfident, trade excessively, and tend to have poor investment performance.[6]

The formation and persistence of beliefs occurs not only at the level of the individual, but also on large scale where entire populations become consumed by it. How errors in belief can gain mass appeal, sometimes quickly and sometimes persistently, is an exciting area of inquiry that I will review briefly in the next chapter. For now, consider what Charles Mackay wrote as far back as 1841:[7]

> In the reading of history of nations, we find that, like individuals, they have their whims and their peculiarities; their seasons of excitement and recklessness, when they care not what they do. We find that whole communities suddenly fix their minds upon one object, and go mad in its pursuit; that millions of people become simultaneously impressed with one delusion, and run after it, till their attention is caught by some new folly more captivating than the first. We see one nation suddenly seized, from its highest to its lowest members, with a fierce desire for military glory; another as suddenly becoming crazed upon a religious scruple; and neither of them recovering its senses until it has shed rivers of blood and sowed a harvest of groans and tears, to be reaped by its posterity.

Students of financial history are, of course, familiar with financial manias that have periodically wreaked havoc in the lives of millions.[8] History books are filled with such memorable events as the tulip craze, the Mississippi scheme, and the South Sea Bubble—and now the tech mania and the housing bubble. From the periodic stock market booms and busts of the last century to the recent housing market crisis in our own times, we are well acquainted with what confirmation bias, combined with other human frailties, can do to us.

Investors Are Human

Modern psychologists have uncovered a plethora of systematic biases that appear to be as much a part of human heritage as anything else. In addition to belief persistence and confirmation bias, there is a tendency for people to be overconfident about their own abilities and to be too optimistic about the outcomes of their actions. Similarly, people tend, on the one hand, to overreact to chance events and, on the other, to think that they could have predicted that which has already occurred.

Of course, entire treatises exist about the biases and visceral drivers that influence our choices; I will touch upon some of these insights in the pages that follow. My intent is to highlight that the utility-maximizing rational investor is a caricature of theory; perfect rationality, even if we know what that means, holds only for normative models. The idea that markets are efficient and that broad diversification accomplished under the dictates of modern portfolio theory is the answer to their unpredictability is as entrenched now as Ptolemy's earth-centric theories once were. The sooner we acknowledge that we are biologically and psychologically predisposed to make poor choices, and that markets are more unpredictable than they are efficient, the better able we will be to accommodate our vulnerabilities when making investments and building investment programs.

In the following chapter, I show how individual errors and poorly thought-out choices aggregate into mass delusions. In later chapters, I develop the techniques of manipulation, the "dark arts" I call them, that are practiced upon us while we go about our daily lives as consumers, voters, and investors—even as we hold the illusion that we are independent thinkers free of all and sundry influences.

CHAPTER TWO

Correlation of Errors

ON FRIDAY, OCTOBER 24, 2008, panic gripped the financial markets. The Chicago Board Options Exchange (CBOE) volatility index (VIX),[1] also known as the Fear Index, reached an all-time high during trading that day. Having remained under 30 for most of the preceding year, and since its inception in 1990 having hovered between 10 and 20, the Index suddenly began climbing in early September, quickly surpassing the previous historical high of 44, and, on October 24, exploded to 89. The fear reflected in the VIX was clearly evident in the panic selling in the stock market.

In just one month, the market as a whole, as measured by the S&P 500 Index, dropped 26 percent and wiped out more than $2 trillion of equity investment in large publicly traded firms.

The economic news had been growing increasingly worse since the summer, but the speed of the market crash caught even the professionals by surprise. The newspapers were replete with stories about savvy institutions and big brokerage houses losing tens of billions of dollars and more. Many companies saw their market values plummet like a rock dropped from on high, and scores of people saw their life savings disappear in what seemed like the blink of an eye.

The remarkable thing about the sudden panic in the financial markets was that just a few years earlier, the sentiment had been quite the opposite. The S&P 500 Index had reached a historical high of 1,552 in October of the previous year, and the housing market had been booming for several years. The aggregate Case–Shiller Index of housing prices had risen from 125 in January 2002 to a peak of 251 in May 2006, at a rate two and a half times the rate of growth for the preceding four years. The euphoria that had been building for the previous half-dozen years was, in the fall of 2008, quickly and suddenly replaced by panic. Along with the decline in the stock market, housing prices plummeted, too: the Case–Shiller Index plunged more than 15 percent in one year.

Clearly, the euphoria and panic of the first decade of the century were not without precedence. Yet, unlike many others that are usually confined to a region, this particular upheaval was global. Instant news and rapid globalization had so connected the markets globally that what previously would have been somewhat contained now quickly spread throughout the world.

For the month of October through day 24, as the stock market indexes dropped precipitously in the United States, stock indexes around the world saw similar or worse losses. Brazil was down 48 percent, Peru 42 percent, Great Britain 31 percent, Germany 35 percent, Japan 23 percent, South Korea 46 percent, and India 36 percent.[2]

All the stock markets globally had been riding high barely one year earlier; now it seemed as if people the world over were experiencing a collective panic attack. As I revised this chapter in June 2015, both the S&P 500 Index (2,105) and NASDAQ (5,095) were at new historical highs. A few months later, in February 2016, panic seemed to be setting in once again.

Booms and busts have been with us as long as there have been markets, and in some ways even longer. In spite of the best efforts to contain them, such cycles have persisted in their unpredictability. It is understandable, therefore, that many theories seek to explain why economies and markets go to excesses in both directions. These theories are mostly technical in nature and thrive in such explanations as aggregate demand, money supply, interest rates, debt, and inventory. For the most part, they imagine the economy to be a machine, as if the fix is in pushing this button or pulling that lever.

The technical explanations force us to question why the aggregate demand explodes or crashes, the money supply goes astray, debt gets to excess, or inventories get bloated. Why do such mishaps happen with such speed and surprise even the savviest of investors?

There are few answers to these questions, in part because the technical reasons don't quite reflect real, ground-level human feelings and emotion; they miss the larger human story at play in such periodic but unpredictable swings. Technical explanations miss the crucial point that economic activity is not an island unto itself; life outside the realm of dry theory influences what happens in the markets.

Participants in the markets are, after all, human. We are the same species that routinely creates flash riots and long-enduring movements, street disturbances and convulsive revolutions. We are the same psycho-biological beings whose collective follies are entertainingly catalogued by many authors such as, more than 150 years ago, Charles Mackay.

Although the world of finance provides a fascinating and highly visible example of collective mood swings, it is but one instance of multitudes acting as though in unison. Both in finance and beyond, the combined fears and hopes of millions take on a life of their own, answerable to no one, relentlessly moving to extremes in any given direction until their eventual, often forceful, dissolution.

In order to understand what happens in the financial markets, therefore, it is instructive to look to the larger human experiences in which we, the people, participate through mass actions. Below, I briefly discuss two examples of mass follies for insights into some of the emotional propellants that may also be at the root of behavior in financial markets.

The Atkins Diet

Consider the Atkins Diet craze that swept across the United States a few years before the market crash of late 2008. As is well known, obesity and its related ills have long concerned Americans, prompting a never-ending search for cures and quick fixes that would magically help people lose weight. As a result, different approaches to dieting have been in the American lexicon for more than a hundred years. Today, there is a well-developed cottage industry, including several thriving corporations, with many products and much advice about how to shed weight without the pain of regular exercise or the disappointment of small portions at mealtime.

The first recorded modern diet therapy came about in the late 1890s, when a man named Horace Fletcher claimed that for healthy eating it was necessary to chew 32 times before swallowing. He made a bundle preaching his own package of ideas, convincing scores of people to masticate diligently. Mastication became quite a craze for a while, in fact, until it yielded to the calorie-counting approaches to dieting that began to emerge around the end of World War I.

All through the twentieth century, a wide variety of diet plans followed one another in rapid succession, each claiming to solve the weight problem, and each doing its part to modify the eating habits of many. The medical profession weighed in with warnings of the dangers of obesity; insurance companies got into the game, linking premiums to weight; drug companies joined in with pills that would do the trick; corporations tapped into a growing market for diet products by developing sugar substitutes and selling consumables they claimed did not add to body weight. Interest in the problem grew, begetting its own momentum.

Virtually everybody seemed to be persuaded that the problem of obesity had to be confronted, and there was a general consensus, varying over time, as to what was the most appropriate solution to the problem. For the most part, by around mid-century, the default thinking was to lower the intake of fat and sugar.

Then, in 1972, a cardiologist named Robert Atkins published a controversial book, challenging the prevailing wisdom that a low-fat diet was necessary for shedding excess weight. Instead, he claimed that the real culprits were high-carbohydrate foods because of the stress they placed on the insulin-producing mechanisms in the body.

Contrary to what most of the medical community had been recommending, Dr. Atkins lifted almost all restrictions on high-fat foods and encouraged people to eat as much protein as they wanted. But he counseled people to severely restrict their intake of carbohydrates to a daily amount much lower than what most other experts insisted was the necessary minimum for good health.

The controversy persisted for years after the publication of the book, as most nutrition experts remained skeptical of the low-carbohydrate, high-fat, and high-protein diets Atkins was recommending. The American Heart Association warned repeatedly that high-fat diets increased the risk of heart disease, stroke, and several types of cancer. High-protein diets, they warned, could trigger kidney and liver disorders and osteoporosis.

Still, Atkins stuck to his claims, publishing in the early 1990s a highly successful revised edition of his book. Millions of people read it and were relieved to learn that they could eat all the fat and protein they wanted and still lose weight. Even so, the conventional wisdom remained unshaken, and the Atkins Diet remained on the periphery of mainstream nutritional advice.

Around 2001, almost 30 years after the publication of Dr. Atkins's first book, interest in low-carbohydrate diets began to grow for no discernable reason. Within the next three years, the buzz surged to such a degree that the Atkins Diet became a virtual craze.

Suddenly, people were avoiding carbohydrates as if they were poison. Office talk was filled with comparisons between low-carbohydrate and low-fat diets. People talked knowingly of this diet and that. Everybody seemed to have a story about their own dietary choices or those of others they had heard about. People were glad to be eating steak without guilt. They were ordering hamburgers without buns. Pasta was out, meat was in. Fruit had to be consumed sparingly, but cheddar cheese omelets were fine. Eggs and bacon were back on the breakfast menu; toast and bagels were off it. *Dr. Atkins' New Diet Revolution*, published back in 1992, now became a phenomenal bestseller.

By 2004, the low-carb revolution was in full swing. Millions changed their habits, revising their meal plans even as they ignored decades of expert advice to the contrary.

The new patterns of food consumption had real consequences, of course. Restaurants had to change their menus to accommodate the movement now afoot. Those that resisted putting low-carb items on the menu saw their sales plummet. Large food companies got into the act with new product lines to meet the new demand.

As doughnuts and pastries lost their appeal, thousands of small bakeries went out of business. In just one year, the market value of Krispy Kreme, the famous doughnut maker, dropped 75 percent from $2.2 billion to $542 million.

Two of the largest makers of pasta, the New World Pasta Company and the American Italian Pasta Company, declared bankruptcy and wiped out their investors. Other businesses barely held on as people by the millions removed bread and pasta from their pantries and took them off their weekly grocery shopping lists. All carbohydrate-containing foods were suspect, and the infrastructure that had over time developed around delivering such foods seemed to be suddenly under enormous stress.

Prospering in this environment was, of course, Atkins Nutritionals, the company that Dr. Atkins had founded in 1989 to promote his theories. The company had grown rapidly, and by 2004, it had more than 350 products sold through a variety of outlets. It was developing a continuous stream of new diet plans and working with restaurants and food companies to incorporate low-carbohydrate items into their menus and product lines. The burgeoning demand for low-carbohydrate foods presented good opportunities, and Atkins Nutritionals was well positioned to capitalize on those.

Then, almost as quickly as it had come, the Atkins Diet craze was over. Dr. Atkins died in 2003 from a slip and fall, and a rumor began to circulate that cardiac arrest had played a role in his death. But the rumor was vigorously contested, could not be verified, and likely did not play much of a role in changes in public opinion.

But the following year, for no apparent reason, interest in low-carb diets waned significantly and with astonishing rapidity. People now suddenly repudiated the beliefs that had propelled the craze, switching back to the more traditional methods of weight loss; they slowed down on the rich creams, butter, and meats. Pasta was back in business, and bread and bagels again appeared in the kitchen.

Unable to withstand the reversal of the tide, Atkins Nutritionals declared bankruptcy in 2005. Within a few years, the storm had come and gone. By 2008, only quiet residues of Atkins remained in diets across America.

Genocide in Bosnia

Diet crazes aside, we can learn about collective emotions by peeking into other spheres as well. The case of genocide in Bosnia provides another illustration of how emotions build up on a large scale to influence the thoughts and actions of individuals, creating the context in which ordinary people make decisions and justify deeds that would be unacceptable under normal circumstances.

Bosnia-Herzegovina was one of six republics within the Socialist Federal Republic of Yugoslavia. Its large Muslim population had a long history of coexisting with populations of other religions, mainly Slavic Christians and Roman Catholics. Josip Broz Tito's authoritarian rule had held the different religious groups together in the federation since the end of World War II, but strains became apparent very soon after his death in 1980. Rising nationalism among the various ethnicities had created political turmoil, as the desire of Serbian nationalists (primarily orthodox Christian) to centralize power met with resistance from the others, such as the Albanians, who wanted greater autonomy. It was in this context of nationalism and power struggle that a mass of emotion began to develop, with drastic consequences for all involved.

We pick up the story on June 28, 1989, when, by some estimates, about one million people had gathered around the Gazimestan monument in central Kosovo.[3] They had come from all over Serbia and other parts of the world to commemorate a battle long ago, one in which the medieval Serbs had fought the invading Ottoman Turks, one in which their legendary hero, Prince Lazar, had fallen. The battle had marked the end of a once-prosperous Serbian kingdom and the beginning of five centuries of subjugation by foreigners of a different religion.

June 28, 1989, marked the six-hundredth anniversary of the Battle of Kosovo, fought on the site now considered the holiest of places for all Serbs. The monument, made of stones the color of blood and shaped like a medieval tower 100 feet tall, sat on a hill about four miles north-northeast of Kosovo Polje (Field), where the bloody battle had been fought. For nationalists, it was a symbol of Serbian identity and evoked emotions that resided deep in their psyche. It was a reminder of the heroes who had laid down their lives, and of the great power that Serbia could have been were it not for the Ottomans.

Of all the legends out of which the Serbian nationalist narrative was constructed,[4] the heroism of Prince Lazar in particular had attained an aura of mythic proportions. He was the hero who had pulled together a force to oppose the more powerful enemy; he was the martyr who had sacrificed himself in defense of his people, choosing to die in battle rather than to live as a vassal of a foreign power.

The anniversary celebrations had started two years earlier, when a coffin said to contain Prince Lazar's mummified remains started making its way from the patriarchate of Belgrade toward the mostly Albanian province of Kosovo.[5] The procession went through monasteries in areas that the Serbs claimed to be their new state, at each stop drawing large mourning crowds dressed in black. Repeatedly during the journey, Prince Lazar was symbolically buried at night and reincarnated in the morning, until he was finally reburied at Kosovo Polje.[6]

By the time of the million-strong rally around the Gazimestan monument, emotions were at fever pitch. This was the day to remember and be proud, Serb leaders told the crowds before them. Representatives of the Orthodox Church were up there on the podium along with anybody who was somebody, including Slobodan Milosevic, the president of Serbia. This was the day for reiterating the conviction that the Serbs were a wronged but great people, whose day was yet to come.

It seemed as if those gathered imagined themselves as direct descendants of Prince Lazar's people, who had made the ultimate sacrifice defending themselves against the Muslims and who, according to a nationalist narrative, had defended the rest of Christian Europe. The emotions of one were as if the emotions of the whole; the million acted as if a single being, with unity of feeling and unity of purpose. The commemoration appeared to have succeeded in prompting solidarity among Serbs everywhere—those present this day on the holy site and those following events from elsewhere—convincing them that they shared not only a common history but also a common destiny. On this day, 600 years after the battle that had triggered their decline, the Serbs were one proud people.

For 600 years, those present seemed to feel that the rest of Europe had remained ungrateful for Prince Lazar's ultimate sacrifice. Were it not for the resistance of their ancestors, who knows how far deep into the continent the invaders from the east would have gone? Yet, there had been no acknowledgement from other Europeans of the bravery and sacrifice of so many of the Serbs' forebears who had perished defending Christianity.

For Serbian nationalists, the lost battle of long ago provided the basis for a powerful narrative of heroic victimization; it formed an interpretive framework in which demands for autonomy by Albanians came to be seen as acts of aggression against the Serbian nation—a perception justified, no doubt, by the fact that those making the demands were Albanian nationalists.

Increasingly, the Serbian nationalists conflated all Muslims living in Kosovo with the invading Turks of long ago, accusing them of plotting to take over the lands that "rightfully" belonged to the Serbs. Slowly but surely, collective memory turned collective pride into collective paranoia; demonization of the "other" took hold. Collective emotions intensified quickly and, encouraged by the political elite, resisting the "enemy" became a dominant preoccupation of a whole nation.

Of course, not all Serbians bought into the narrative that was shaping the collective opinion against non-Serbs. Sure, there was dissent against this rising tide of emotion, as antiwar groups openly opposed what seemed like an unstoppable march toward war. But the narrative of heroic victimization was so powerful and the mass of emotion so immense that the dissent was marginalized.

Just two years after the million-strong gathering on Kosovo Polje, bitter ethnic wars broke out, and the Serbs were accused of committing ethnic cleansing across what was then Yugoslavia; some years later, in 1995, they were accused of genocide against the Muslim population of a Bosnian town less than 100 miles north.

The twin tragedies of ethnic cleansing and genocide were neither solo acts nor the responsibility of any one person; they were the result of the direct action of thousands and the indirect support of millions. They were, in fact, collective actions inspired by intense collective feelings, subsuming millions of people in a mass of emotion and inciting them to behave as if they were one body carrying out a single act.

Obviously different from each other in any number of ways, millions nonetheless joined the growing chorus of feelings about themselves as Serbs, about their history and their destiny, and about others who were different. Basic distinctions among the Serbs, differences of personality and social class, were all overwhelmed by the surging emotion and smothered into sameness. Even organized opposition by the antiwar groups and dissent from those Serbs who opposed the nationalistic fervor could not contain the emotional mass that had built up for aspirations of a Greater Serbia.

Such was the context in which scores of everyday people committed incredibly brutal deeds. Good citizens and patriots, kind in many other ways, were drawn, by the mass of emotion, into killing thousands of their compatriots, including women and children, not for what they may have done but simply for who they were.

Large-Scale Swings

The story of Atkins is vastly different from the one of violence in the former Yugoslavia. One is about butter, the other about guns. Despite the job losses and broken dreams, those affected by the consequences of the Atkins wave lived for another day; those on the wrong side of live ammunition in the former Yugoslavia are now dead or living a life of trauma.

Whereas concerns about personal health propelled the diet craze, anxieties about collective identity and collective recollections of events long ago propelled the forces leading up to genocide. Yet, these differences are largely superficial. Despite their surface appearances, these two episodes reveal several deep similarities. For instance, it is clear that unalterable objective truths could not have driven the behavior of people in either case, simply because there were no such truths.

Most dieters could not quite have grasped the science of dieting and the complexities of how different foods interact with the chemistry of the body. Those are nuanced scientific issues that remain mired in debates among specialists. Similarly, the myth of Prince Lazar had undergone numerous subsequent embellishments since the Battle of Kosovo six centuries earlier. By 1989, a hitherto disputed version had taken hold, one that was convenient for the sentiments then prevailing.

Both episodes arose not from thorough analytical evaluation of incontrovertible evidence, not on rational calculus of data at hand, but from stories that had been in circulation for years before they suddenly generated intense interest. The collective fascination with the Atkins Diet faded soon after the sudden death of Dr. Atkins; the Serbian emotion dissipated soon after the wars.

Both episodes followed a rough cycle of rapid buildup after a long period of gestation, and both then experienced a relatively quick dissolution following a peak of intensity. They were storms of sorts that for a period ensnared the attention of millions and then quickly passed through, leaving behind a swath of destruction and unsavory consequences.

Though extreme, the Atkins craze and the Balkan brutality are examples of behavior that is all too common in human affairs. The story of humanity is in fact a manifold story of behavioral storms. Large numbers of people on occasion become highly energized about a narrow set of issues, feeling and acting as if in unison, creating a mass that erupts seemingly unannounced. Having done its work, the mass then dissolves, leaving dispersed individuals and residues of their collective action deposited as fresh layers on the scale of time, only to be followed by yet another surge of a different variety in another place.

Granted, aggregate patterns of human behavior are many and varied. But there is something common, something fundamentally human that impels people to think alike and act alike, to produce similar behaviors that quickly aggregate into patterns with meaningful consequences. Consumer fads and fashion, public opinion and political sensibilities, religious beliefs and ethnic identities, wars and insurgencies:

these are very much part of the human experience. Human experience is social experience; people think alike and act alike in a wide range of social endeavors. Why should markets be any different?

What we know is that behavioral storms arise in part by our collective hopes and anxieties, which remain subject to powerful undercurrents of social memories and narratives. Individual choice is not simply a matter of rational calculus of facts computed in the moment. Choice arises largely from how we frame facts in the context of normative scripts or stories lodged deep in our minds. These scripts shape what information we pay attention to and what we do with that information.

The Visceral Market Hypothesis

Scripts and social memories that lurk beneath conscious awareness also shape our investment choices. The script that told us mortgage bonds were safe because homeowners wouldn't default on their most significant investment helped fuel the housing bubble, the effects of which we're still feeling years after it burst. That broad diversification across asset classes is the best way to reduce risk is yet another widely shared script that shapes investment choices among professional and lay investors alike.

These scripts enable us to take things for granted and pay selective attention to information that agrees with those scripts. It is for this reason that investing choices are subject to powerful pressures of which we may be only dimly aware. In order to learn how to invest well, therefore, we must acquire clear insights into our social and inner lives.

It is not simply that we as individuals make mistakes; more important is the fact that individual errors often become highly correlated to produce large-scale moves and collective errors. Shared feelings and impassioned stories are the key ingredients that transform a collection of individuals into an active mass that erupts with notable impact. Investors, too, are prone to bouts of euphoria or panic when emotions of greed or fear, built on powerful underlying scripts, overwhelm sound analysis.

This tendency is markedly different from the rational choice and equilibrium models that define modern academic finance. Those models derive from a fundamental script about price formation that runs through the economics profession: the efficient markets hypothesis. Yet, we know that the assumptions driving these models—the atomistic, asocial, and undifferentiated individual; fixed preferences; and utility maximization—are unrealistic. They are made to transform finance, an utterly human phenomenon, into physics, an utterly hard science. Given the unrealistic assumptions that undergird them, these models focus attention on the wrong things and often misdiagnose events leading up to catastrophic events such as the Great Recession of 2007–2008.

Perhaps we are stuck in a script that is an accidental product of scholarship in a particular time and place. Market efficiency, for instance, is a term of choice imposed by mathematically inclined financial economists and by operations researchers whose main preoccupation appears to be with optimizing physical systems; "efficiency" invokes the engineering image of a machine. This is partly because economists take deep inspiration from the mother of all sciences, physics, and seem to be forever searching for regularities and laws that are free of human intervention. Yet, markets are human constructions comprising people and algorithms made by people. Conceiving markets in the image of efficient machines hides what may be most interesting about them: they are prone to excesses and instability.[7]

Given the unpredictable ways in which people behave in different spheres, financial markets are perhaps more visceral than efficient. After all, we scratch when we feel the itch, get irritable when hungry, and choose when we must. When we begin to look closely at what people really do, efficiency goes out the door and messiness comes to the forefront. In this way of thinking, the humanities provide a more useful perspective than does mathematics, giving feeling more weight than thinking. It has been our loss that, given the path we have been on since the 1950s, the humanities and softer disciplines have been almost wholly missing from how we educate those preparing for careers in finance.

I submit that we can better understand markets through, for instance, the smudgy lens of crowd psychology than through the precision of high-order mathematics. This different way to conceive markets would compel us to incorporate into our thinking disciplines such as psychology and history, the arts and theater, in equal or perhaps greater measure than mathematics.

Unfortunately, finance departments in most business schools are not equipped to take on this challenge—for both institutional and ideological reasons. The efficient markets hypothesis and modern portfolio theory are the core intellectual foundations of finance education today, and they are deeply entrenched in the training, hiring, and rewarding of finance professors. Academic journals are highly skeptical of claims of markets not being efficient. Ideologically, too, it is presumed that efficiency demands freedom from regulatory intervention, and this belief is politically palatable to many in the finance profession more broadly.

In light of the above and as a small step in the direction of reconceiving investment education, I develop in this book a decision-making framework and associated techniques that respond to the fundamental unpredictability of financial markets. First, however, we must grasp how the inclination of people to herd and, by implication, of investors to get caught up in speculative manias, has been understood through history.

CHAPTER THREE

The Dark Arts

IT'S BAD ENOUGH that we're prone to making errors in judgment and so very vulnerable to holding all variety of faulty opinions and beliefs; it's worse that our built-in biases open us up to manipulation. The big secret of modern societies is that armies of operators make a living using our habits and ways of thinking to influence what we believe, to shape which products and services we consume, which choices we make in local and national elections, which causes we choose to support and oppose, and where we look to invest. What is perhaps most disturbing is that knowledge about our systematic biases and psychological vulnerabilities is sometimes used to instigate behaviors that are against our very own interests.

Years of thinking by philosophers and psychologists about human reasoning and mental processes has helped build powerful insights into how to influence people en masse so as to modify our choices and behaviors. These insights have generated a wide array of practices that sometimes use our common biases and collective errors to someone else's advantage, even to the point of undermining our own interests. Because these mass-persuasion practices rely on effective manipulation of psychological factors that reside below the level of awareness, I call them the "dark arts."

Below I briefly review the history of the techniques of mass suasion. It is important for investors to understand how dark arts are practiced upon us, as such an understanding will help develop and deploy methods to defend against them when investing.

We will learn that the practice of the dark arts is through the medium of language and symbols, through the clever use of words and images to focus our attention on some issues over others and then to integrate the message with our natural subconscious tendencies. Let's start at the beginning.

The Ancient Foundations of the Dark Arts

The art of persuasion was already well developed in classical Athens by about 400 B.C. Plato explores, for instance, differences between substance and form, between seeking truth and avoiding falsity. In one of his works, *Gorgias*, Plato creates a dialogue in which he pits Socrates against a sophist named Gorgias to explore the difference between truth and mere belief. Sophists were the wandering intellectuals of the period, and they were much in demand as teachers because of their skill in making compelling arguments irrespective of the facts at hand. Plato was distrustful and contemptuous of the sophists, as he saw them as conjuring up language to prove or disprove whatever caught their fancy.

Gorgias was one of the pre-eminent sophists of his time: a pioneer who practiced rhetoric as a performance art that included plays on words and the specific manner of their delivery. Like other sophists, but as one of the first among them, he argued that rhetoric was a supreme art of persuasion that enabled mastery over others and could move people to action.

Sophists believed that there was no absolute truth, only what one made of the facts at hand. They were skilled at arguing both sides of an issue. For this, many saw them as amoral, nihilist, and obstructionist, and accused them of using clever rhetoric to muddy the facts and lead people away from truth. Sophistry acquired a derogatory connotation; in our own time, we equate it with deceptive, slippery reasoning used to accomplish unpalatable ends.

Sophists made a living instructing students on how to use words to produce desired emotions and effects in others. In a democratic and litigious society such as Athens, skills of persuasion were highly sought after by elites, statesmen, and orators (demagogues), and they were widely used in debates and jury trials. Much in demand as teachers for hire, sophists fine-tuned the techniques of oral persuasion and gave their disciples general arguments that could be adapted to a variety of purposes. One common technique of persuasion was to flatter the audience in order to gain their favor. Also in the training were techniques such as voice modulation and projection, humor, and an even-balanced use of the body and gestures to accompany carefully chosen words and arguments. The sophists emphasized not only logic and reasoning but also emotions, such as anger, fear, pride, and pity, as the occasion demanded.

Plato was afraid the sophists were not only practicing but also teaching their arts of persuasion and techniques of manipulation. That, to him, was immensely dangerous, as masses could easily be led and prone to respond to skillfully made but false arguments. To Plato, the sophists were tricksters and mere opinion shufflers; they taught for pay and were, therefore, corruptible. More importantly, by selling their tricks of manipulation, sophists were hurting the reputation of true philosophers.

From a modern perspective, we can see sophists as viewing knowledge as a social construction, requiring flexibility of thought and social discourse. In that sense, they anticipated some of the more advanced social thought of our own time: that there is no absolute truth, only our perceptions of it. They seemed to believe that we live in a subjective world that has objective things in it; perception and interpretation are at the core of how we experience the world. But back in their time, the newly found fascination with the search for absolutes lowered people's tolerance for relativistic doctrines, viewed as dissent against the established order. So, little by little, the sophists faded from the scene and did not survive the strife that followed the Peloponnesian War.[1]

Largely in response to sophistry, Aristotle formalized the art of persuasion. In *Rhetoric*, he noted three essential elements of effective persuasion: ethos, indicating the credibility of the source; pathos, indicating the emotion of the audience; and logos, indicating logic and reasoning in the arguments. Even though personal credibility and logic were important, Aristotle insisted that the emotions of those in the audience also counted a great deal. He described each emotion in detail and encouraged the persuader to use these to stimulate desired responses. Like the sophists, Aristotle understood the powerful effect that a good speaker has on the emotions of audiences.

What the Greeks started, the Romans built upon. The renowned orator and lawyer Cicero is famed for advancing the techniques of rhetoric and is still very much present in high school curricula across the country. Well versed in the works of Plato, Aristotle, and other classical Greeks, Cicero developed an expansive style that he practiced in courts, in the senate, at funerals, and on other public occasions. He relied not only on logos, or pure reason, but on a range of formal techniques to appeal to the pathos, the emotions, of his audience. He used storytelling, humor, digression, and imagery to bring the art of persuasion to new heights.

A more lasting contribution came later from Rome in the works of Quintilian, also a lawyer, who became the first officially funded teacher of rhetoric. He founded an institute to train orators, where he formalized rhetoric in education and emphasized the doctrines and practices of earlier influential rhetoricians. The program of study included the staged process for learning to become an accomplished, ethical, and virtuous orator who would serve the public good.

Rhetoric quickly spread through Rome and found its way into the broader culture, social critique, and entertainment. Reminiscent of Plato, Quintilian saw the broader use of rhetoric as crass and an unfortunate victory of style over substance, and as the second coming of the sophists.

The Middle Years

Formal study of rhetoric faded into the background for centuries after the breakup of the Roman Empire, yielding to more formal training with an emphasis on repetition and rote learning. But remnants remained in letter writing and found expression in sermons. Although considered a pagan art, the study of rhetoric was nevertheless continued by the likes of St. Augustine. If the techniques of rhetoric helped plead right and wrong, then why not apply it for just causes? Rhetoric in sermons became commonplace and, justified by the righteousness of the cause, formalized over time into homiletics, the application of rhetorical ideas to preaching.

Rhetoric began to regain prominence in the early sixteenth century in the works of a Dutch Catholic priest, Erasmus, and his friend, Juan Luis Vives, a Spaniard living in England. A century later, the formal study of rhetoric became established in England, but shifted from Greek and Latin scholastic traditions to vernacular English. There was a movement to discard eloquence and linguistic elegance in favor of more straightforward words and sentence structure. Fine speaking was a disease, John Dryden said, and ought to be replaced by simplicity and directness, taking into account the occasion, the subject, and the audience.

The rise of democratic institutions in the eighteenth and nineteenth centuries spurred a revival of rhetoric in education. The increasing importance of language and persuasion was instrumental in this revival; knowledge gained over the previous centuries provided a good deal of ammunition that could be subjected to serious study using the emerging methods of scholarship.

By the twentieth century, as in classical Athens and Rome, rhetoric was once again indispensable to liberal education in Western Europe and the United States. Today, the art of rhetoric is well developed and firmly ensconced in education and the culture at large.[2] Many universities offer a doctoral-level specialization in rhetorical studies that emphasizes not only research but also teaching and practice—carefully developing theories and techniques for creating messages such that they have the desired effects on the intended audiences.[3]

Practicing modern rhetoricians are increasingly interested in the role that cultural symbols and images play in their suasory approaches. Speeches, essays, and poetry aside, the modern world is now full of persuasive messages that are packaged with a full complement of audio and visual aids. Far from the world of Plato and Aristotle, ours is a world ripe with rhetoric in its varied forms, and through all possible mediums. Whether trying to convince another individual, a small group, or masses of people, those trained in rhetorical techniques are constantly at work. Lobbying groups, law firms, public relations firms and corporations, marketing and advertising agencies, newspapers and magazines, television, radio, and the Internet—these are some of the most eager employers of those who have a mind for, training in, and sensitivity for rhetorical techniques.

The Vulnerable Investor

Madison Avenue is more than just a street in New York; it is an intellectual home for the vast number of professionals in advertising and public relations everywhere. It is ground zero for the art of mass persuasion, with individuals focused on creating and delivering messages designed to influence beliefs and generate action. Just as the sophists in ancient Greece had long ago discovered, these modern-day sophists understand that emotion is a key lever in the design of persuasive or dissuasive messages.

The rapid rise of financial news media in the last few decades has brought Madison Avenue lock, stock, and barrel into the world of finance. Print, radio, television, and now the Internet and social media are common channels though which much information, news, and opinion are packaged and delivered to the masses of retail investors; advisor networks, offices, and customer support centers are geared to deliver advice and financial products in a more personal fashion.

All of this creates opportunities for potential investors to access—and become easy targets of—large amounts of relevant and useful information that would have remained mostly inaccessible only, say, two decades ago. Yet, useful information comes embedded in noise and with hidden messages that make investors even more vulnerable to suasion or manipulation on a large scale—inducing them to make choices that are products of questionable influences rather than careful analysis.

So, let's turn to understanding how the techniques of mass suasion have developed over the last century in order to illuminate how and why investors are vulnerable to acting against their own interests, and what they can do about it.

CHAPTER FOUR

Purveyors of the Dark Arts

PRACTICAL INSIGHTS INTO how to manipulate mass audiences have been part of elite discourses for centuries. But formal thinking on this matter originated in late nineteenth-century France and quickly made its way across Europe and to the United States.

In this chapter, I tell the story of mass psychology through reviews of three seminal books on the subject. Separated by geography and time, and operating independently of each other, three authors popularized the theories and practices of mass persuasion. Their influence is very much with us today and it behooves students of investing to understand what these writers made visible through their labors.

The Psychology of Peoples

The nineteenth century was one of much turmoil in Europe in general and in France in particular. After the bloody revolution of 1789 and the dark days following it, the country fell under Napoleon's rule and entered into a series of bloody and ultimately disastrous wars with its European neighbors. When Napoleon was finally removed from power in 1815, things settled down for a few years, but massive upheavals returned with the revolutions of 1830 and 1848, followed by a particularly devastating war with Germany in 1870 and then a bloody civil war the following year. Also starting in midcentury, the industrial revolution brought millions of people from the countryside into Paris and other big cities, making the streets fertile grounds for all nature of disturbances. In this context of recurring revolutions and wars, and an increasingly assertive industrial proletariat, many thinkers posed this question: Why do people behave so badly when in large numbers?

Starting in about 1870, several different arguments began to emerge about the psychological characteristics of large human aggregates such as crowds. Especially influential in this debate was Darwin's *On the Origin of Species*, published in 1859 and translated into French in 1860. Darwin had connected humanity to the animal kingdom and to the belief that we are the product of hundreds of millions of years of biological evolution: humans are a product of deep time, in which the primordial core has been overlaid with the more recent layers of civilization in succession up to modern times.

Soon, the psycho-biological view of humanity gained rapid currency: that powerful psychological and biological forces governed human behavior. Many of the French intelligentsia were convinced that, while behavior could be somewhat modified with strong discipline, education, and selective breeding, humans were animals at their core. Civilization, according to this view, was but a fragile and thin veneer, barely containing strong primordial impulses.[1]

This jaundiced view of humankind was put forth to explain social upheavals. Many argued that large crowds of people were more dangerous and destructive than individuals because they multiplied people's innate animal impulses. Reminiscent of how the classical Romans saw them, crowds were seen as beasts that, if left unchecked, could destroy everything in their path, including the very institutions that made civilized social life possible.

Worse, demagogues and enemies of the state could manipulate crowds if they so chose. So, the race was on to understand how crowds could be controlled. Control, it became evident, was possible because of the susceptibility of people to manipulation by skilled rhetoricians and other students of human behavior. This was the origin of crowd theory, which became hugely popular during the last two decades of the nineteenth century.

The most popular rendering of this kind of crowd theory was that of Gustave Le Bon, the French writer who used this theme to produce four international bestsellers in just eight years, from 1894 to 1902. Le Bon was strongly ideological and vehemently opposed to the increasing tide of socialism sweeping through France, arguing for the need for ruling elites to manipulate the masses so as to be able to preserve social order. He was (and remains) a highly controversial figure and was rightly accused of being an elitist and a bigot because of his open contempt for all non-elites.

Along with many of his compatriots, Le Bon wrote that because of the savagery hidden deep within them, humans could not be rational. Volition and conscious choice were no match for animal passions. Not rational thought but instinctual life, or the urges and feelings from "below," were fundamental to the human condition and governed daily existence. Le Bon and other conservatives maintained that humans are essentially irrational creatures, driven largely by instinct and habit and prone to mental imbalance.

Social controls restrained the animal within all humans, he argued. When in a crowd, however, humans become mad as their beastly impulses break through. The social pressures of belonging to a group make the civilized individual a dumb animal; careful, deliberate, conscious thought goes out the door, and animal cravings dominate behavior. That is why, Le Bon said, crowds were extremely dangerous to social stability, and elites needed to control them through manipulation. He argued

> Man is only dimly aware of the diverse jumble of unconscious aspirations that dominate his mind. Such aspirations are touched by fleeting images that remain elusive and outside the grasp of consciousness. These forever-passing images produce anxiety from which people seek relief by holding onto whatever beliefs are easily accessible. Carefully chosen words evoke and crystallize grandiose images that flow in and out of the mind.

The need for relief from anxiety creates such a strong need to believe that, Le Bon wrote, "Were it possible to induce the masses to adopt atheism, this belief would exhibit all the intolerant ardor of a religious sentiment, and in its exterior forms would soon become a cult."[2] The object of sentiments may change, but people need to believe in something and to be fascinated.

Any sort of synthesis of the fleeting jumble of images and the hope of their realization is what gives the demagogue power over people. Regarding how people behave in crowds, Le Bon wrote

> as they [humans] must have their illusions at all cost, they turn instinctively, as the insect seeks the light, to the rhetoricians who

> accord them what they want. . . . [T]he masses have never thirsted after truth. They turn aside from evidence that is not to their taste, preferring to deify error, if error seduce them. Whoever can supply them with illusions is easily their master; whoever attempts to destroy their illusions is always their victim.

Le Bon argued that the leader of a crowd instinctively relates to the unconscious aspirations of his fellows. He is himself hypnotized by a single dominant idea and becomes its apostle, preaching it to those who listen, speaking to their aspirations, helping them imagine its realization. Strong conviction, not reasoning, is his strength: opposition or contempt only makes his cause greater, slowly but surely leading him to exercise despotic control over the masses. For the qualifications of such leaders, Le Bon had choice words: men of action, not gifted with foresight; morbidly nervous, excitable, half-deranged, bordering on madness; immune to contempt and persecution; without instinct for self-preservation; seeking martyrdom.

Because a crowd has no reasoning power, Le Bon argued, not reasoning but rather sharp images and shrewd words are the best tools for persuasion. Le Bon argued that stirring up an already expectant crowd requires imagery and suggestion by a prestigious person. A crowd needs affirmation of vaguely felt aspirations, for someone to give form to formless ideas and to stabilize those unconsciously fleeting images that torture people's minds. Affirmation by itself is not enough, however, as any mildly tangible images just beginning to take root are liable to be washed away by torrents of chaotic and unformed notions. Affirmation must be repeated:

> The repeated statement is embedded in the long run in those profound regions of our unconscious selves in which the motives of our actions are forged. . . . [W]hen an affirmation has been sufficiently repeated and there is unanimity in its repetition—as has occurred in the case of certain famous financial undertakings rich enough to purchase every assistance—what is called a current of opinion is formed and the powerful mechanism of contagion intervenes.

Once affirmation and repetition give an idea traction among the most susceptible, the idea spreads through contagion, gaining in strength with an increase in the number of converts. Not logic but rather blunt messages to the unconscious capture the attention of crowds; such is the modus operandi of successful crowd manipulators:

> Logical minds, accustomed to be convinced by a chain of somewhat close reasoning, cannot avoid having recourse to this mode of persuasion when addressing crowds, and the inability of their arguments always surprises them.

In fewer than 100 pages of his short book *The Crowd*, Le Bon speculated at length on the psychology of the masses and presented plausible arguments about how to control them.

Although Le Bon was despised by some progressives as a reactionary, he was a hero to conservatives. He was also much in demand by political figures wanting to learn his theories for their own advantage. Eager followers applied his ideas in business, and for a time up to World War II, his thinking also found its way deep into the battlefield doctrines of both the French and American militaries.[3]

Le Bon died in 1931, but his influence remained. Modern thinkers question many of his assertions, believing them to be colored by bigotry. Still, he had planted the seed of an idea that influenced a large number of political figures and intellectuals in his own time. His ideas also found their way into the writings of other influential figures of the twentieth century. One such person was Edward Bernays.

Engineering Consent

Bernays came to Le Bon's writings through those of his uncle, Sigmund Freud. He accepted the premise that people become less intelligent and less rational when they are part of any human aggregate, whether a committee, jury, assembly, or crowd.

Bernays carried many of Le Bon's ideas into politics and business in the United States; he was the one to coin the term "public relations" and was instrumental in developing the field through the mid-twentieth century. He took Le Bon's prescriptions indirectly from the theories of his uncle and turned the manipulation of the masses into a highly successful art form that is to this day widely practiced and now deeply institutionalized in many parts of the world.

Bernays wrote several books on public opinion, but the ones that made him famous were *Crystallizing Public Opinion* (1923) and *Propaganda* (1928). Like Freud, he agreed with Le Bon that the group has "mental characteristics distinct from those of the individual, and is motivated by impulses and emotions which cannot be explained on the basis of what we know of individual psychology."[4] Paraphrasing Le Bon, he wrote:

> The group mind does not think in the strict sense of the word. In place of thoughts it has impulses, habits and emotions. In making up its mind its first impulse is usually to follow the example of a trusted leader.
>
> . . . But when the example of the leader is not at hand and the herd must think for itself, it does so by means of clichés, pat words or images which stand for a whole group of ideas or experiences.

Bernays noted the immense success of the techniques of mass manipulation, such as that of the Committee on Public Information set up by the Wilson administration to gain support for America's entry into World War I. Much later, Bernays was to acknowledge that his early work had helped the Nazis build up their propaganda machinery. He was at the vanguard of public relations as a new profession that to this day continues the very old practices of using clever rhetoric to persuade the masses.

Bernays developed the technique of using focus groups to uncover the habits that were developing among people and the concepts of product placement for deftly placing the products of his clients in the media and tie-ins for associating related themes. He was among the first to advertise products simultaneously in multiple channels. He also pioneered the practice of celebrity endorsements and fake authority, such as when a spokesperson dresses as a doctor.

Among the most famous of Bernays's campaigns was to make public smoking acceptable for women. At a time when smoking by women was a cultural taboo, the American Tobacco Company hired him to study the issue. He uncovered deep aspirations for liberty, as well as strong social undertones that supported more rights for women and immigrants. Bernays deftly combined these at the 1929 Easter Parade, during which a group of debutantes marched down Fifth Avenue lighting up Lucky Strikes. The campaign, shrewdly labeled "Torches of Freedom," was immensely successful, in one fell swoop breaking down an age-old taboo against women smoking in public.

"Torches of Freedom" was hardly the only campaign in which the master manipulator applied the ideas of Le Bon and Freud to have his way with the masses. Over a 40-year career, Bernays ran numerous successful campaigns for big-name corporate clients, such as General Electric, but also for nonprofit institutions, such as the National Association for the Advancement of Colored People (NAACP). He even helped President Calvin Coolidge by transforming his dour public image. To his credit, once the harmful effects of tobacco became clear, Bernays also worked to support antismoking campaigns.

Promoting himself as America's number-one publicist, Bernays repeatedly leveraged existing cultural beliefs and social symbolism to build a lucrative business. The key to his success was uncovering social undercurrents through focus groups. Then, using vivid images and simple language, he orchestrated the discoveries in his messages. The final message of a campaign was artfully constructed, and its delivery was a culmination of much work; it was a production. Logic could be seen in hindsight, but logic was always secondary to and in the service of emotion. Clearly, Bernays was more Gorgias than Plato.

The Hidden Persuaders

By the time Bernays retired from active work, the practice of mass suasion was already becoming entrenched in some quarters. The methods he had pioneered and used were now widely applied in politics, business, and elsewhere. Marketers and advertisers were going full throttle trying to get people to buy this way or vote that way. Americans were under constant bombardment, with appeals for everything under the sun, some loud but many soft and some in the form of insistent whispers.

An air of cynicism soon developed among the public. They knew they were being sold to, and they generally took the sales pitches for what they were worth: as innuendo, half-truths, or outright lies. Although it was accepted that American culture was a consumer culture, there was an underlying anxiety that there was more to it than met the eye.

Perhaps the most impactful of the critical analyses of the period appeared in 1957 in the exposé *The Hidden Persuaders* by Vance Packard, which unmasked (if in a somewhat wild-eyed, scandalous way) how aspects of the social sciences were being used by marketers to treat consumers and voters like "Pavlov's conditioned dog." In spite of some shortcomings by academic standards and vehement criticisms by the advertising industry, *The Hidden Persuaders* had a strong public impact. By 1975, three million copies were in print, and it remains an indispensable read today for those interested in the art of mass suasion.

Packard's words resonated with people because of a pervasive sense that something was not right; in the book, readers discovered some of the methods marketers used to develop their pitches. Packard told readers

> about the large-scale efforts being made, often with impressive success, to channel unthinking habits, our purchasing decisions, and our thought processes by the use of insights gleaned from psychiatry and the social sciences. Typically these efforts take place beneath our level of awareness; so that the appeals which move us are often, in a sense, "hidden."

Based largely on Freudian psychoanalysis, the techniques of commercial mass suasion had been in practice since the 1930s. Packard discussed the use of psychological techniques by marketers and advertisers and gave examples of what these individuals were doing to induce beliefs and manipulate behavior so that people would buy as told.

Packard explained that many of the manipulators, indoctrinators, thought controllers, persuaders, and probers, as he variously called them, were "systematically feeling out our hidden weaknesses and frailties in the hope that they can more efficiently influence our behavior." They were using psychiatric probing techniques on little girls, on graduates, and on everyone in between, he lamented. Nothing was sacred, no one off limits:

> Typically they see us as bundles of daydreams, misty hidden yearnings, guilt complexes, irrational emotional blockages. We are imaged lovers given to impulsive and compulsive acts. We annoy them with our seemingly senseless quirks, but we please them with our growing docility in responding to their manipulation of symbols that stir us to action.

Packard wrote that the persuaders were learning their tricks "by sitting at the feet of psychiatrists and social scientists." Researchers from well-known universities such as California, Chicago, Columbia, and Harvard were eagerly working with the people-manipulators or setting up their own private consulting practices. Packard had reason to be concerned. The American Psychological Association had only recently (in 1953) published its first edition of the *Ethical Principles of Psychologists and Code of Conduct*; the monitoring of personnel in the field was still in its infancy, and appropriate codes of conduct were neither fully developed nor uniformly enforced.

Many in the industry were, however, skeptical about Packard's account of the new methods of persuasion. Critics argued that the depth approach was a pseudo-science and that motivational researchers was overselling themselves to Madison Avenue and, perhaps, exploiting the exploiters. Even the most enthusiastic practitioner of motivational research, Vienna-born Dr. Ernest Dichter, was cautious. He agreed with the critics that explaining why people made the decisions they did was extremely difficult.

Still, the use of motivational research continued to grow unabated. The pull of the hidden persuaders was just too great. The very perception that the depth approach helped sell products and services was validation enough. That people seemed to respond to subtle manipulations indicated the usefulness of probing techniques. In spite of the mysteries surrounding it, both supporters and detractors agreed that probing into the psyche of the masses had much potential and staying power.

The use of the social sciences to invade peoples' privacy troubled Packard, however. Of the "psycho-suaders," he wrote:

> They are mostly decent, likable people, products of our relentlessly progressive era. Most of them want to control us just a little bit, in order to sell us some product we may find useful or disseminate with us a viewpoint that may be entirely worthy.
>
> But when you are manipulating, where do you stop? Who is to fix the point at which manipulative attempts become socially undesirable?

Packard had brought to light the techniques first noted by Le Bon and then, through others such as Freud and Bernays, had found their way deep into the political and commercial culture. To an average person, all this validated the suspicion that there was more to advertising than met the eye; it was a frightening thought that the seemingly free choices were not free after all.

Where previous writers had mostly wanted to impress the social elites by helping them accomplish political and commercial goals, Packard's wild-eyed exposé opened up the techniques of mass manipulation to the masses themselves. He showed how deeply institutionalized such techniques had become in the commercial culture of the United States. It was no longer just a few elites manipulating the ignorant masses; a broad swath of society, including professionals and academics, were now engaged in practicing the art and refining it further for better effect. The practice had evolved into a multifaceted and formidable weapon in the arsenal of those who understood its true potential.

Persuasion Everywhere

More than 50 years after Vance Packard's exposé, the practice of mass suasion is an inextricable part of our culture and economy. The channels through which we received messages have proliferated far beyond those available during Packard's time. Not only have print, radio, and television expanded their reach, but cable and satellite television are now well established. Further, the widespread availability and use of the Internet, smartphones, and wireless technologies are making it possible to deliver customized messages to millions in an instant.

Large professional organizations now support the persuasion industries, with the teaching of necessary skills deeply institutionalized in the educational system and in various workforce training programs. Smart and ambitious individuals compete on career paths where success depends on one's skills in creating persuasive messages. Modern living, as media theorist Douglas Rushkoff's documentaries show, is saturated with messages.[5]

If the din was growing louder during Packard's time, it is now deafening and getting louder still. The persuaders are coming straight at us through our smartphones and soon will be through our glasses and wristwatches. Ironically, the din is not all just sales pitches or even irrelevant noise; in it are truly effective messages that tug at our secret fears and desires, sometimes at wants and aspirations that we don't even know exist. Plus, most effective messages are entertaining and informative. They attend to real needs. In fact, the messaging industry is at the center of economic life: it creates demand that keeps factories humming, workers employed, and societies functioning. However difficult it may be to see this, contemporary artists such as political consultant Frank Luntz and cognitive linguist George Lakoff play a legitimate role in such an enterprise.

Yet, persuasion is a double-edged sword. It can be used for good but also for not so good. Persuading people to give up smoking or to contribute to charity surely is desirable. In contrast, persuasive messages that urge gambling or other forms of addiction do a lot of damage. As the sophists understood at the dawn of civilization, the unfortunate fact remains that there is no clear line separating socially desirable from hurtful messaging.

Clearly, mass suasion is here to stay, and we will remain vulnerable to manipulation. We may now be more educated and technologically sophisticated than those whom Le Bon observed in the late nineteenth century, but we share with them our basic bio-psychological makeup. Moreover, given refinements to the practice of mass manipulation since then, we are perhaps more deeply enmeshed within the manipulation matrix than were our nineteenth century counterparts.

CHAPTER FIVE

Victims of the Dark Arts

TO UNDERSTAND THE subtle influences that impinge upon us as decision makers, imagine wanting to eat well. To that end, let's say that you factor in nutrition, quantity, taste, aroma, color, presentation, and perhaps other considerations like with whom you eat and the environment in which you dine, and things such as service and comfort.

In normal circumstances, you will try to be consistent with your desire to eat well. There will be times when you may splurge, but mostly you will follow your plan. Now suppose that you are very hungry. Let's say you haven't eaten all day. What will happen to your plan to eat well? Chances are you will be slightly irritated, in a somewhat bad mood, and ready to eat what is available. What if you are extremely hungry and on the verge of starvation? In that case, you will likely be very irritable, and hunger will become an all-consuming drive, so much so that you will reach for any food.

Cravings for food, drink, and sex, psychologists say, are visceral factors. So is a smoker's need for cigarettes and an addict's need for drugs; so are moods such as happiness and sadness; emotions such as anger, fear, and greed; and the sensation of physical pain. Especially at high levels of intensity, these factors make us behave in a manner that is not in our own long-term interest, even though we know at the time that our immediate actions are not good for us in the long run.

As residues from our animal past, these visceral factors are always present. Under normal conditions, they remain muted but lurk in the background and powerfully shape our daily routines. After all, our need for food has to be periodically satisfied and subtly governs where we go during the day. Similarly, recurring thirst reminds us that that we cannot be too far away from water for very long.

Yet, at high levels of intensity, these same visceral factors tend to dominate our very being. George Loewenstein of Carnegie Mellon University has proposed that the first effect of intense visceral factors is the very strong urge to satisfy them.[1] An intensely hungry person wants to satisfy hunger above everything else. The focus narrows to food, and all other considerations fade into the background, having little or no impact on decisions made in the moment.

The second effect of intense visceral factors is the need to satisfy them immediately. The time dimension shrinks to such an extent that long-term thinking goes out the window. Even when we are aware that a choice made in the moment will be against our own long-term interest, the need to satisfy the powerful urges simply trumps those remote considerations. The here-and-now reigns.

The third effect of intense visceral factors is that they go away as quickly as they come. Once hunger is satisfied, there is no way to remember the power it had over us until the next time it comes around. The intense craving makes us blind to life outside the moment. A starving person cannot quite recall how he or she felt when not hungry; a satiated person cannot recall how it felt when he or she was last starving. Because we cannot remember the previous intense experience of hunger, it is very difficult to anticipate and prepare for moments of intense hunger in the future; it is also difficult to comprehend the behavior of someone else who happens to be in the grip of hunger.

As with hunger, so it is with other visceral factors such as anger and fear, envy and greed, and extreme sadness. The result of these cravings, moods, and emotions is that when active in their full intensity, they override rational deliberation, or cool-headed thinking. People who are deliberative in normal circumstances make incredibly odd decisions when in the grip of a visceral urge.

In this way, along with psychological obstacles, such as belief persistence and confirmation bias, our biology also at times works against us when it comes to making good decisions. Together, all these factors make us highly vulnerable not only to making bad decisions by ourselves but also to being sold to or being taken advantage of by unscrupulous others. Let's discuss some of those situations.

Manipulation in Practice

In reporting the results of a survey conducted in 2005, the Federal Trade Commission (FTC) noted that 30.2 million people, or 13.5 percent of adults in the United States, self-reported as victims of fraud.[2] Weight loss products garnered the highest number of frauds reported at 4.8 million. Other frauds on the list were foreign lottery scams (3.2 million), unauthorized billing and buyers' clubs (3.2 million), prize promotions (2.7 million), work-at-home programs (2.4 million), credit card insurance (2.1 million), unauthorized billing for Internet services (1.8 million), advance-fee loans (1.7 million), credit repair scams (1.2 million), and business opportunities (0.8 million).

Of the medium used to reach their marks, perpetrators of fraud used print advertising (27 percent), Internet and email (22 percent), television and radio (21 percent), and telemarketing (9 percent). About 30 percent of the frauds reported occurred by other means, such as word of mouth. Victims in the study were mostly vulnerable populations, such as the elderly and the lonesome, usually in lower economic strata. Yet, even relatively affluent and sophisticated people routinely fall prey to fraud.

Consider the Ponzi scheme, made famous by and named for Charles Ponzi. The fraud involves the age-old trick of taking from Paul to pay Peter and swindling them both in the process. The usual modus operandi of Ponzi schemers is to manipulate emotions, especially greed, by promising very high returns with no risk. In reality, a Ponzi scheme works because money taken from later investors is used to pay the earlier ones, and the scheme collapses when new investors cannot be recruited any more or when existing investors want their money back in a hurry, as during panics or steep recessions.

Perhaps the most well known of recent Ponzi schemes is the one operated by Bernie Madoff. Unlike the usual victims of such schemes who are poor, elderly, and uneducated, those whom Madoff swindled were wealthy and financially sophisticated: hedge fund managers, royalty in Europe, and affluent retirees. They all fell victim to an elaborate ruse. Taking advantage of his high status in the financial community, Madoff conned his marks with the promise of moderate but steady and relatively risk-free returns. More important, he seems to have cruelly manipulated their trust in him, their apparent greed, and their lack of ability or motivation to do their own due diligence.

Like other master manipulators, Madoff seems to have been well versed in such common human emotions as greed for more money, desire for security, awe of authority, fear of asking questions, hope that everything was all right, and blind faith in a prestigious figure. Working deftly as if an expert puppeteer, he manipulated his associates and clients and bilked them of their life savings.

Madoff's bluff is famous because of the wide coverage it received in the media. But the Ponzi scheme is a common fraud perpetrated on unsuspecting victims with frightening regularity. The Securities and Exchange Commission (SEC) routinely reports such cases on its website.

In May 2014, for instance, the SEC charged Chicago investment fund manager Neal V. Goyal for employing a Ponzi scheme in which he raised over $11 million from unsuspecting clients. While his clients thought that he was productively investing their monies, he in fact used the funds to buy two homes, pay down mortgages, and generally invest in his own lavish lifestyle. In the same month, the SEC also charged Sarasota-based Gaeton "Guy" S. Della Penna with running a Ponzi scheme in which he raised $3.8 million from three investors—to whom he sent false statements of profits. In actuality, he had used $1 million of their money to pay down mortgages and spend on his girlfriend.

Reading through the SEC's website is sobering if for no other reason than seeing the frequency with which people in search of high returns are manipulated by unscrupulous operators. Even though the SEC was asleep at the wheel while Madoff built his fraudulent empire, the cases they do bring to light reveal the dangers we face from those who prey on our vulnerabilities.

Particularly disturbing is the fact that Ponzi schemes are now sophisticated operations involving teams of people working as if in a formal organization. Unlike the solo operation of Charles Ponzi, the scams nowadays are in many ways similar to the organized efforts that companies put in place to sell genuine products and services. This insertion of organization into the Ponzi scheme creates a special danger to the unsuspecting public.

Yet the Ponzi scheme is just one of its kind. The world is full of swindles such as pyramid schemes, affinity scams, pump-and-dump operations, and virtually infinite variations in which people willingly part with their money.

As Arthur Leff once argued in his brilliant book *Swindling and Selling*, there is little difference in the tactics that good salespeople and shrewd fraudsters use. Both are masters at gaining confidence and subtly manipulating the emotions of their targets. Given our vulnerabilities, the lack of distinction between the genuine and the disingenuous creates difficult problems for investors everywhere.

The Art of Manipulation

In a Fraud Forum organized by the FTC in February 2009,[3] researchers noted that even though the persuasion tactics used in frauds come in a wide variety of forms and mutate over time, their underlying structure is amenable to study. Forum participants presented the results of a project in which they used data from, among other things, 300 undercover audio recordings compiled by the American Association of Retired Persons (AARP) and the Financial Industry Regulatory Authority (FINRA).

According to the FTC analysis, the most common tactic used by fraudsters is "phantom fixation," which involves creating a phantom reward and telling one's marks that they have won something big. By fixing their attention on the reward, marks inhibit careful evaluation of the offer. The trick here is an old one: to raise the emotions of hope and greed and suppress the ability to reason.

The second psychological tactic used by fraudsters is to create a perception of scarcity: insisting that the deal of a lifetime is available only for a limited time. The psychological trick here is to make the mark feel rushed, again inhibiting the ability to logically evaluate the veracity of the offer.

The third psychological tactic used by fraudsters is to gain credibility in some way. As Le Bon long ago noted, prestige impresses people. Swindlers know this instinctively. Madoff, of course, had prestige. Swindlers sometimes fake prestige by claiming far more education and social status than they have and by outward displays of wealth through living an expensive lifestyle.

The fourth psychological tactic used in committing fraud is to use a comparison. The comparison may be genuine but is more likely to be fake, and fraudsters use it to create the impression that their offer is much better than anything else the mark could get. The psychological trick here is to create an anchor or benchmark against which the phantom offering looks much better—once again interfering with the reasoning process and forcing attention away from the offer, hiding it in plain sight.

The fifth psychological tactic used by fraudsters is to create imaginary social proof by strongly hinting that there are lots of other people already buying the opportunity or waiting for a chance to buy it. The psychological trick of this tactic is to give the impression that others have already evaluated the offer favorably so there is no need to evaluate it further.

The study also showed that not all five persuasion tactics worked equally well in all situations. Source credibility and phantom fixation were, for example, most common in investment frauds, although social proof and scarcity also played a role. In travel-related frauds, source credibility appeared to play no role at all, whereas phantom fixation and scarcity dominated as tactics. Fixation and scarcity were also common in sweepstakes and lottery frauds.

Fraudsters often take advantage of our inclinations to trust others and take things at face value. This trust instinct is, of course, important for living a stable and happy life, but it is one that unscrupulous operators deftly exploit. Then there is the illusion of control or invulnerability, with some thinking they are just too smart to be outsmarted, not realizing that this illusion itself creates the vulnerability, as fraudsters feed a sense of self-importance, navigating their way into a relationship of false trust.

As shrewd manipulators of emotions, con artists appear to be well aware of human frailties, not to mention the visceral factors that so powerfully influence our behavior. Loewenstein notes that they are experts at "rapidly invoking greed, pity, and other emotions that can eclipse deliberation and produce an override of normal behavioral restraints."[4]

Moreover, knowing that visceral influences subside rapidly, skillful fraudsters emphasize immediate action. Get on board now, they say, because the train is leaving the station; this a limited-time opportunity; this house will be snapped up, so buy now. Students of human behavior, as con artists are apt to be, they understand that visceral factors are their best friends, readily leveraged or deftly invoked to their advantage.

In the Stock Market

Aside from direct one-on-one fraud operations against them, people also lose money because they are swayed on a large scale to make poor choices. Whereas Ponzi schemes and other swindles typically involve operators who select their marks and organize to fleece them, the general climate, as portrayed in the media, can result in similar effects for those who invest in the stock market.

In a series of well-constructed studies over more than a decade, Professors Brad Barber and Terrance Odean presented strong evidence about how investors make bad choices. In a 2006 paper, for example, they showed that individual investors generally purchase only attention-grabbing stocks—those that are in the news, perhaps pitched on television or in cyberspace, and those that become noticeable because of high trading volume or recent extreme price movements.

The authors have built on the work of behavioral psychologists to argue that people make identifiable, systematic mistakes in their stock market decisions. For instance, they've shown that investors have a strong desire to avoid regret, which leads them to sell their winners too soon but hold on to losers too long. The authors have also shown that people are unnecessarily optimistic and overconfident in their abilities to make the correct decisions, which is why they may be subject to easy manipulation. Barber and Odean report that people trade too much and lower their returns; in one study, their returns were lowered by as much as 7 percent per year compared with what they could have attained by simply purchasing a market index.

The authors were more concerned with investor behavior than with motivation and did not delve more deeply into why people thought they could do better by trading more. Yet, it is no secret that our airwaves are filled with urgent pitches that flatter and encourage the gullible, tantalizing them with the possibilities of quick riches. In addition, the marketplace is overflowing with easy-to-use tools that facilitate trading. For those willing, not only is there a good deal of encouragement but also the means with which to do the buying and selling; a couple of key strokes, and the monkey is in the market!

To a lesser or greater extent, we are all capable of making bad decisions and being taken advantage of, especially when in the grip of any of the visceral factors. Deep biases in decision making and the ease with which persuaders penetrate our minds make for formidable obstacles for investors.

So, we need to understand how to overcome the various obstacles to good decision making, to guard against our emotional vulnerabilities, and to build good defenses against manipulative attacks originating in the financial media or elsewhere. In the next few chapters, therefore, I develop a conceptual framework for countering our many biases and vulnerabilities so that we may become better investors.

PART TWO

Verity

CHAPTER SIX

Logic—Data—Doubt

IN THIS CHAPTER, I briefly review four thinkers who wrestled with and clarified the process with which to separate truth from falsehood. You may wonder why I am continuing with, even belaboring, abstract philosophy when this book is really about the very practical problem of investing wisely. Bear with me.

The thinking reviewed here is crucial to understanding how to invest well. Finding, evaluating, and recognizing good investment opportunities is about thinking clearly and seeing potential investments for what they really are. By understanding how people over the centuries have tried to separate fact from illusion, investors can develop the mental processes necessary for separating genuine investment opportunities from those that only seem to be so. Investing is a mind game; learning how philosophers have thought about how the mind works is important for investors to learn and appreciate.

The desire to distinguish truth from falsity, reality from perception, substance from form, and value from hype has been with us since at least the time of the ancient Greeks. Sophists were skilled at blurring the lines between seemingly polar opposites and frustrating the claims of what seemed like straightforward truth. Perhaps instinctively, they recognized that a thing or idea could look very different depending on the perceiver. So, let's begin by reviewing early efforts to sort fact from fiction.

Logic and Deduction

"That some reasonings are genuine," Aristotle wrote in *Sophistical Refutations*, "while others seem to be so but are not, is evident.

This happens with arguments, as also elsewhere, through a certain likeness between the genuine and the sham."[1] In order to help separate valid arguments from tricks, he identified 13 fallacies that clarified the structure of the word plays and tricks that sophists used. To ward off such attacks, he suggested, we must understand the kinds of tricks the sophists used.[2]

Aristotle then went on to develop a systematic approach to creating knowledge in order to formally arrive at conclusions that could be defended against false attacks. To that end, he insisted that philosophical claims of knowledge were an enterprise in which the method was really the key and much more important than knowledge itself.

In a collection of six writings, which his followers later compiled as *Organon*, Aristotle offered a system of logic for making formal inferences. Now called term or traditional logic, this system consists of three parts: (1) terms that represent something, such as "tree" or "stock," but don't by themselves indicate right or wrong; (2) a major premise and a minor premise; and (3) an inference that necessarily follows from a logical combination of the term with major and minor premises.

That is, Aristotle argued that if you define terms properly and then take some things as given, then you can draw conclusions that are different from those suppositions but which naturally follow from them. So, if you suppose that all men are pious (major premise), and Rob is a man (minor premise), then Rob is pious (conclusion). Conversely, every valid conclusion must have within it underlying premises that are held to be true, and those premises must themselves be built on well-defined terms.

Syllogism, the kind of logic developed by Aristotle, has been influential in Western thought ever since it was first developed; it was the dominant mode of thinking until it was eventually supplanted by modern versions of logic, most notably by predicate logic and other higher logics that encode much more complex reasoning and make liberal use of mathematical notation. Still, syllogism persists and remains valid today.

Syllogism was also crucial to how Descartes developed his method. Calling his method deductive reasoning, Descartes extended Aristotle's argument that a conclusion is valid if it necessarily follows from a set of two or more premises. That is, deductive reasoning involves drawing a conclusion based on a combination of existing statements that we take to be true.

So, up until the early seventeenth century, and the time of Descartes, the dominant mode of trying to understand reality continued to be strongly influenced by the Aristotelian doctrine of deriving conclusions from presupposed statements taken as given. Yet, the syllogistic or deductive method of knowledge discovery was nonempirical—driven by pure logic and thinking alone. That is, the premises used in deductive logic came from conceptions of reality and not direct experiences of it; premises could be subject to biases and prejudices, as they often were—and yielded conclusions (often delusions) largely unsupported by reliable facts. This meant that you could justify a preferred conclusion by simply choosing to use any premises that supported that conclusion.

If it turns out that not all men are pious, the conclusion from the original syllogism that Rob is pious would be wrong, even though it is consistent with the (faulty) premise that all men are pious. In other words, if the major premise is taken as a given but is, in fact, a faulty product of your imagination or some pernicious bias, then the conclusion will be logically correct but still an outright mistake.

Data and Induction

This prescientific approach to knowledge creation remained chronically burdened by an overreliance on premises based on mystery and myth. For an eternity, passions and pre-existing beliefs incited human action. Once the public decided that an accused woman was a witch, as in Salem, Massachusetts, for example, it was then easy to come up with supporting but faulty premises to confirm that the accused was indeed a witch and, therefore, deserving of torture and execution.

But the significance of sensory data was not lost on all. Among those who put faith in observation and data was the English polymath Francis Bacon. A restless intellect and a brilliant thinker, Bacon applied his significant talents to the dissatisfactions he had with the Aristotelian dogma. He questioned the validity of conclusions derived purely through deductive reasoning. Where the establishment bowed to Aristotle, Bacon felt it was time to move on.

Playing on Aristotle's *Organum*, in 1620 Bacon published *Novum Organum* (*The New Instrument*), in which he presented the method of induction and detailed how to create scientific knowledge through a formal process of verification. Instead of ignoring data because of concerns about sensory distortions, he argued that systematically gathering, organizing, and evaluating data was at the center of building sound knowledge. Instead of taking premises for granted and deducing conclusions from logic alone, Bacon insisted that real data be used to verify premises. Empirical verification was to be at the center of scientific inquiry.

"Those who simply assert the laws of nature do great injury to science and philosophy," Bacon wrote in the preface to the book.[3] Inducing belief through professional affectations, with claims that cannot be verified outside of pure logic, was harmful; it created empty dogmas and quashed inquiry. Empirical verification was necessary, he argued, precisely because the human mind is highly vulnerable to sundry influences; claims of knowledge derived from pure logic could be grossly misleading.

Pure deduction was inadequate for true understanding, Bacon explained, because deep-rooted false notions beset people's minds. He clarified false notions as idols of the tribe, idols of the den, idols of the marketplace, and idols of the theater; he discussed each in detail to show how difficult it was for people to filter out influences and see things for what they truly were. It is natural for people, Bacon argued, to look for more order and regularity than may exist in the world. This need for order creates dreams and fancies that reinforce both false notions and rigidity. Once people adopt an opinion, they are drawn to all evidence that supports and agrees with that opinion, and they despise that which is contrary to their opinion.

The human mind is unquiet, he went on, and always in motion; we continually seek something beyond, for explanations about universal laws when in fact we are confined by the natural limits of our own understanding. Humans, Bacon argued, are inclined to believe readily whatever they wish:

> He [Man] rejects difficult things from impatience of research; sober things, because they narrow hope; the deeper things of nature, from superstition; the light of experience, from arrogance and pride, lest his mind should seem to be occupied with things mean and transitory; things not commonly believed, out of deference to the opinion of the vulgar. Numberless, in short, are the ways, and sometimes imperceptible, in which the affections color and infect the understanding.

The limitations of the human mind are so extreme and deeply entrenched, Bacon insisted, that simply willing them away is impossible. The only way to prevent such limitations from corrupting the scientific enterprise is to develop sound methods that systematically attend to them. He agreed with Aristotle that the focus ought to be not on knowledge per se but on the method of its production, but he strongly disagreed on what those methods ought to be.

Bacon's insights are important for investors to understand because deeply embedded human flaws are often the reason for costly mistakes in investing. The most pressing problems in investing, it is evident, are within us. Given that we are prone to distorting facts to our liking or ignoring them altogether, the principal task for investors is to understand how to manage and correct the deep flaws that lie within themselves.

Once he had shown the difficulties in seeing clearly and thinking independently, Bacon went on to discuss how to overcome those difficulties. Instead of relying on pure thought, he argued, real-world data are central to producing knowledge. Instead of ignoring the world around us, we need to develop methods to make sure that our data are not corrupt. A robust, data-driven method is the key.

The necessary defense against the natural distortions in our thinking, Bacon argued, is in what he called inductive reasoning. Instead of basing premises on opaque beliefs or relying on priors based on faith or tradition, he urged that we base our premises on empirical evidence, on data. Results are invalid if underpinned by faulty premises or shoddy evidence. Wholly empirical, the Baconian (or scientific) method was different from deductive reasoning, which it sought to supplant. Although he did not entirely reject syllogism and deduction, Bacon urged empiricism, in which direct observation informs premises, which, being data driven, then logically combine to produce valid conclusions.

Suppression of Belief

Bacon's insistence on planned procedure constitutes an indispensable element of scientific inquiry to this day. Of course, the scientific method has been much refined over the centuries, but the basic acknowledgement of natural biases and the need to guard against them we owe to

Bacon. Yet, inductive reasoning, too, has drawn a strong contingent of skeptics who oppose it on two grounds. First, they argue, the supposition that you can uncover general laws by marshaling empirical evidence is suspect. How can universal truths be uncovered from particulars? When you collect evidence, how are you to know that the particular sample you are examining adequately represents the entire population to which the results may be generalized? How much evidence do you need to be able to say that what you see really does reflect an underlying truth?

If there have been no devastating accidents in the nuclear arsenal of the American military, can we be sure that there will be no such accidents in the future, or even in the very next moment? Nassim Taleb provides an example: The more white swans the Europeans saw over the centuries, the stronger became their taken-for-granted assumption that swans were of no other color. Yet, as is now widely reported, a Dutch explorer eventually discovered the black swan in the southern hemisphere.

In effect, the first objection to inductive reasoning is that all the empirical evidence you collect may mislead you by drawing attention to available evidence at the expense of truly important facts that are simply unavailable or unobserved at the time of analysis. Even if your methods are sound, in other words, the evidence may be insufficient for you to draw conclusions; worse, it may be sufficient for you to draw wrong conclusions.

If stock prices have generally gone up in the long run, does it mean that they will always go up? Could past occurrences be the exception to the rule, not a reflection of future events?

The second, stronger objection to inductive reasoning is in the strong confirmation bias that plagues decision making. Bacon clearly saw the tendency for people to try to confirm what they already believe. But he still underestimated the strength of such bias and overestimated the ability of induction to overcome it. The method of induction fell short of overcoming the very biases and distortions that Bacon had outlined with his four idols.

The Falsification Way

Objections to induction were forcefully articulated by such eighteenth century thinkers as David Hume. But it was the Austrian living in twentieth century England, Karl Popper, who formally articulated the chief solution to the problem of induction. Reminiscent of Aristotle's desire for separating good reasoning from false argumentation, Popper was concerned with "distinguishing between a genuinely empirical method and a nonempirical or even a pseudo-empirical method—that is to say, a method which, although it appeals to observation and experiment, nevertheless does not come up to scientific standards."[4]

In a 1953 chapter on how he solved the problem of induction, Popper explained that data collection and analysis alone did not make something valid as scientific knowledge. Astrology, for example, was not a science even though it was characterized by a stupendous amount of data. It was more myth than science.

To argue his point, Popper used examples from Marxism, Freudian psychoanalysis, and Adlerian individual psychology. These he described as being less science, like astronomy, and more primitive myth, like astrology. This is how he explained his thinking:

> I found that those of my friends who were admirers of Marx, Freud, and Adler were impressed by a number of points common to these theories, and especially by their apparent *explanatory power*. . . . [T]he study of any of them seemed to have the effect of an intellectual conversion or revelation, opening your eyes to a new truth hidden from those not yet initiated. Once your eyes were thus opened you saw confirming instances everywhere: the world was full of *verifications* of the theory. . . . [T]he most characteristic element in this situation seemed to me the incessant stream of confirmations, of observations which "verified" the theories in question; and this point was constantly emphasized by their adherents.

To Popper, this was a grave problem: How do you distinguish claims based on legitimate empirical methods from those that may be corrupted by our many human frailties?

Popper's response to this long-standing problem of inductive reasoning was to turn the tables on Bacon. Instead of collecting evidence to prove your hypothesis, Popper argued that the correct scientific approach is to try to falsify your expectations. In a brilliant twist, he noted that whereas there is always a strong incentive, but never enough evidence, to conclusively prove your hypothesis, a single counterexample may be sufficient to disprove it. So, instead of justifying or verifying, we must falsify.

What distinguishes science from nonscience, Popper reasoned, is not simply that one is empirical and the other not. The real difference is that we must clearly express scientific knowledge so that we may empirically falsify it. We must be able to take the risk of disconfirming our knowledge. The emphasis is still on observation and data, but the shift is in what to do with those data.

Empiricism says nothing about the quality of thinking involved. Instead, scientific knowledge requires that we use data to challenge our beliefs. The reason that psychoanalysis is not science, Popper wrote, is that therapists use data gathered during clinical sessions to apply or verify, rather than falsify, the basic premises of psychoanalysis. The more you see data confirming what you already believe, the more likely it is that you may be falling prey to confirmation bias, and the greater is the caution warranted through empirical falsification.

By insisting on falsification, Popper also made truth inaccessible. You can never be sure about the truth of a situation. The inability to falsify a thesis at a given time does not mean that the next effort to falsify it will not succeed; even repeated failed efforts to falsify do not mean that the next effort at falsification will not succeed. All scientific laws or "truths" are subject to the risk of disconfirmation, in other words, and all scientific knowledge is tentative by its very nature.

The Investor as Philosopher

Through the labors of a long line of thinkers, we now understand that good decisions require the careful application of logic, data, and doubt. Together, these provide some protection against the many corrupting influences on our ways of thinking and making choices.

Logic and data best serve the path to knowledge when we use them not to confirm but to challenge our beliefs. What we need is a mental orientation of skepticism, a constant search for well-constructed empirical evidence that challenges or negates what we think we already know. Systematic empirical skepticism, or falsification, incorporates both careful logic and good data.

More than 2,000 years removed from the labors of Plato and Aristotle, half a millennium after Bacon wrote his masterpiece, and nearly a century after Popper began his studies, we now have a method with which to tackle the frailties of the human mind. As investors, we must take heed.

So, negation is the approach we will take to frame investment decisions. In the chapters that follow, I show how to set up an investment hunch as a thesis and how to then try to cast doubt on that thesis using both quantitative and qualitative data. If the investment thesis survives serious efforts to create doubt and disconfirm it, we then have a good basis for confidently making investment decisions.

CHAPTER SEVEN

Investing as a Negative Art

IN *SECURITY ANALYSIS*, Benjamin Graham and David Dodd discuss the psychological problems of investment analysis, problems that become daunting because of the array of confusing cues emanating from the churn of the markets and the noisy coverage of the media. Their approach to solving those problems is noteworthy because how they define the task of analysis is as important, if not more so, than what they may think about any particular investment situation.

For instance, when discussing the principles of bond selection, the authors emphasize that bond selection is a negative art because, given the limited upside, losses can be costly without the corresponding potential for high gain.[1] I submit that this cautious approach is valid for all securities, including stocks, because the hope of gain intensifies confirmation bias, easily leading investors to throw caution to the wind and behave like speculators.

It is for this reason that clear thinking when investing rests largely on our willingness and ability to disconfirm the prior beliefs we bring to an evaluation. That is the method of the philosopher and, arguably, a method for sound investing. This method of analysis is the key, as it incorporates not only good technique but also the correct temperament to seek and approach data with appropriate skepticism.

Given the noises of the market and the hubbub in the psyche of the analyst, like Graham, we, too, need to be suspicious of pure deduction, of logic alone. Like Francis Bacon, we should insist on empiricism, on collecting data, on quantifying, and on establishing standards and benchmarks. Of course, data can be faulty and misleading, but a good analyst should have the skills to detect faults in the reported information. Investors must learn to make decisions based not on conjectures and vague premises but on guarded judgments grounded in good data.

Precisely because analysis is vulnerable to corruption from confirmation bias and its many cousins, a mental orientation of refutation and disconfirmation is paramount. Instead of trying to verify that a given investment is good or bad, as we may be inclined to believe from hearsay, half-truths, and initial impressions, we must use sound, data-driven judgments to sort through to the core truths about an investment candidate. Investors must be quantitative and, aware of the hazards of investing, guarded in their evaluation and interpretation of facts. Disconfirmation is key, method is king, and a conservative orientation is indispensable for investing wisely.

It is impossible, of course, to know for sure the incontrovertible truth about an investment opportunity. Still, perhaps more than any other method, a systematic process of disconfirmation can get us closer to correct evaluation because it forces our attention on facts that challenge our beliefs, facts that we'd rather ignore because they are so psychologically painful for us to confront.

Graham did not explicitly mention disconfirmation as an approach to investment analysis. I suspect he knew about it instinctively, but not enough to articulate it as succinctly as Popper did when he identified empirical falsification as being central to scientific rigor. Born in 1894, Graham was a practical man of money; born in 1902, Popper was an academic philosopher. The need to cut through the noise inspired Graham, and he excelled at working through the haze of the markets. Understanding the nature of knowledge inspired Popper, and he excelled at working through the problem of intellectual integrity. Graham wanted to solve the age-old problem of trying to make a buck without being run over by the herd; Popper wanted to solve an age-old philosophical problem of knowing: How do we know what we think we know?

Two very different men, Popper and Graham, but both had the same deep desire to find and draw that line of demarcation: between science and nonscience for the philosopher; between investment and speculation for the investor.

Investment Versus Speculation

Popper used falsification as a line of demarcation between science and nonscience, arguing that while knowledge comes in many forms, *scientific* knowledge demands testability and empirical falsification. Similarly, for those seeking to make good investing choices, testability and disconfirmation mark the line of demarcation between investment and speculation.

Investments are opportunities that risk being rejected because they may not live up to specific criteria. Opportunities are speculative when they do not risk rejection; they may be justified in one way or another, but they cannot formally be set up for refutation.

It's important to note that Popper articulated the method of empirical falsification to help strengthen scientific research in natural sciences such as physics and astronomy, which aim to uncover fixed laws that are unalterable by human action. We can only approximate his methods in the social sciences and the humanities. Unlike the natural sciences, where we collect and analyze a plethora of replicable, objective data, in the social sciences—and in investing—data are transient products of human behavior. Some have claimed that social phenomena are objective social facts,[2] but they don't go further to claim that social data are as objective as, for example, observations of magnetic waves and solar radiation.

Popper's falsification is but one example of the larger *principle of negation* that has been a consistent theme in Western thought. It is a particular form of doubt and draws from a broader orientation of being skeptical and cautious about beliefs. This inclination to doubt, especially self-doubt, has clearly been present among thinkers since at least the age of the sophists in classical Greece. Skepticism and doubt remain relevant outside the natural sciences,[3] too, such as in investing endeavors. Modern researchers agree that good decisions require a deft combination of tentative verification and outright disconfirmation to build confidence in a given point of view. Sound logic and relevant data are the keys, but both in the spirit of trying to negate whatever the initial and emergent beliefs may be.

Still, given the variability of data and subjectivity intrinsic to social phenomena, rejecting an investment thesis on a single observation is naïve. Instead, disconfirmation is a process that formalizes a mental orientation of skepticism—one that helps an individual attain a deep and holistic understanding of the investment under scrutiny. If it turns out, for instance, that the firm under consideration has low profitability or high financial leverage, these factors are not by themselves sufficient reasons to refute the investment thesis. Instead, disconfirmation analysis helps one develop judgments about the safety, suitability, and potential of the investment under scrutiny. Investors should reject a thesis when it violates some key principle of good investment (e.g., poor leadership). They may also reject a thesis when several different tests weaken it to such an extent that it is no longer viable in light of available evidence.

For instance, if you have a thesis that a particular stock is a good investment, you would evaluate that thesis by setting up a series of subtheses about, say, the financial strength of the company. You test this subthesis by examining a set of quantities (e.g., cash flows and debt capacity) that indicate the financial strength of the company. You may choose not to reject the subthesis if only one of the many quantities indicates financial weakness, with all others being indications of strength. Financial weakness will, however, cast doubt on the thesis, and this doubt will carry through the analysis eventually to be evaluated in light of the overall sense of the company under scrutiny.

In essence, rather than reject a thesis based on a single quantity or even a set of quantities, you try to disconfirm it on an overall judgment based on the totality of tests. It is important not to lose sight of the overall picture when applying this approach. Disconfirmation is also an exercise in sorting through a large number of investment candidates that may look equally attractive.

Descartes, you may remember, doubted everything and used doubt as the key to uncovering and rejecting false knowledge. In a similar vein, disconfirmation can weed out investment candidates that only seem attractive but are not truly so. Refutation is an inductive method of doubt; when used well, it leads you to investment opportunities that are truly attractive, having survived well-calibrated skepticism.

The tasks ahead of us are to define the criteria we should use for disconfirming investment theses and then to outline how we should apply such an approach in practice. Before we do that, however, I present thoughts on how to generate falsifiable investment theses, how to think about errors, and how to look for potentially good investment ideas.

CHAPTER EIGHT

Shaping the Investment Thesis

TAKE A QUICK glance at the figure below. What do you see? Now take another slower look. Start at the bottom left corner, and trace the line along all the edges. What do you see now?

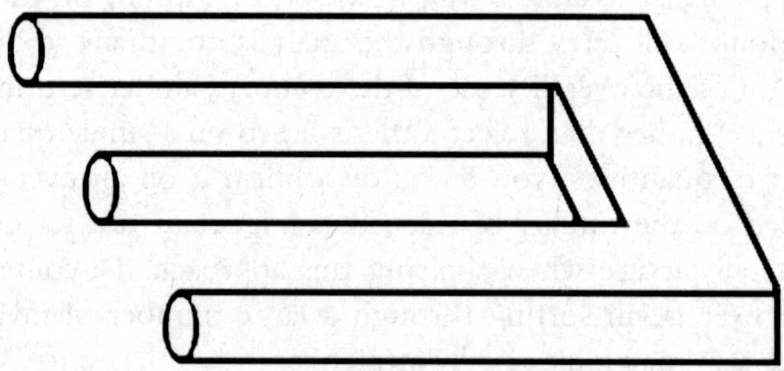

The figure is an optical illusion[1] that shows three prongs when the eyes fix on the left and a U-shape when fixation shifts to the right. Only when the eye sweeps horizontally or along the edges does the impossibility of the figure become evident. Among other things, the figure shows that the mind, always in motion, readily supplies the information necessary for forming the patterns we expect or want to see. That is, as if in a hurry, the mind wants to jumps to conclusions. Yet, this exercise also shows that, by shifting focus and closely following the facts of the case, we can correct the wrong impressions.

In this chapter, I briefly discuss the native and powerful tendencies of the mind to generate ideas and patterns, both real and imaginary—and the ongoing need for us to sort through those to form correct impressions of reality. For investors, such tendencies of the mind suggest that we must always be on guard against settling on wrong impressions, but also that we can leverage the powerful processes of the mind to strengthen the investment process.

Clearly, sciences of the mind are vast and rapidly evolving fields of study; we cannot fully evaluate those here. I will, therefore, simplify and extract a few intuitions directly relevant for us as investors—especially about how we may be able to intervene in the natural processes of the mind to sharpen our thinking and uncover useful insights.

Discovering the Falsifiable

As we have seen, the falsification framework exhorts investors to exercise disciplined skepticism that, when backed by sound logic and suitable data, seeks to disconfirm entrenched beliefs that could distort thought and corrupt analysis—forcing unforced investment errors. As a method rooted in the principle of negation, falsification encourages a cautious frame of mind with which to evaluate an investment thesis and see if the underlying idea is worthy of confident commitments of capital.

Making good investment decisions is not simply about falsifying, however; it is most of all about generating worthy ideas. Wise investing requires, in fact, a two-step mental process: (1) generating investment ideas; and (2) sorting good ideas from bad ones. Without the editing function of falsification, a stream of ideas quickly deteriorates into incoherence. Yet, good ideas are the medium through which the principle of negation operates, so idea generation remains at the heart of the investing process.

Good investment theses do sometimes emerge from actively trying to falsify obviously entrenched beliefs. For instance, consider the once entrenched belief that noninvestment-grade bonds defaulted at a much higher rate than investment-grade bonds, so much so that the former were considered simply too speculative for investors seeking safety. Formal analysis of reams of data revealed, however, that default rates for the former were much lower than conventionally believed. This insight led to a booming market in "junk" bonds and, in spite of some notable excesses, facilitated the financing of many worthy projects. Similarly, those who saw in empirical data reasons to question and then break away from the long-held belief that mortgage bonds do not default benefitted handsomely when the market for mortgage-backed securities (MBSs) collapsed during the 2007–2008 financial crisis.

Yet, an investment thesis rarely emerges fully formed. The examples of junk bonds and MBSs seem brilliant in hindsight, but there is more to it than the retrospective accounts suggest. Why did some investors question the entrenched beliefs? How did they even think to look for breaks in those then conventional notions?

Where Popper focused on empirical falsification as the engine of scientific progress, he was mostly silent about how to develop and nurture new ideas. In practice, falsification as he conceived it is too strong an instrument to apply to ideas in their infancy. New ideas are often initially vague and hard to grasp because they run counter to native intelligence; even good new ideas are easily nipped in the bud because they cannot stand up to the harsh, data-intensive scrutiny that proper falsification demands.

The Idea Machine

Most scientific discovery begins as a hunch, from a sense that something is amiss, that something interesting is up. This inner world of insight and intuition, what Michael Polanyi called tacit awareness because we cannot articulate it, is the fountain of creative thought. As students of investing, we must understand this inner world of discovery so that we may learn to nurture and shape the best ideas emerging from such a fountain into credible investment theses—which we may then evaluate using the formal method of empirical skepticism.

The starting point for understanding the creative process of developing investment ideas is to become aware of how we handle information in our environment. Researchers have long argued that we simply do not have enough bandwidth—neural capacity—to handle the innumerable cues that relentlessly bombard each of our senses.[2] There is just too much information around us. So, a key function of the brain is selective attention: we pay attention to something by ignoring everything else. What do we pay attention to, and what do we ignore? Without active acts of will, habits are what drive attention; in scientific terms, habits are simply well-worn neurological pathways encoded in the physical brain, as markers of past experiences.

Even though we pay attention to only some information, the vast streams of unattended sensory impressions hover just outside our consciousness and exert unrelenting influence on what we are directly aware of. Even as you read these words, for instance, you are aware of so much more: sounds, smells, skin sensations, objects in our peripheral vision, and so forth.

This *fringe*, as William James once called it, influences us in ways both subtle and obvious, leaking in and out of consciousness as our attention wavers, shifting with context, and constantly changing our perception of focal objects. Cues in the fringe come into focus when we explicitly pay attention to them, only to push the object previously in focus into the background to merge with the silent, shadowy context.

Direct awareness and the fringe sit atop deep layers of the unconscious, the incredible machinery of the brain of which we have no conscious awareness. Yet, the unconscious is strongly implicated in how we perceive and relate to the world around us. Both the fringe and the unconscious have strong bearing on focal awareness, on what we see and how we see it.

Researchers estimate that the human brain has upward of 100 billion nerve cells. The cerebral cortex alone comprises up to 55 billion neurons, each pulsating electrochemical signals at an average of 40 per second—to produce up to 6,000 billion events per second through hundreds of millions of fibers.[3] The massive information processing capabilities of the brain come from a highly decentralized structure comprising millions of specialist clusters of neurons, all engaged in innumerable interlocking tasks and routines. Although out of reach of conscious awareness, these deep capacities of the brain do the yeoman's work in helping us deal with and sort through the vast amounts of information in which we are always embedded. Left on their own, these brain functions remain focused on tasks necessary for the routine functioning of the brain; when harnessed intelligently, they can be powerful generators of insights and creativity.

The Logic of Tacit Inference

Michael Polanyi once noted that understanding how the mind works can teach us a lot about how scientists discover breakthrough ideas. He explained that nonexplicit thought and intuition propel new ideas;

while conscious awareness sets direction, the fringe and the unconscious provide the energy to power the discovery process.

For Polanyi, perception is the result of tacit powers of the mind integrating millions of small cues into coherent patterns. Perception, or the comprehension of an object, is not just what we see with our eyes; it is the integration of visual cues with subliminal cues, such as those from the inner ear, and marginal cues, such as those from the corner of the eye. We do not directly pay attention to these peripheral or subsidiary cues, but without them, we cannot really comprehend the object of our attention. Perception is, by definition, cue integration and pattern recognition—a product of automatic and fluid mental processes that are beyond the level of conscious awareness. Creativity requires actively harnessing such mental processes.

Like science, investing advances by shrewdly harnessing processes of the mind to develop new ideas and evolve them into testable theses. Falsification plays a role, of course, but much later in the process; it is best to use falsification for editing and managing the fountain of patterns, not for snuffing them out in their infancy.

Idea Generation: Processes and Pitfalls

With this background, let's review how investors can bring creativity to the investment process. Actively seeking new ideas requires that we avoid rigidly fixating on just a few facts, instead fluidly scanning both focal and peripheral facts and being aware that some facts will remain outside our conscious awareness. For instance, novel ideas emerge from consciously engaging in mental exercises such as the following: seeing sameness and distinctions between concepts, seeing relationships among concepts, noticing similarities or analogies between pattern fragments, shifting boundaries by grouping and ungrouping concepts, and generalizing from facts to build abstractions such that specifics begin to be seen as special cases in some conceptual template.[4]

Idea generation, furthermore, is not simply a dry analytical skill but invokes a sense of aesthetics, an artistic flair for making connections and generalizations, for fluidly moving between the abstract and the concrete, between theory and data, in ways that allow fresh insights into the seemingly mundane. It is perhaps for this reason that Polanyi was dissatisfied with Popper's focus on explicit inference and insisted, instead, that tacit powers of integration and pattern making were central to generating new insights.

At its most advanced level, creatively developing fresh insights about investment prospects requires mentally exploring patterns, combining them with other patterns or disaggregating them, and conceptually juggling ideas. Indispensable in all this is having a sixth sense about which pathways are most promising and most likely to be productive for the task at hand.

Analogies are central to perceiving patterns and new ideas. They leverage perceptual processes to mentally scan objects of interest by, for instance, requiring the mind to slip from object sameness to abstract resemblances. For instance, 4 and 6 are different digits but also similar in that they both are single digits divisible by 2; they are the same in that they both belong to the same class of (even) numbers. This ability of the mind to shift or "slip" between different, similar, and the same, allows generalizations and pattern sensitivity. Such slippage can be a small skip, as in the above example, or a deep shift, as when you see abstract resemblance between two very different situations such as, say, structural similarities between two companies in different industries. Actively slipping from one situation to another can reveal interesting possibilities that would otherwise not be visible. So, analogies allow smooth transitioning from a central idea or concept to contiguous ones, creating what Douglas Hofstadter calls the commonsense halo.

Consider an illustration. As oil prices rise, you begin to sense the positive impact on oil exporters, such as Iran and Russia, and on producers of alternative forms of energy. You begin to see the negative impact on oil-importing countries, such as India and Japan, and on oil-dependent industries, such as trucking and plastics. You may begin to anticipate airfares going up and air traffic suffering, which will also negatively impact rental cars and hotels. You may see the suppliers into these industries feeling the pressure but suppliers to oil companies benefiting from increasing demand for their products or services in anticipation of oil producers reinvesting fattening cash flows.

Such an expanding conceptual sphere, or expansion of thinking from the core observation of increasing oil prices, may continue ad nauseam, the central concept slipping fluidly via analogies into areas that are further and further away from the initial thought.

Yet, lurking in this fluidity are dangers for those seeking concrete investment theses from the ever-expanding jumble of ideas that the mind so easily creates. The pattern-making proclivities of the mind expand in all directions through slippage and chains of connections with ever-larger sets of seemingly similar mental objects. Unless actively controlled, this process is prone to expand one's thinking so much so that later ideas connect at best tenuously with the original idea. Each idea becomes a candidate for a new core, forming the basis for another abstract chain of connections.

Not only is the mind prone to meandering and wandering, in fact, the patterns that take shape may themselves be imaginary or incorrectly track a reality that ought to be grounding the investment process. As we saw in the geometrical illusion presented at the beginning of the chapter, it's easy to see patterns where none exist, or different ones from those that do. Unlike the concrete figure in that example, however, the problem becomes more acute when the object of imagination is an idea or concept not directly in contact with any of our five senses.

Shaping the Investment Thesis

On the one hand is the vast potential that we carry in our craniums, and so is the fluidity with which we deploy incredible mental capabilities in varieties of daily tasks. And on the other hand are the in-built biases, peculiarities, and breakdowns of mental processes. Our mental machinery is powerful but prone to serious error.

Given the vastness of the investment world, we can form many different varieties of investment theses. Given the type of security or investment objectives or orientation of the investor, the specifics of the ideas to build into testable theses will vary. Below I develop some general principles based on the discussions above, so that we can, over time, learn to apply those to form credible and testable investment theses.

Conceptual Context

Limitless wandering of the mind does not necessarily mean limitless possibilities. Uncontrolled slippage from idea to idea has the potential to throw up lots of false impressions, dissipating attention and energy through fact checking ideas that ultimately prove unproductive. Hence, it's important to control the idea-generation process by establishing a context or theme in which to contain our mental wanderings. Such containment does not have to be within airtight boundaries, as reaching elsewhere to make associations remains important, but some broad limits to wandering are necessary.

Usually, the context is always already limited because the fringe and the unconscious greatly influence what we see and how we see it. These out-of-awareness limits become operational through what psychologists call *priming* and *fixedness*.[5]

Priming is the notion that whatever we are thinking about in one instance influences how we interpret the very next concept that comes along. The fringe and the unconscious simply absorb the events, ideas, and concepts we come across and automatically make meaning of them in our "inner" context. For instance, we interpret the word "cold" differently depending on whether we are thinking of beer or weather or emotional disposition. A fundamental psychological process that can sometimes limit understanding, priming is also central to the learning process; it indicates the commonsense view that we make meaning of new information based on what we already know.

Fixedness refers to rigidity arising from unconscious assumptions that provide the backdrop against which we interpret sensations and information. Fixated on a few salient facts, we jump to conclusions before all the evidence comes in and, now captured by the inner context, tend to resist changing our initial interpretation. We may think, for example, that the spectacular historical record of a company makes it a good investment candidate and resist changing that view even though the competitive landscape has significantly changed. Without critically evaluating the company afresh, we are liable to fall into the trap of getting fixated on past records and ignore relevant new information. In the extreme, fixation is the opposite of slippage.

When generating falsifiable investment theses, therefore, investors must try to systematically leverage priming effects and avoid extreme fixedness or extreme slippage. This requires setting the conceptual context for one or more closely related investment themes, loosely defining the boundaries within which to explore those themes, and then using priming and analogy to critically evaluate central facts that define the subject matter at hand.

As an illustration of this process, imagine that you want to explore investment ideas in the transportation sector. You immerse yourself in the subject matter by reading deeply into industry reports and company literature. Once so primed, you then let loose with ideas but keep coming back to the core theme of transportation. As you get deeper into the theme, priming and slipping to develop nuanced understanding, you begin to lightly fixate so as to gradually narrow and sharpen the theme to, say, freight carriers. Continuing to hone ideas so generated may eventually lead to those that are sharp enough to shape into testable theses, yet broad enough to remain open to further analogies.

Mental Orientation

Along with the conceptual context, the correct mental orientation must guide idea generation to channel the mind toward high-potential pathways. What those pathways specifically are depends, of course, on the objective at hand, but the purpose of such containment is to preserve attention and energy for the most promising potential investigations. While free-associating and following hunches wherever they may lead can be productive, putting up self-imposed limits on which pathways to follow concentrates mental resources and provides deep insights into a delimited set of possibilities.

Mental orientation is the direction in which you want to move your mental energies and how you choose to do so. For instance, while the broader theme of transportation could take you in many different directions, you may choose to follow the narrower pathway of "moving stuff" rather than "moving people," or you may decide that a particularly appealing direction to pursue is moving stuff internationally, by sea. Directionality brings you closer to sharp, testable theses.

How you move along the pathway of choice is important as well. You may choose to be experimental and aggressive, or you may choose to act more defensively. You may throw up many ideas without regard to quality and roughly test multiple theses to narrow down a smaller list, or you may obsessively fact check at every turn and be selective about what to investigate with great depth and vigor. How you move down your chosen pathway depends on where you are in the search process, but it is often governed by temperament.

Given the potential for errors in judgment and the associated costs, it's helpful to have a realistically skeptical and defensive orientation when moving on a pathway of ideas. Remember that the end goal of such an exercise is still only an explicit thesis, which you will try to forcefully and empirically falsify. Even so, a defensive mental orientation early in the search process will yield testable theses that are robust and credible, and which will make later evaluation more productive.

Data and Patterns

Given that the mind is forever seeking patterns where none may exist, it is easy to spin fanciful stories and then get lost in those. What we need is a sophisticated sensitivity to data and an affinity for fact checking that encourages us to look for meaningful facts that ground investment ideas in concrete reality. Such data may be secondary, as in databases, or primary, as those obtained via interviews and direct personal observation.

More important than isolated facts is the ability to leverage proclivities of the mind to uncover deep patterns. Uncovering interesting and nonobvious patterns in the data, and the dynamics within those patterns, is what separates great investors from those who are merely good.

The importance of this pattern-uncovering ability is clearly on display in many places outside investing. A casual football fan, for example, is unlikely to see the deep patterns visible to, say, experienced defensive coordinators. In fact, of all the capabilities that high-quality coaches bring to their craft, the chief among them is their ability to sew the skill attributes of individual players into different patterns as the situation demands. High-performing coaches are highly skilled at reading the patterns thrown at them by opposing coaches and constructing their own in anticipation. Seen this way, more than the result of the talents and skills of the players, a good football game is a highly complex interaction between patterns of offense and defense.

Pattern recognition is more complex in as abstract an endeavor as investing, of course. Unlike football, investing involves a great variety of players acting out their hopes and fears in an abstract space and with much ambiguity about the rules. Even so, pattern recognition remains an important ability, and the quality of the patterns uncovered greatly influences the quality and testability of the investment thesis. For this, investors require some ability to work with large quantities of data and to sort through multiple lines of narratives. High-level play in any field of endeavor demands strong pattern recognition as the price of entry. Investing is no different.

Major and Minor Theses

A plausible way to develop the investment process is to nest minor theses about sharply specified situations within a major thesis about broad trends. Often, a sound major thesis emerges from mismatches in clearly identified macro patterns, such as those between patterns in supply of and demand for broad categories of products and services or commodities. For instance, in highly liquid markets where trading is unhindered, fluid price adjustments quickly correct minor supply–demand mismatches; prevailing prices seamlessly clear the available supplies. Sometimes, however, major disruptions in supply or a sudden change in demand upsets the balance, thus providing openings for alert investors to step in even as the bidding processes in relevant markets bring the two rapidly back in line.

Starting in the second half of 2014, there was a seemingly sudden major mismatch between the supply and demand for crude oil. Anemic growth in most of the developed economies outside the United States and longer-term trends of increased production from new sources such as shale oil both caught the oil markets in the cross-squeeze of dropping demand amidst plentiful supply. Although these trends have been visible for some time, financial markets responded with a rapid drop in crude oil prices within a few months, from a high of over $110 per barrel to under $40 per barrel. Most of the world seemed surprised by the rapidity with which this came to pass, in large part because demand for oil is incredibly difficult to predict.[6] Yet, those who are immersed in the business and routinely track the supply–demand volumes are better positioned to anticipate such mismatches, develop appropriate investment theses, and allocate capital accordingly when occasionally they do have clear insights about emerging mismatches.

Similarly, the mismatch between the supply of housing and demand for it had created opportunities for those who were actively monitoring emerging patterns. In the later years of the most recent boom, speculators had inflated housing demand to unsustainable levels. High-interest variable-rate loans made to suspect borrowers were going to come due at the end of known-in-advance maturity dates, and with it a day of reckoning for those buying up large quantities of mortgage bonds.[7] For those paying close attention to data, the observable mismatch was between cost-to-own versus cost-to-rent, with the own/rent ratio in many regions very different from historical patterns.

Investors who actively sought out such data to monitor changes in demand patterns benefited handsomely when the mismatches eventually led to a sharp adjustment in prices.

Depending on how slow or fast the demand and supply patterns shift, mismatches can be imperceptible, except to those who remain deeply connected to the data. Even though the supply-side pressures from the emergence of shale oil were several years in the making, for instance, the recent fall in crude prices seemed to come out of nowhere—in part because, in spite of slowing demand, big suppliers such as Saudi Arabia were unwilling to lower production for both economic and political reasons. To casual observers at least, mismatches are often difficult to anticipate because important actors obfuscate the data, or the forces driving supply and demand become lost in the noise. For those not paying close attention to the data and actively looking for pattern mismatches, such missed opportunities are perhaps a source of frustration. More committed investors can benefit, however, from staying close to data in their domain of expertise, and looking there for pattern mismatches.

Patterns for developing a major thesis often emerge from large-scale material trends that take shape amidst changing demographics, large-scale shifts in consumption behaviors, and technological evolution. These forces are complex and dynamic, suggesting that they are amenable not so much to statistical techniques but to good intuitions about trends in the data.

Larger pattern mismatches usually reverberate outward from the focal markets through overlapping economic activities—and so lead to minor or specific investment theses. For instance, with oil prices dropping precipitously, oil-producing regions suffer from depressed economic conditions, as do those industries, such as steel and housing, which had served the erstwhile oil booms in those regions. Both steel and local housing industries are then ripe for explorations for disruptions in patterns specific to those regions. Similarly, falling oil prices translate into lower gas prices, which puts discretionary dollars into the hands of consumers in non-oil-producing regions. The freed-up dollars flow to satisfy pent-up demand for, say, automobiles and consumables, thus generating a search for investment theses related to operators in those industries.

In effect, macro-level pattern mismatches help generate investment theses in a range of affected areas. Alert investors following such mismatches for pattern disruptions may be able to generate additional theses in areas where they feel competent. In such endeavors, setting boundaries to the common sense halo, a defensive mental orientation, and remaining close to the data remain paramount.

In the chapters that follow, I make a simplified case based on the long-term pattern of economic inequality that has been taking shape in the United States, low and stagnant median household earnings in the United States,[8] and the importance of low prices on everyday items for a vast majority of the population (discount retail). Based on these data, I develop the falsifiable investment thesis (Walmart) and try to systematically disconfirm it using both quantitative data and qualitative analysis. The intention here is to build and illustrate an intellectual framework for deliberately exploring ideas and developing testable investment theses. Not for the faint-hearted, this process is rigorous; it demands immersion, patience, and care.

CHAPTER NINE

How to Be a Wise Investor

FOR A BEGINNER to think that he is a smart investor just because he knows how to buy and sell stocks is like imagining that one can execute a battle plan just because one knows how to shoot a gun. The truth is that however talented someone may be, investing wisely demands mastery of certain analytical skills, understanding the particulars of a potential investment opportunity, and, more importantly, a sound method to help control destructive internal urges and external inducements for thoughtless action.

New investors often start out with wild, frenzied buying and selling. They are attracted to popular names, impressed by the seemingly infallible expertise of commentators, and fascinated by the thought of striking it rich. They alternate chaotically between hope and fear, fixate on one stock after another in quick succession, and trade too much. Their distracted, disjointed plays inevitably lead to steep losses, sooner or later, and the realization that investing is more complex than it may at first seem. Eventually, drained of resources and in financial pain, they begin to develop an appreciation of the complexity of the endeavor. Caution follows, and alert novices begin to learn the importance of reasoned restraint when investing.

As novices mature into investing "adolescence," they become more deliberate in their choices. But they still chase too many ideas simultaneously and remain enamored of quick wins—buying when excited by the prospect of a sure thing and selling when gripped by fear of loss. They lack a systematic approach and have little by way of an overall game plan that gives coherence to their actions. Intermediate-level investors still don't quite grasp the importance of organized buying and selling to build positions that transcend daily fluctuations in prices and periodic bouts of euphoria or panic. Slowly, they realize that personal experiences by themselves are insufficient to master investing. As Jesse Livermore once said, there are just too many different mistakes that investors can make to ever be confident that experience alone is sufficiently educational. Hence, the most alert investors eventually recognize the importance of sound conceptual frameworks that help decipher the complexities of investing. They begin to see the value of playing for position and the need to develop appropriate emotional and analytical skills.

As investors mature and habituate to playing for position, they learn that investing wisely is not just about clever buying and selling. It is about making sound positional plays such that each trade firms up the foundation of their investment program and sets them up for future investing actions, both deliberate and opportunistic. That is, each trade is part of a larger investment program, even if that program evolves as the investor matures through experience and reflection. In order to accomplish this, advanced investors become interested in developing a method—a conceptual framework—to guide them through the chaos of the financial markets.

The path from ignorance to wisdom in investing can be long and arduous, and not everyone who embarks ends up at the right place. But those who acquire the correct analytical skills and mindsets will find that the self-knowledge they gain along the way pays very good dividends, with both outsized investment performance and personal satisfaction.

Investment Errors

A large part of investing wisely is to understand and manage the errors that are inevitable when making decisions under uncertainty, as investment choices are apt to be. The principle of negation can certainly help reduce self-inflicted mistakes that investors are liable to make. But even as cautious an approach as one guided by the negation principle cannot eliminate mistakes altogether; there are just too many factors to fully account for in even the most comprehensive analysis. Hence, good investing requires broadly framing the kinds of errors that investors are likely to make in spite of good analysis.

Conceptually, investing mistakes are of two kinds: errors of commission and errors of omission. In order to understand how these errors come about, consider the following simplified example.

Assume that you are considering a major commitment to buy a particular stock price of P per share. You figure that buying the stock is a good idea and make the investment. You later find out that the stock did very well; your thesis turned out to be correct. In figure 9.1, that puts you in cell 1: you thought that buying the stock was a good idea, and it turned out to be so. If it so happened that your investment did poorly, your purchase would have been a bad idea. That would put you in cell 2: you thought that the stock at price P was a good investment, but it turned out to be a bad one.

On the other hand, your initial thesis could have been that investing in the stock was a bad idea. If the investment turned out to be good, you would be in cell 3: you thought that the stock was no good, but it turned out to be good. Conversely, if it turned out that the stock was a bad investment, then you're in cell 4: you thought that it was a bad stock, and it turned out to be so.

So, four possibilities exist in the combination of your thesis (Good or Bad) and the outcome (Good or Bad): (1) Good—Good [Gain]; (2) Good—Bad [Pain]; (3) Bad—Good [Regret]; and (4) Bad—Bad [Relief].

Cells 1 and 4 are where your expectation was consistent with what actually turned out to be the case. You either make an investment gain or are happy that you avoided a loss.

The other two scenarios are much less rosy. In cell 2, your disconfirmation analysis led you to think that the stock was a good idea, but it turned out bad. You made a false-positive, or Type I, error: incurring an investment loss by mistakenly not disconfirming the thesis that this was a good investment. This mistake would be as if you had invested in the likes of Enron, Lehman Brothers, AIG, or any other of the busts over the years that looked good but were, in fact, bad investments.

Cell 3, on the other hand, is where you disconfirmed the thesis that the stock was a good investment. You decided not to make the investment, only to find out later that it was indeed a good investment. You made a false-negative, or Type II, error: you disconfirmed what was, in fact, a good investment, and you suffered the regret of not having invested. This error would be like letting go of the likes of Home Depot, Dell, Microsoft, or one of many other breakout companies

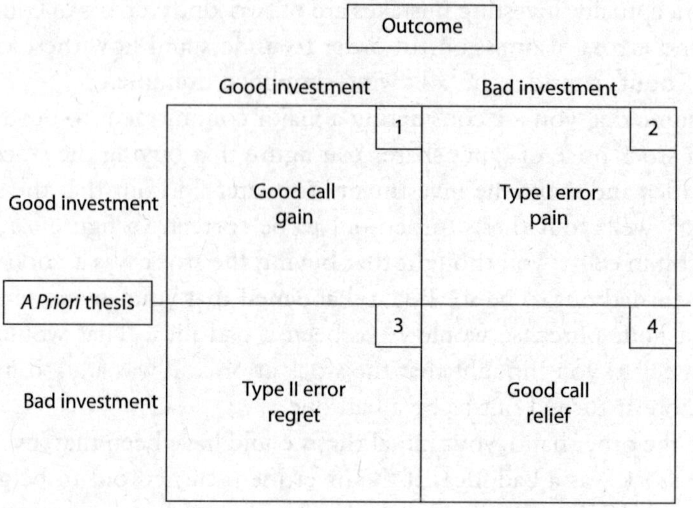

Figure 9.1 Error trade-off: errors of commission (pain) versus errors of omission (regret)

in their early years. With Type II errors comes the emotional cost of regretting not catching a winner.

The problem for investors is that the type of error committed is a function of how the disconfirmation analysis is set up and executed. If you design loose filtering screens (in which the investment thesis is hard to disconfirm), then you increase your chances of committing a Type I error. If, on the other hand, you design stringent screens (in which the investment thesis is easy to disconfirm), you increase your chances of committing a Type II error. Loosening the screens will allow more garbage into your investment program; conversely, tightening the filtering screens will squeeze out good opportunities.

Error Trade-Off

A further problem for investors is that the two types of errors are the exact opposites of each other. Reducing the chances of making a Type I error increases the chances of making a Type II error and vice versa. Sure, you'd like to reduce the chance of making both errors by doing good analysis, but you can do so only up to a point; you will still have an unavoidable trade-off between Type I and Type II errors. You have to decide which of the two for you is the more egregious error that you'd like to avoid most, and which of the two types of errors is more acceptable to you.

We will see in chapter 24 that you may be able to use portfolio logic to improve performance by having an appropriate mix of potential for the two types of errors. Your orientation toward errors of commission (Type I) or errors of omission (Type II) plays an important role in how you invest.

Note that errors occur in spite of good analysis—when, for example, the market price is driven largely by sentiment or other extraneous factors that did not factor into your analysis. Some amount of irreducible uncertainty remains in all investing endeavors.

Still, this framework for error trade-off brings a measure of control to investment decisions. It also helps clarify your own personal approach to and style of investing. If you find Type II errors acceptable but want to avoid Type I errors at all cost, for example, then your approach to investing is likely to be strongly defense oriented. Conversely, if you find Type I errors acceptable but want to avoid Type II errors at all cost, then your approach to investing is likely to be aggressive and perhaps even adventurous. In either case, you will calibrate your approach to the mix of possible errors that is right for you.

In this sense, wise investors shape their investment programs in accordance with their underlying preference for, or the ability to withstand, either of the two types of errors. Even when seeking outsized investment performance, advanced investors usually develop well-conceived filters to avoid at least the most egregious errors that have the potential to deeply undermine their otherwise carefully conceived investment program.

CHAPTER TEN

The Art of Looking

MUCH OF WHAT happens in investing seems to be driven by people's strong inclination to focus too much on what others say and not enough on their own analysis of the facts at hand. Both professional and lay investors fall easy prey to this tendency to rely on what others think and do in the stock market.

Blithely following others is so rampant among analysts and money managers, in fact, that researchers now recognize imitation as a central feature of the financial markets.[1] Sometimes called rational herding, imitative behavior among professional investors is said to arise from, among other things, the pressure to produce returns for anxious clients who demand quarterly performance when, in fact, the nature of markets is such that performance simply cannot be guaranteed.

The problem of not paying attention to facts and relying instead on what others say is much more pronounced in lay people, who typically don't have the time or skills to do their own confident analysis. Most lay investors, therefore, look to media personalities and other authority figures in order to form opinions about where to invest and how.

The Urge to Imitate

What encourages copying and complicates investing is that, in the short term at least, driven largely by the unpredictable forces of demand and supply, prices move randomly.[2] Even those investors who think they're doing good analysis can suffer poor results because prices can move sharply against well-informed expectations. There is little if any connection, in other words, between careful analysis of fundamental factors and investment performance in the short-term.

Then there is the chance that the analysis itself is incorrect because of misinterpretation of facts, leading to investments that turn out to be mistakes. Since prices do move randomly in the short term and analysis can be wrong, reasonable people may think that it's easier to just ignore the facts and follow what everybody else seems to be doing. Going along with the herd can be profitable, after all, even if getting caught going in the wrong direction can create losses.

Imitation is also an easy, if dangerous, solution to the problem of noise in the markets. With so many stocks, bonds, and other securities to choose from, and with so many opinions and marketing pitches to sort through, potential investors are vulnerable to utter confusion. As they gaze over the noisy markets, a sense of paralysis can set in and induce either no action at all or one that is drastically against their own self-interest.

If undisciplined in the art of analysis, both lay and professional investors can easily succumb to the impossible task of trying to understand everything and, as a result, see nothing. Such a state of confusion and bewilderment is an inducement for many investors to try to imitate what they think others are doing, especially when those others have prestige and credibility.

Together, a focus on the short term and an inclination to copy others go hand in hand with the facts that prices are unpredictable in the near term and markets are incredibly noisy. These are reasons enough for people to succumb to blind imitation and, as a result, engage in gambling and unfettered speculation.

It is no surprise, then, that imitation and speculation drive the markets. With the lay following the experts and the experts following each other, investing often becomes an exercise in which everyone follows everyone else with few, if any, carefully evaluating fundamental drivers of economic value. It is easy, in such an environment, for fragments of disjointed data and opinions to so fill the airwaves that facts get inextricably mingled with fantasy and thoughtful analysis becomes increasingly difficult. The sea of noise that surrounds the would-be investor drowns out, in effect, the important nuggets and insights. It is not easy in such an environment to look for, find, and stay focused on key facts that may be salient to the investing opportunity at hand.

Already disoriented by the maddening cacophony, aspiring investors are further misled by modern finance theory, which says the markets are efficient and prices incorporate all relevant information. The unfortunate, if unintended, implication of this theory is the persistent and strong message that analysis will not help because efficient markets make it impossible to find profitable opportunities.

The overwhelming noise and inclination to imitate together induce people to herd, perhaps with the thought that others might know something they themselves do not. It is when the gaze shifts from facts about the investment to the behaviors of those around an individual that speculation becomes pervasive. What others will do next or where prices will go next becomes a question of supreme importance.

Not doing careful analysis appears to have become so widespread that people hardly know much about what they trade or own. Those who buy mutual funds don't usually know what mutual fund managers really do, let alone what they own. People who buy stock index funds or exchange traded funds seem not to care or are unable to keep up with the stocks that make up the funds they own. Hedge funds and their practices are black boxes. The millions of individuals who buy stocks often do ad hoc analysis of poorly organized data or know very little about the companies in which they invest. Still many more simply get a thrill from chasing prices up and down and couldn't care less about what they're trading.

From Imitation to Analysis

Yet, for thoughtful investors interested in opportunities to put their capital to use in fundamentally sound businesses, ignoring important facts is foolhardy. Fundamentally sound businesses produce good and growing profits over a period of time and, when carefully chosen, have the potential to create great wealth.

Certainly stock prices of even good companies fluctuate a lot and are essentially unpredictable in the short run. But good managers and their enduring ability to generate strong returns on invested capital make good companies worth careful scrutiny. Investing in such companies can be highly profitable over the long term, but this requires the investment thesis to be clearly set up and subjected to a rigorous process of disconfirmation.

As opposed to gambling or speculation, investing requires that investors re-learn the art of looking, of honing in on important facts, and then cobbling together an array of clues into a well-informed thesis about each entry in their investment portfolio. Intellectually demanding though good analysis is, it is only as good as the diligence, analytical skills, and the temperament that the analyst brings to the task. The process demands consistent focus on facts and their patient evaluation.

It pays for investors to learn to dig into the facts precisely because most people care not to do so. Where others may be focused on prices and trying to figure out which of a plethora of opinions to follow, those with the correct temperament and analytical skills have a leg up in the world of investing; their choices are anchored in the enduring fundamentals of wealth creation rather than in the fickle sentiments of the moment.

Investors need to learn, therefore, how to evaluate companies, to know what to look for, to know how to dig up useful data, to interpret the data and make guarded judgments from their analysis, and to patiently wait for good results to come over time. Good investors are capitalists—they invest on the basis of sound data and analysis, with an eye for what could go wrong.

Yet sound analysis is not easy. As discussed in earlier chapters, the many biases we have in our ways of thinking easily distort perceptions and lead us astray. A key to looking, therefore, is to be aware of the inclination to confirm beliefs and to counter that inclination with formal skepticism: a systematic process of disconfirmation, a way of seeking and approaching data so as to try to refute whatever hopeful thesis you may have begun to form.

The formal process of disconfirmation acts as a check on fascination with price movements or with the careless pronouncements that so fill the airwaves. It forces attention on crucial facts with which to try to refute the thesis that the quoted price of a stock is sufficiently different from reasonable expectations of its economic worth. Trying to refute and disconfirm wishful thinking brings forth important data that analysts may secretly want to ignore for any of many reasons. It encourages a careful but cautious look, fully acknowledging the possibility that the eagerness to prove a point, bolstered perhaps by hopes for quick riches, can get investors to do foolish things. A skeptical orientation and the process of disconfirmation help investors make good choices.

How to Look when Investing

Investing is the search for divergence between valuation and sentiment and the ability to clearly see such divergence when it does occur. It is based on the view that, at least for some stocks, reasonable estimates of economic worth can be made independent of both market sentiment and the prices at which those stocks trade. Investors must keep three things in mind:

1. Estimates of the economic worth of a stock may be ascertained with a reasonable degree of confidence, although never with precision;
2. Such estimates of economic worth must be made without factoring prevailing price into the equation, so that it may be possible to compare market price directly against worth; and
3. Investors can make estimates of economic worth for some, but not for all, securities.

As discussed in later chapters, the techniques of valuation—for estimating economic worth—are only moderately complex. The arithmetic that drives valuation analysis is straightforward, and most investors can learn it with a modicum of effort. The assumptions behind the numbers that go into the analysis are an altogether different matter, however. As we have seen, assumptions are powerfully shaped by personal biases and emotions overlaid with the seductions of the marketplace. Bad assumptions can make analysis pointless or, worse, dangerous.

The first task in the process of disconfirmation is to formalize the hunch by setting up the investment thesis that, in any particular case, price has indeed deviated far from reasonable estimates of intrinsic economic worth. This thesis may arise for a variety of reasons. You may think that shares of Home Depot, for example, have fared poorly of late because of apparent reasons that have little to with the fundamental attributes of the business. A market-wide panic or overreaction to new information that is only seemingly harmful could have driven the prices down. You may think that you must formally investigate a tip you received from a respected friend. Whatever the reason, you begin to form a hunch that Home Depot is undervalued, or priced much below economic worth. So, you set up a formal thesis that the stock of the company is an attractive investment.

Next, instead of trying to prove or confirm the thesis that Home Depot shares are an attractive investment, you try to disconfirm that such is the case. If the process of disconfirmation is successful, then you know that your initial hunch was incorrect, and you reject the thesis about undervaluation. By doing so, you avoid making the mistake of buying Home Depot, thinking that it was underpriced when, in fact, it was not. If the disconfirmation is not successful, on the other hand, then you accept the thesis tentatively; still, you remain cautious and continue trying to disconfirm the thesis. If repeated attempts to disconfirm fail, then you have a degree of confidence in your initial thesis, and, perhaps, you commit and invest.

The important point of setting up a clear thesis and executing tests to try to disconfirm it is that by doing so, you risk the outcome that the belief you had begun to form about the stock could be rejected. This very *risk of rejection* makes it helpful for you to evaluate the investment as a possible opportunity. What is also useful about engaging in this process is that it forces you to pay attention to inconvenient facts of the case that you would have likely ignored were you not actively looking for them during the disconfirmation analysis. This means that even if you were ultimately to reject the investment thesis, the work you did greatly enhanced your understanding of the factors that contribute to the economic worth of the company you were evaluating.

Refutability Is the Key

Unlike an investment thesis, a speculator's thesis requires no risk of rejection. Speculators base their thesis on hope or expectation that prices will move up or down within a certain time period. There may be good or bad reasons for expecting such price movements, but no easy way to set up adequate tests in order to refute such expectations.

Consider gold, for instance. If you were to think that the price of an ounce of gold would rise 10 percent, how would you disconfirm that thesis? Forces of supply and demand drive market prices of gold. While it may be possible to approximate supply with some effort, the demand for gold is in large part driven by noneconomic factors, especially fears and hopes about the unknowable future. So, absent any reasonably firm estimate of worth against which to evaluate the price of gold and the inability to set up a clear, refutable thesis that risks rejection, it is in practice not possible to disconfirm claims about what the price of gold might be in a given period of time.

Disconfirmation is possible, on the other hand, for stocks whose approximate intrinsic worth investors can estimate with inputs based on a good understanding of the economics and leadership of the companies in question. In such cases, pitting the prevailing price against estimates of worth derived from careful valuation and related analytics allows the possibility that you can disconfirm the investment thesis.

As we discussed in the previous chapter, the risk of rejection, or disconfirmation, is the fundamental difference between investment and speculation; it is the line of demarcation between them.

Indeed, for some stocks and in certain situations, intrinsic economic worth is indeterminate. In those cases where you simply cannot make reasonable estimates of worth from available information, the prevailing prices are without an anchor. That is the realm of speculation.

That is, stocks whose worth is equated wholly and squarely with the quoted prices are purely speculative in character. This would be if no record of steady performance exists, for instance, or when the underlying economics are simply those of uncertain supply and whimsical demand, or when the business model is opaque too complex to clearly articulate. Investible stocks, on the other hand, are those that have enough of a historical record and such information as would help ascertain the approximate economic worth with a reasonable degree of confidence.

Ironically, the same stock could qualify both as a speculation and as an investment. An investible stock is one whose approximate value you may be able to estimate with credible data and analysis but without reliance on the prevailing market prices at which it is selling at a given time. The same stock would be speculative, however, if there was no reasonable data-driven conception of its potential intrinsic value independent of the prevailing prices.

So, imagine that you were to purchase shares of Home Depot at a given price with the expectation that the price was about half the approximate estimate of intrinsic worth. In this scenario, you are an investor evaluating the legitimate opportunity. If, on the other hand, you were to purchase the same shares of Home Depot with no conception or estimate of intrinsic value but with the hope that the price would go up in the future, then you would be speculating. The ability to make and the very act of making reasonable estimates of economic worth separates investment from speculation.

Yet, worth and value are elusive concepts. As such, the conventional tools of valuation are liable to be misused to justify preconceived notions of what the underlying value of a stock might be. Estimates themselves are shaped by hope, fear, and greed; commentary by television personalities and the plethora of well-written, "free" advice available in print and on the Internet all have powerful effects on investors trying to make estimates of economic worth.[3]

So, what separates investing from speculation or gambling is the ability to be deliberate and measured through the use of a formal process of refutation. Logic, data, and doubt are the three key ingredients of this process. Formally trying to refute or disconfirm your investment thesis is, in essence, the art of looking.

PART THREE

Foundations

CHAPTER ELEVEN

Price and Value

IN OUR CAUTIOUS approach to investing, we are making the essential assumption that we can compare prices of a given stock with robust estimates of intrinsic value, or true economic worth. That is, we assume that price and value are distinct concepts, that we know one and can estimate the other. Not knowing the worth would throw the entire enterprise of investing into disarray: How would you then know what the correct price ought to be? If each share of Walmart sells for, say $55, how do you know that it is worth that much? How would we know that it is not worth $25, or $95, or any other amount for that matter?

In this chapter, I show that value is an elusive concept and precisely computing it is not necessary for making smart investment choices. The key to investing wisely is engaging in the process of valuation in order to make reasonable estimates of approximate economic worth. Good investment opportunities arise when prices seem to have significantly diverged from such estimates of worth.

Some argue that expectations and counterexpectations about capital appreciation are the only things that drive prices—such that they go up or down as expectations about the future change. But what are those expectations based on? Are expectations driven solely by hope or fear, or are they anchored on identifiable economic factors? Even if sentiment plays a role, should expectations and prices not have some basis in economics so that markets can function and transactions may occur? Otherwise, driven by the mood of the moment and periodic amplification of emotions to either extreme, the markets would experience spectacular booms and busts and, ultimately, seize up. Program trading that so defines our times would likely make such oscillations even more frequent than they are now.

As John Burr Williams long ago pointed out in *The Theory of Investment Value*, economic fundamentals must play a role in pricing.[1] Identifying and assessing those fundamentals, their impact on economic worth, and their relation with prices is, therefore, essential for investment analysis. Once robust estimates of economic worth are available, then it is a matter of comparing those with prevailing prices to see if the two are sufficiently divergent to create a possible opportunity to invest profitably. The theory is that, under specific conditions when markets are functioning smoothly, prices will be correlated with their underlying value, and the two will converge, more or less. Under certain other conditions, however, sentiment or other extraneous factors may drive prices far and away from confident estimates of true economic worth. It is under those conditions, when prices diverge from robust estimates of value, that investors may find attractive opportunities to deploy their capital.

The confusion for those who wish to invest arises from the short-term fluctuations in prices and, given the many uncertainties about future prospects, a lack of confident estimates of economic worth. Seeing value as distinct from price and then understanding the complexities inherent in making robust estimates of value are, therefore, at the crux of making good investment choices. So, let's take a moment to reflect on what value means and how investors should think about it.

Value Is Elusive and Unstable

As David Graeber has shown, there are three accepted conceptions of value.[2] Some see value as a property that is good or desirable, recognizing that value changes with social norms. What is desirable in one time and place may not be so in a different social context. Others consider value as indicating something that is meaningfully different. As the distinctiveness of something fades, so does its value because we can no longer articulate it as separate from other things. Still others think value is associated with use or trade, or as Adam Smith long ago argued, value-in-use and value-in-exchange.[3] That is, value is economic worth based on the utility from use or the price from trade.

Investment (intrinsic) value denotes economic worth but with a specific meaning. As conventionally understood, the investment value of an asset is the net present value (NPV) of expected future cash flows. That is, if you invest $1 in an asset and that asset then generates a stream of cash in the future, then the investment, or intrinsic value, is simply the present value, or that future stream properly discounted to the present. Simple in principle, such estimates are at best approximate and often a difficult endeavor. Since NPV depends on estimates of future flows as well as assumptions about the rate at which they ought to be discounted, worth and value are essentially subjective judgments of the analyst. Because they are subjective in nature, such estimates are vulnerable to considerable variation among investors. Such differences in estimates of value are not all bad because, as Friedrich Hayek and Fischer Black[4] both noted on different occasions, they create the incentive for transactions and, ultimately, are critical for the proper functioning of the markets.

Yet, subjectivity also means that intrinsic value is inherently unstable. Expectations about future flows and the rates at which to discount those are both prone to drift depending on the state of mind of the analyst. In optimistic times, such as roaring bull markets, for instance, analysts are inclined to inflate the expected future flows and use low discount rates to reflect collective hopes of a rosy future. In pessimistic times, such as recessions or bear markets, analysts may be inclined to have just the opposite orientation, thus depressing valuations across the board. Not only individual valuations by individual analysts but also the collective mood in the broader markets may be subject to a bold or fearful reading of the specifics of the company or asset being valued.

Hence, as Edgar Lawrence Smith once wrote, measures of intrinsic value are neither fixed nor constant. Unlike a yardstick that measures length in fixed units, value is an elusive concept that expands and contracts with the mood of the analyst and especially with the broader social mood that prevails at any given time. Psychological or mental context greatly influences estimates of value.

Even if the psychological context were constant, market prices exert considerable pull on estimations of value. As George Soros once noted, changes in price affect economic worth by way of the operations of the markets.[5] For instance, the rising price of a stock increases the issuing company's debt capacity and also in other ways allows the raising of capital for productive endeavors—which, when managed well, have the effect of raising prospects for stronger cash flows in the future. Conversely, falling prices lead to a decreasing value of collateral and a lowered debt capacity, thus shrinking the availability of credit and forcing retrenchment or starving promising projects. In this sense, prices create incentives or disincentives to consume and invest that, in turn, affect value.[6]

Such mechanisms are visible at the aggregate level as well. Rising prices invite speculators, whose buying pushes prices even further and sometimes leads to bubbles. Falling prices encourage selling, which pushes prices down even more and sometimes leads to crashes. In this sense, prices are endogenous to the actions of buyers and sellers, who trade in anticipation of what they think others will do and how prices will move in the short run.[7]

The psychology of traders may also interact with the economic mechanisms at work. As the stock market rises, individual portfolios expand and investors feel richer and become prone to consume more; increasing aggregate demand invites business investment in productive capacity, which raises wages and encourage more consumption—thus setting up the virtuous cycle of consumption–investment–employment–consumption. Rising prices, both at the level of individual company and across the board, can, therefore, trigger a positive dynamic of higher valuations, leading to even higher prices. Similarly, falling prices shrink the wealth of investors at large and suck demand out of the system, triggering a negative dynamic of lower demand, leading to curtailed investment, which then push valuations lower again.

So, as a result of both subjective psychological reasons and the adjustment operations of well-functioning markets, intrinsic values do not remain stationary; they fluctuate moderately up and down—sometimes by the very market prices that are supposed to only reflect value. In normal circumstances, such fluctuations are self-correcting, both at the level of individual companies and at the level of the economy as a whole. As prices and values pull each other on an upward trajectory, for instance, the cost of money begins to rise, and the set of productive opportunities begins to shrink, thus putting breaks on expansion. Conversely, as prices and values pull each other on a downward trajectory, costs of borrowing money begin to fall (partly because central banks lower rates to counter the shrinking demand for money), and productive opportunities begin to open up to induce expansion. In such normal circumstances, therefore, valuations rise and fall to reflect the normal economic and psychological forces at work. Prices and values remain tethered and moderately mutually fluctuating.

Every so often, however, the subtle dynamic balance between price and value ruptures because of an internal or external shock. The technological revolution of the Internet raised expectations to such a level in the late 1990s that prices rose rapidly and pulled valuations up dramatically—only to come crashing down when reality set in a few years later, jerking valuations down as well. Similarly, the housing crisis and the Lehman Brothers bankruptcy created such a panic that prices dropped sharply in the fall of 2008 and sank valuations across the economy. Rising values because of, say, technological breakthroughs, push up prices dramatically and create an virtuous upward cycle; falling values because of, say, a demand shock, drive prices sharply down and create a vicious downward cycle.

From time to time, similar extreme movements can occur when prices of the shares of individual companies suddenly rise or fall because of forces that have nothing to do with their economic realities. An extreme rise in stock prices also pulls up, for a time, the intrinsic value of the company—only to bring both down sharply when reality catches up. Similarly, a sudden fall in stock prices can do grave damage to the economic value of the company—until managers can stabilize operations to begin building the business back up again.

The circular relationship between cause and effect, between value and price, is what makes investing challenging. Such a dynamic is all the more complex because, whereas changes in economic value are usually slower and longer term in nature, prices move much more fluidly and quickly, as traders seek profits and shun losses. In well-functioning markets, for every small fluctuation in value, the movement of prices is much faster and sharper. This is what Robert Shiller long ago observed, and it is consistent with the overreaction hypothesis of behavioral finance.[8]

Such instability of intrinsic value obfuscates the distinction of value from price. It also calls into question the very notion of efficiency, which assumes that value is fixed and markets simply find the correct or clearing price. Instead, trading itself may sometimes drive prices irrespective of underlying economic worth, and prices, in turn, may influence estimates of value.

Hence, as Soros once so insightfully observed,[9] value is dynamically, if loosely, tethered to price via feedback loops, in normal times rising and falling gently with the ebb and flow of economic and psychological forces—but at times breaking the band, so to say, when prices move disruptively up or down outside the normal range.

To complicate matters even more, intrinsic worth sometimes does not figure at all into buying and selling transactions of both traders and investors alike. It is common, for example, for mutual funds and money managers to sell a stock when it goes off an index and buy another when it gets on, largely on the expectation that inclusion in the index raises demand, with little or no consideration for underlying economic fundamentals. Similarly, individuals and institutions often buy and sell stocks to rebalance their portfolios. Some may sell stocks to cover margin calls or to send their kids to college or for any number of other reasons. Market participants buy and sell stocks and other securities for a range of economic and noneconomic reasons, in other words; in practice, many such transactions may or may not have anything to do with robustly estimated economic worth.

From Value to Valuation

But instability and elusiveness by themselves do not mean that value is not a useful concept when investing. Whereas estimates of value may vary depending on the mental orientation of the analyst and the general climate of hope or fear, the very process of trying to make the estimates encourages careful evaluation of forces that influence future flows and rates of discount. Estimates of future flows require a keen understanding of the factors that directly or indirectly affect economic performance; trying to determine the appropriate discount rate requires a keen understanding of key uncertainties about future flows. In this sense, although value itself may be elusive, the very act of trying to understand the intrinsic value of an asset directs attention to facts and processes that create wealth.

The act of engaging in valuation creates opportunities to clarify not only what the cash generation potential of an asset is but how that potential may be enhanced and managed. More than the estimate itself, in other words, the process of valuation helps one make good investment choices.

Furthermore, because subjectivity pervades the process, valuation is really an argument. It is an argument in which you bring estimates of economic worth to the negotiating table, to haggle with all the other buyers and sellers about the price at which you are willing to do business. If you get the price that makes sense in light of what you think is a good deal, then perhaps you do business. If you don't like the price, then perhaps you have the courage to walk away. That is the value investing discipline.

Price on Demand, Value on Fundamentals

Note that it is not one's analysis that drive prices but the acts of multitudes of people buying or selling. As for any other product or service, the laws of supply and demand remain relevant in the pricing of financial assets, be they shares of a publicly traded company or some other security.

Specifically in the stock market, since the supply of the shares of a company is limited at any given time to the number of shares outstanding, demand has great influence on prices. There may be instances in which buying and selling by large shareholders or institutions affects the supply of securities, but it is the demand side of the equation that mostly drives prices.

Yet, we know that a variety of motivations and perceptions influence demand for a given security. Hence, it is not just economic fundamentals that influence prices; prices remain vulnerable to a variety of noneconomic influences and manipulations.

As investors go to the market with their analysis and valuation in hand, they find that other parties may or may not be as prepared. Some may have better information or maybe a different analysis, giving them widely varying assessments of worth and value. Some may not even look at the fundamentals, relying only on the movement of prices, tips from friends, or the urgings of an influential television personality. Others may not do any analysis at all and may be acting on a hunch, or even no hunch at all but simply on hearsay, hope, or hype.

The theory is that the buyers and sellers of all stripes will somehow negotiate prices so as to make trades that clear the available supply—such that underlying worth is ultimately discovered through the actions of free agents. The errors that may exist are assumed to be both on the upside (overpricing) and downside (underpricing); in this theory, those errors simply cancel out in the aggregate to reveal clearing prices that mirror the correct value of the shares.[10]

Now, the law of large numbers does apply when millions upon millions of shares change hands following thousands upon thousands of decisions. Yes, liquid markets comprising large numbers of independent agents do provide good estimates of economic worth. But, critical for markets to function properly is a wide diversity of opinions. This is because the law of large numbers works only when enough decision makers are independent of all others—in which case independent errors (white noise) cancel out, such that, over time, prices find their central or correct value. That is the theory.

But we also know that buyers and sellers in the capital markets are not independent of each other; they are exposed to a lot of the same information and influences, often from the same sources given the concentration of media in the country. As such, market participants often suffer from common source bias and, especially during times of crisis, lose their independence of thought.

In spite of the great diversity in preparation and motivations, in other words, large numbers of people are drawn to think and act similarly, and, as we saw in chapter 2, errors tend to become highly correlated. As a result, instead of converging on whatever may be true worth, prices can diverge from reasonable estimates of value for varying periods of time.

Now, some argue that smart money corrects such correlation of errors by betting against deviating prices. It seems reasonable that, seeing a deviation, investors may want to take advantage of the situation and arbitrage the gaping difference in prevailing prices and what they see as underlying worth. Such a mechanism, assumed key to market functioning, should discover and regulate prices so they remain close to intrinsic worth.

Yet, there are several reasons such arbitrage may not be possible without serious risks to the arbitragers. After all, if thousands of investors are driving billions of dollars in one direction, what arbitrager can effectively resist that? Individual or even institutional arbitragers do not have much of a chance, no matter what their resources; successfully reversing the tidal wave of deviating prices is about as likely as standing on a beach and trying to stop a tsunami. It is more likely that savvy traders will ride the rising or falling tides and, when the momentum has run its course and the directional move begins to falter, they will ride the wave in the other direction as well.

So, market efficiency is not a constant; it is a variable. Under certain conditions, markets are efficient; in others, they are not. That markets are always efficient is a myth that relies on omniscient investors, the law of large numbers, and phantom arbitragers successfully fighting valiant battles to bring prices back in line with some underlying economic worth.[11] In fact, prices do not so much as correctly reflect the true underlying worth as they are endogenous to fluctuating estimates of worth based largely on the sentiments of buyers and sellers at a particular point in time.

What the pricing mechanism does do is find and clear the supply. Remember that value is elusive and unstable, so price discovery may sometimes be in vain. In fact, if value is elusive, what are prices driving at? What is the meaning of efficiency when value itself is not fixed and, sometimes, even unknowable?

The difficulty of elusive and unstable value does not mean that there is a better system out there for finding the approximate economic worth of assets and for allocating resources in the economy; the pricing mechanism is still a much better and more equitable system than, say, central planning.[12] It's just that the best system we have is still so vulnerable on many levels.

So, what use is valuation analysis? What use, especially, is the kind of analysis we will be doing in this book going forward? If prices move hither and thither chasing elusive value, often under the influence of emotion and noneconomic considerations, then what good is careful analysis going to do for you?

The power of analysis is in the fact that it forces investors to ground their decisions in the facts of the case, allowing them to control their impulses, to slow down before committing. Given the tricks that the mind can play, and given that a whole army of influencers is trying to persuade people to do this or that, even well-informed investors can succumb to the emotions of the markets, be seduced by the stories of how this stock is going to go up and that one down. Careful and rigorous analysis helps investors resist the temptation to do foolish things.

Careful analysis helps investors focus on meaningful facts and ignore the noise; it enables investors to seek and process relevant information deliberately. Analysis allows for caution so that the cerebral cortex catch up to the impatience of the brain stem. Analysis makes the value investor.

Valuation and Negation

In the following chapter, I show how to approximate the economic worth of a business. We will see that the techniques of making the estimates are only moderately complex; most people can learn these with little effort, with perhaps no more than simple algebra. Yet, the techniques can be misused easily, as small changes in the key assumptions produce big differences in estimates.

As such, approximations of value must be made cautiously and with care, defensively and with humility in the knowledge that valuing a business is, in the end, more an art than a science. It is more about maturity and emotional control than about complex mathematics. It is about using assumptions that are consistent with observable facts and are logically defensible.

More to the point in relation to what we have done in the first part of the book, the key to good valuation is that you try to refute your thesis that the asset you want to evaluate offers an attractive investment opportunity. That is, since emotion and the desire to justify a particular price can corrupt analysis, the key to good valuation is a careful application of the principle of negation.

You must try to refute.

CHAPTER TWELVE

How to Value a Business

ALTHOUGH MANY DIFFERENT techniques exist for estimating how much a business may be worth,[1] I focus here on two common ways to do so: market valuation and intrinsic valuation.

For an intuitive grasp of the issues, let's start by examining those involved in a housing purchase. Say you want to buy a house for $100,000. You apply for a mortgage to finance the purchase; the bank gets an appraisal; and the appraiser collects data on similar houses sold in similar neighborhoods in the recent past and makes adjustments based on space, location, number of rooms, quality of construction, and so on. All this results in an estimate for the market value of the house.

This appraised value indicates how much similar houses have sold for in the recent past. The bank then lends money, perhaps about 80 percent of the appraised value, in order to have a bit of a cushion in case housing prices drop. The appraiser may also give you a replacement value for how much it would cost to rebuild if fire or other serious damage destroyed the house. Sometimes called cost-basis value in housing parlance, insurance companies use the replacement value to write homeowners' insurance policies. If you were to rent out the property, then you could estimate the intrinsic economic worth by appropriately discounting the future cash flows, net of costs, from rental income.

Similar logic applies when valuing the stock of a publicly traded company. Replacement value is rarely used in such transactions, but it is common to use the market value or comparable method, where value is estimated using the sale prices of similar businesses. You may also approximate the economic worth, or intrinsic value, of the stock, appropriately discounting the expected future net cash flows.

Market Value: Capitalization Ratios

It is common to base market appraisals of a stock on the pricing of stocks of "similar" businesses using certain normalized ratios. The challenge in this kind of analysis, however, is to find market transactions involving businesses that are similar to yours in such terms as specialization, geography, demographics, size of markets or clientele served, size, and profitability. No two businesses are exactly alike, and trying to find an identical twin in the world of business is quite difficult indeed.

Hence, once you locate several transactions involving similar businesses, you then make necessary adjustments to account for unique attributes or circumstances. As in housing appraisals, moreover, the adjustments are a result of subjective judgments based on the particulars.

Typically, therefore, we assess the market value of equity using ratios such as price/sales, price/earnings, price/book, price/cash flow, and so on. That is, we capitalize the variables in the denominator to get a sense of how the market is pricing each dollar of sales, earnings, book value, or cash flow. Which particular ratio is best in a given situation depends on the business. It may be, for instance, that similar businesses have been selling at a price that equals revenues. In valuation parlance, this means that the market is capitalizing revenues by a factor of 1. On the other hand, the market may be capitalizing not revenues but free cash flows and by a factor of, say, 4. In that case, the market value of a business with, say, $10 million in annual free cash flows would be approximately $40 million. It helps to be familiar with the nature of business and with ongoing transactions in the marketplace to know which ratios to use as rules of thumb in particular cases.

Let's take Walmart for example. Table 12.1 demonstrates what some of these capitalization ratios looked like as of July 25, 2015, when the company was trading at $71 per share.

As shown in the table, at the then prevailing price per share of about $71, the market value of Walmart's common equity was just

TABLE 12.1

($mm)	July 2015		
Market value (MV)	293,651	Ratio	
Revenues (Rev)	483,521	MV/Rev	0.47
Net income (NI)	16,363	MV/NI	14.01
Common equity (CEQ)	81,394	MV/CEQ	2.82
Free cash flow (FCF)	16,390	MV/FCF	13.98

under $230 billion. For the most recent fiscal year ending January 2015, the company had reported sales of $483.5 billion, net income of $16.4 billion, and $16.4 billion in free cash flow. The company had $81.4 billion in common equity (also called net assets or book value).

As the right-most column of the table shows, in July 2015, the market was valuing the company at 0.47 times sales, about 14 times earnings, just under 14 times free cash flow, and under 3 times common equity.

To put these valuations in perspective, let's also look at corresponding numbers at three different times in the company's history: when prices were high in 2014, in 2004, and, for further perspective, in 1999, when investors were particularly optimistic about the stock market in general (table 12.2).

Clearly, the company has grown substantially from annual revenues of $166 billion in 1999 to $483 billion in 2014, and from $2 billion in annual free cash flow in 1999 to more than $16 billion in free cash

TABLE 12.2

($mm)	2014	2004	1999		2014	2004	1999
Market value	293,651	259,587	313,204	Ratio			
Revenues	483,521	286,103	165,639	MV/Rev	0.61	0.91	1.89
Net income	16,363	10,267	5,377	MV/NI	17.95	25.28	58.23
Common equity	81,394	49,396	25,834	MV/CEQ	3.61	5.26	12.12
Free cash flow	16,390	2,151	2,011	MV/FCF	17.92	120.68	155.70

Note: MV, market value; Rev, revenues; NI, net income; CEQ, common equity; FCF, free cash flow

flow in 2014. The optimism baked in 1999 valuations is also evident in the capitalization ratios. In 1999, the market was pricing the company at 1.89 times book value, almost 60 times total net income, above 12 times net assets, and 155 times free cash flows; in 2014, those valuations were much more sober at just 0.61 times annual revenues, under 18 times net income, 3.6 times net assets, and under 18 times free cash flow. Clearly, investor perspective changed dramatically in a span of about 15 years, such that valuations were actually lower for a much bigger and much more profitable company.

It is certainly possible that investors in 1999 were expecting rapid growth and that the high prices reflected their optimism about Walmart's prospects going forward. They valued Walmart as a high-growth company, and the company did, indeed, deliver on that optimism. Yet, those who paid more than 12 times net assets in 1999 perhaps paid too much, and, if they had held on to their shares until 2015, would have earned total returns (including dividends) of under 2 percent. Current valuations at $71 per share, as shown in table 12.1, reflect much more pessimistic expectations about the company's prospects going forward, but they also are historically low valuations at well under 3 times net assets and just below 14 times the free cash flow reported for 2014.

Along with the comparison of historical valuations, we also must do a cross-sectional evaluation of the focal company with another in the same industry. Although Walmart is a company unlike any other, let's compare it with Target in order to illustrate a point.[2] Although the two companies are much different in size, the ratios on the right-hand side of table 12.3 show that they were priced differently as of 2015 (WMT $71/share; TGT $80/share). For each dollar of sales, the market price of Walmart is 0.47 and of Target is 0.63. Walmart shares sold for 14 times net earnings, whereas Target reported an accounting (Generally Accepted Accounting Principles [GAAP]) loss for the preceding two years. Walmart sold for 2.8 times the common equity and Target at about 3.25 times common equity. Walmart sold for under 14 times annual free cash flow and Target over 17 times free cash flow.[3]

Using such cross-sectional comparisons between the two companies indicates the degree to which the market pricing of a company may or may not be in line with how investors are pricing other similar companies.

TABLE 12.3

($mm)	WMT	TGT		WMT	TGT
Market value (MV)	229,188	45,455	Ratio		
Revenues (Rev)	483,521	72,618	MV/Rev	0.47	0.63
Net income (NI)	16,363	−1,636	MV/NI	14.01	−27.78
Common equity (CEQ)	81,394	13,997	MV/CEQ	2.82	3.25
Free cash flow (FCF)	16,390	2,653	MV/FCF	13.98	17.13

The technique of capitalization and comparable metrics requires a good deal of guesswork about which ratios to use and which companies to compare with. Although capitalization ratios give a quick sense of how the market prices a company, numbers show that the market can value the same company very differently.

Capitalization ratios can provide investors with insights into the reasonableness of prices. But if valuations across the market are low or high, it will be difficult to judge the reasonableness unless investors can evaluate the capitalization ratios both historically with previous valuations and cross-sectionally in comparison with those of other similar companies.

Intrinsic Value: Discounted Cash Flow (DCF)

Let's now turn to the most common method of getting at the economic worth of a business. In this secion, I demonstrate using a hypothetical private business. Valuation of publicly traded companies requires a similar thought process, and I will illustrate such with a specific example in the next chapter.

Say you wanted to buy a small medical practice for $1 million from a friend. You figure that the practice is well established, although by no means at its full potential. You would like to update the capital equipment with an additional $300,000 by the end of the first year. Then, with some savvy marketing and tie-ins with large hospitals, you believe you could grow the practice at an average rate of at least 10 percent a year for the foreseeable future. Your dear friend Leon Shaky is willing to lend you the $1 million at a 20 percent annual interest charge plus a 25 percent stake in the business. You think you'll try to make the business profitable for about 10 years, at the end of which you'll re-evaluate.

Your due diligence shows that the practice was financially healthy. It generated about $1 million in annual revenues and about $300,000 in free cash flow; the business had no debt. You figure that additional investments, increased expenses, and new interest charges will reduce your free cash flow to $247,000 at the end of the first year. Growing this figure at 10 percent a year for the next 10 years, your free cash flows will look like what is shown the second row of table 12.4.

Note in the "Nom" (Nominal dollars) row that the first year includes a $300,000 cash outflow from the equipment update. Since you expect the company to generate $247,000 in cash flow, you expect net free cash flow during the first year to be –$53,000. After that, starting from a base of $247,000, you expect free cash flow to grow at 10 percent a year for the following 10 years.

With the cash flows estimated, you then have to determine the rate at which to discount those future expected cash flows. You decide that since you are putting a lot on the line, you want to be sure that the investment makes sense at an annual rate of 25 percent. So, using a discount rate of 25 percent, you estimate the present value (PV) of future cash flows as shown below.

Adding all discounted present values for the first 10 years gives a net present value (NPV) of –$51,932. What this means is that, given your sense of business uncertainties as captured in the discount rate of 25 percent, you expect the project to lose money over the next 10 years. So, you think, why do all this work only to lose money?

Then, you realize that you could probably sell the practice at the end of 10 years. But how do you estimate this terminal value? To do that, you assume that if you keep the practice in good order and can keep free cash flows growing at 5 percent a year for a very long time starting year 11, then your business will be worth over $3 million in year 11. This you then discount at 25 percent to bring back to the present, and the residual value turns out to be $275,100 in current dollars.

Including the residual value, the NPV for the business now turns out to be a positive $223,227, provided your assumptions hold. You own 75 percent of this value, and your friend Shaky owns the rest. Does it make sense for you to buy the practice given this analysis? What would you do? Is this enough of a profit for you to make the investment? Are there ways in which you could improve the value of this business?

TABLE 12.4

Year	0	1	2	3	4	5	6	7	8	9	10	Residual
Nom*	−1,000	−53.0	271.7	298.9	328.8	361.6	397.8	437.6	481.3	529.5	582.4	3,203
PV†	−1,000	−42.4	173.9	153.0	134.7	118.5	104.3	91.8	80.8	71.1	62.5	275

*Nom: nominal dollars ('000)
†PV: present value ('000)

This, in essence, is the discounted cash flow (DCF) technique of estimating the economic worth or intrinsic value of a business. It does not give you an answer per se, but it helps estimate ballpark numbers that you can then use to make a business decision. Of course, the final NPV number varies widely depending on the assumptions you use. What the future cash flows of a business are likely to be and how uncertain you think those cash flows are—these can vastly influence the final estimates of value. In such analysis, therefore, precision does little good, whereas reasonableness of assumptions is paramount. The need to understand assumptions then forces a close look at the drivers of profitability.

While the DCF technique is theoretically sound, note two shortcomings. First, since the outcome of such analysis is so much a function of assumptions and gut feel, you get widely varying NPV numbers depending on the assumptions. It is impossible to get a fix on true value using DCF analysis. Second, even if "true" value did indeed exist, and you did somehow correctly compute it, there is no assurance that the sale of the business would fetch the determined amount. Depending on market conditions, businesses sell at prices that deviate substantially from the results of the inherently approximate DCF analysis.

Given the vulnerability of valuation estimates to faulty assumptions, in chapter 14 I will discuss this technique in some more detail—and turn DCF analysis on its head to make it useful for making estimates of the economic worth of publicly traded companies.

CHAPTER THIRTEEN

Risk and Uncertainty

IMAGINE THAT YOU have three bags marked A, B, and C. Suppose you know that bag A contains 30 red balls and 70 green balls. You know the total number of balls in bag B but don't know the proportion of red and green balls. You know that bag C has red and green balls, along with an unknown number of black and white balls, but know neither the total number nor proportions of different colors. Assume also that a green ball is worth +$1 and red ball is worth –$1. Let's say that a black ball is worth +$10, and a white ball is worth –$10. You must decide which bag to draw from to maximize your gain.

Which of the three bags is the riskiest?

If you're like most people, you think that bag C is the riskiest. If so, you are mistaking uncertainty for risk, which, as once explained by economist Frank Knight,[1] are two distinct concepts. You can quantify and measure risk, but you cannot do so for uncertainty, which indicates unknowns and unknowables.[2]

If you know the frequency distribution (how many of each) from which a particular event (color) is drawn, then you can measure risk using statistical terms such as probability and standard deviation. Since you know the count and proportion of red and green balls in bag A, you can compute the probabilities and know what the odds are that you will pull out a particular combination of red and green. Since you know how much each ball is worth, you can also compute the probability of making a given sum of money. You can quantify risk for bag A.

You cannot compute the probabilities for bag B, however, since you know neither the count nor the proportion of red and green balls.

Not knowing the frequency distribution, you face uncertainty. You face even greater uncertainty in bag C, where the black and white balls make the stakes even larger.

If you were an investor, you would reach for bag A because the odds are clear. You would prefer if all the balls were green but would accept the challenge because you can quantify the probability of loss, and the odds are good that you'll make money. Instead, if bag A had 70 red and 30 green balls, you would know that the odds are not in your favor and perhaps choose not to draw at all. If you do choose to draw, then you are simply hoping that you pick green in spite of the odds being against you. In either case, you can quantify probabilities and, therefore, know the risk.

As a speculator, on the other hand, you might be inclined to choose bag B, perhaps in the spirit of experimentation. You accept the possibility of limited losses to see if you might be able to uncover an underlying pattern from the first few draws. That is, you approach bag B cautiously, getting information with each draw, hoping that the true proportions will become evident and be in your favor. Of course, you know that the underlying patterns may not show, or worse, you may infer incorrectly.

Finally, as a gambler, you would favor bag C, where you cannot calculate the odds, but the prospect of drawing +$10 black balls is appealing; the chances of drawing –$10 white balls brings the excitement that makes the game worthwhile. You don't know the risk but like the uncertainty and the possibility of a big payoff if you were to pick black.

So, investors, speculators, and gamblers differ in their tolerance for uncertainty and in wanting to know the risk they're taking. As an investor, you want to know the risk as precisely as possible and shun situations that are clear gambles.

Resolving Uncertainties

In real situations, it's not clear which of the three kinds of bags you're drawing from. In most investment analysis, counts, frequencies, and objective probabilities about key factors are simply unavailable. But by using one-off and situation-specific information that may be available, you try to make educated guesses about whether the odds are comfortably in your favor.

The essential task for you as an investor is not so much to measure risk but to understand the key uncertainties and develop well-informed judgments to try to resolve those uncertainties the best you can. If you cannot resolve key uncertainties, then you must temper the confidence with which you make claims about the attractiveness of an investment.

That is, you begin with a hunch, or maybe just a hope. Then, with diligence and patient analysis, you try to figure out the contents of the bag to the point at which you have a good idea of which way the odds point. Of course, some uncertainty and, therefore, speculation will remain in your choice. Yet, because your analysis has clarified the odds, your behavior is like that of an investor.

Investment analysis, in other words, is the process of uncovering the odds built into a situation, so that you may commit resources where they are heavily in your favor.

It may not be within your power to resolve all of the many kinds of uncertainties that may surround a particular investment thesis. Uncertainties about macroeconomic events and the environment depend on larger forces over which you have no control. However, you must still articulate such exogenous uncertainties in order to clarify how they might influence your investment thesis. Whether or not the European Union will satisfactorily resolve the debt crisis, for instance, is an uncertainty that you cannot resolve—although you must still try to understand how the situation affects your thesis.

Other kinds of uncertainty may surrender to your judgments if they originate not in external phenomenon but in the lack of your own understanding of the situation at hand. Such uncertainties are endogenous to your personal knowledge and diligence; whether you resolve them depends on the skill and creativity with which you approach your analysis. For instance, a company's ability to deliver sustained performance over time may be an uncertainty that you can resolve with an analysis of such things as its historical performance, the sustainability of its business model, and the quality of its leadership.

The focus on uncertainty does not mean, of course, that frequencies and objectivity do not have a role in analysis. Where possible, you must use available data to form baseline judgments. Data on past instances of accounting fraud in similar companies, for example, may be helpful in assessing the likelihood in a particular case. But the important distinction here is that instead of trying to measure the so-called objective risk, you focus on developing processes and skills that will help make sound judgments about uncertainties surrounding key issues that impact your investment thesis.

Quantifying Market Risk

Our emphasis on subjective judgments in investment analysis is in sharp contrast to the vain search for objective measures of risk that has characterized modern finance for over six decades. One such measure of risk relies on the size and frequency of returns. When it first came into common use during the 1950s, this specification, standard deviation of returns, was an advance over the subjective assessments of risk that businesspeople had been making for eons—or so some people claimed.

Many at the time felt that subjectivity was a license to be arbitrary. Subjective assessments lacked precision, and they were difficult to standardize and compare across investments. So, defining risk as standard deviation became widely popular. Using standard deviation as a base concept, people began to formalize the measurement of risk as β (beta), or the degree to which returns of a stock co-vary with the returns of a benchmark index such as the Standard and Poor's 500 Index. The β is, in a way, akin to the relative frequencies of the green and red balls in our example above. In this way, high-β stocks are highly risky; low-β stocks have low risk. Such quantification of risk for individual stocks closely relates to the idea of portfolio risk, or the standard deviation of portfolio returns, as I will elaborate later in the book.

Note that although the theory says to use expected future returns, we necessarily have to compute standard deviations using past returns. In practice, therefore, the statistical measures of risk are measures of how returns have behaved during a window of a few months in the recent past.

It is easy to see the attractiveness of quantifying risk using standard deviation of returns. Since past returns data are plentiful, computing standard deviation is a straightforward application of elementary statistics; it appears to give an objective measure of risk and avoids the need for subjective judgments that could be plagued with vagueness. Defined and computed this way, the risk of an investment is equivalent to the number and proportion of red and green balls that may be in bag A, to use the example above. Once you so quantify risk, investing is simply about figuring out how much risk you're willing to take.

Although β is a good indicator of the volatility of prices in the recent past,[3] quantifying investment risk in this way is misleading. For instance, in standard theory, we assume that the underlying distribution of returns is normal, but that assumption is questionable.[4]

Ironically, the focus on quantifying risk distracts investors and weakens the understanding they ought to have about the formidable uncertainties that may be plaguing an investment thesis. Unlike a bag full of red and green balls, companies are dynamic entities, constantly evolving their business models as they try to adapt to a changing environment. Their past stock returns may say little or not much at all about the uncertainties they face or about their future prospects. The past returns may, in fact, be driven by macro events, fickle investor sentiment, or something else altogether, but they may have little or nothing to do with the underlying uncertainties related to the business, operations, or leadership.

Subjective Probability

Fascination with seemingly objective statistics and past returns is largely owing to a deeper fascination with objectivity and precision. The wide availability of past pricing data fuels this fascination, as does the misplaced envy of hard disciplines such as physics, where objective data seem to allow for the application of standard statistical tools.[5] But the bias toward seemingly objective measures of risk severely limits clear thinking when brought into the world of investing, a world of human affairs in which data themselves change in response to interpretation and action. When rising prices attract hopeful buyers, the demand so created pushes prices even higher; when falling prices induce fearful selling, prices drop even further. So, if price data are endogenous to human action, how is variation in prices objective?

It turns out that the focus on objective probability ignores a long-enduring Bayesian tradition that conceptualizes probability in personal terms—that probabilities are not objective but subjective,[6] that they inhere not in the object or event but in the ideas and expectations of the observer.

Think about the odds of getting heads in a coin toss. Most people would place the odds as one in two, since each of the two possibilities appears equally likely. From a subjectivist's point of view, however, those odds assume that the coin is perfectly balanced, which may not be true. Only after observing the results of many coin tosses can you update your baseline expectations about balance and be able to say what the odds actually are for this particular coin.

Probability does not inhere in the coin but in your expectations about how well the coin is constructed. Subjectivists say that you can start with one-in-two odds of turning up heads, but you must then update that initial expectation (prior probability) based either on new information about how balanced the coin is or from your experiences over several flips. You learn from experience and incorporate this new information to form updated expectations.

Accepting β as a measure for risk depends on your expectation that the markets are perfect assimilators of all available information: that they are efficient. You may base this expectation on your unique definition of efficiency or your subjective feeling or interpretation of empirical evidence related to market efficiency. If you don't believe that markets are efficient in general or in a particular case, then you must discount the suitability of β as a measure of investment risk.

The trouble with β and other statistical measures of risk is that quantification does not imply comprehensiveness; irreducible uncertainty remains in all statistical representations of risk.Worse, the focus on statistics and vast amounts of quantitative data shifts investor attention away from the richness of data in the particulars of individual investments. In the world of investing, where underlying distributions are unknown, where you form beliefs using inadequate or even missing data, where theories usually live in the dark shadow of confirmation bias, having a rigorous way of subjectively assessing probabilities is more helpful than the vain search for objectivity and precision.

As I will show going forward, when evaluating particular companies for their investment potential, you must focus on the many uncertainties that affect future operating performance. You can capture such uncertainties by trying to assess such things as prospects for future growth, sustainability of yields, stability of operating performance, and financial strength. You must also make subjective judgments about such things as the quality of the business model and the competence of the management team.

Uncertainties that affect future cash flows are of fundamental importance to investors. Where a keen understanding of the operations and fundamentals is missing, uncertainties remain high and drive down the valuation because of the need to use a high discount rate, as we will see in the next chapter. Similarly, where strong leadership and a deeply entrenched competitive position reasonably assure future cash flows, intrinsic valuation is high because of the justifiably low discount rate.

Key operating uncertainties are fundamental to grasping economic worth, and they are distinct from uncertainties about market prices. Seeking to derive objective risk using market prices alone undermines the role of judgment in investment analysis, and it diverts resources away from careful analysis of the many business-related issues that are at the heart of making informed judgments.

All this, then, brings us full circle to the example from the beginning of the chapter. We see that investors rarely if ever face situations as well defined as bag A; the search for well-defined risk has misled us all into thinking that we can precisely measure the hazards to our investments. In fact, investors typically face situations more like bags B or C and must then work diligently to figure out what is in those bags before committing to draw from them.

Updating Subjective Probabilities

Of course, subjective judgments suffer from personal biases and possibly ungrounded beliefs, and they can lead to egregious mistakes. But fear of mistakes should not prevent you from trying to develop a well-informed subjective understanding of probable future outcomes. As in any other judgment-driven profession, subjective understanding is unavoidable and indispensable when investing. The key is to form judgments conservatively and to update them in light of new information.[7] Rigorous thinking, rather than precision, is the key to investing wisely.

In order to make good judgments, we need to ensure that our beliefs are reasonable and consistent with well-developed standards of logic and data. More importantly, we need a systematic way of updating our beliefs by seeking and being alert to new information. The principle of negation and the derivative framework of disconfirmation help us make good subjective judgments. They are the basis for making subjective but rigorous assessments of data that pertain to a given investment thesis. Such is the rationale for the quantitative tests I develop in chapters 14 and 15, and for the framework for qualitative analysis I discuss in chapters 16 through 20.

CHAPTER FOURTEEN

The Simple Math of Valuation

INVESTORS USUALLY FACE two kinds of difficulty when trying to estimate the intrinsic value of a company: one from not enough skepticism and another from too much of it.

The first difficulty arises when you seek out a formula to reach a precise answer, which you can take as exact or approximate value. Once obtained, such an answer anchors your mind to it. The very process of computing gives the resulting answer a feeling of credibility and creates a psychological anchor that impedes further nuanced thinking. The formulaic approach perhaps soothes the anxiety that many feel from the ambiguity that surrounds the ideas of worth and value.

But simple formulations like these make investors vulnerable to mistakes or outright manipulation, as any formula, by definition, focuses attention on a narrow set of variables and hides broader considerations from view. Such vulnerability is especially likely if people are also prone to apply the formulae without fully understanding the assumptions or limitations in their derivation.

Consider the supposed Graham formula for estimating intrinsic value, which seems to propose a simple mathematical relationship between the price-to-earnings (PE) ratio, earnings per share, and expected growth rate.[1] The association with Graham gives the formula instant credibility and, for all too many, a license to apply it uncritically. But Graham used the formulation to illustrate the foolhardiness of trying to project the future and the rosy scenarios analysts sometimes conjure up to justify lofty valuations.

The second difficulty arises from a deeply felt skepticism that correctly estimating the economic worth of a company is even possible. After all, valuing a company requires estimating its projected future earnings and the appropriate rates with which to discount those earnings. But the future is unknown and, for the most part, unknowable. In theory, a virtually infinite list of factors could affect the future earnings of a firm. Clearly, it is impossible to anticipate all of them.

Such concerns have merit. Indeed, it is difficult for many people to navigate through the maze of information, uncover and analyze the salient facts, and make reasonable judgments about economic worth. Complexities and an absence of concrete answers lead many into thinking that analysis is hopeless.

But complexity is not unique to investing. Professions such as law and medicine address problems as complex or more so. As in other fields, the problems in investing exist on a continuum from very simple to incomprehensibly complex. Investors can, however, avoid complex problems and focus on simple ones and only gradually, if at all, move up the ladder of complexity. Investors have this flexibility, which perhaps no other profession does: doctors cannot choose which patients they will see, but investors can choose which securities they will analyze and which they will not.

Instead of gullibility or senseless skepticism, investing requires a sensible middle ground where quantitative and qualitative approaches help guide judgments about economic worth and value. The skill that investors need is to recognize and avoid problems that cannot be solved, instead focus on those situations that are amenable to competent analysis, given their skill set at a given moment. The purpose of analysis is not so much to get a single number indicating value but to grasp the essence of a situation and surface fundamental forces that may be driving economic worth.

In this chapter, I show how to apply the principle of negation to evaluate an investment thesis pertaining to the valuation of stocks. Note that stocks are akin to bonds but with indefinite maturity, variable and discretionary coupon, and, perhaps most importantly, residual risk (beyond interest rates and default or downgrade). Let's first value a simple bond and see how that translates into valuing stocks. I will then show how to use the mechanics of valuation to try to set up and refute the investment thesis.

Valuing a Simple Bond

Let's say that we have a bond of $1,000 face value paying a coupon of $50 (5 percent bond yield) at the end of every year. Assume that the bond matures in five years, at the end of which, along with the last coupon of $50, you also receive the face value.

Row 1 in table 14.1 shows the nominal cash flows from this bond. We know from the time value of money that, in an inflationary environment, future cash is worth less than cash in hand. Assuming that the coupons of this bond are mostly reliable, you set the discount rate for future cash flows at a constant 4 percent. This leads to $1,045 as the net present value, or intrinsic value, of the bond. If you set the discount rate at 6 percent, value drops to $958; when the discount rate equals the bond yield of 5 percent, value is $1,000, the same as face value.

Consider the same bond with one difference: assume it has no maturity. That is, the bond has a perpetual coupon of $50 per year. For such a bond, the technique for valuing would be the same as shown in table 14.1, except that the table will keep on going to the right.

It so happens that, in such a perpetual maturity bond, table 14.1 can be approximated by a very simple formula:

$$\text{Perpetual Bond Value} = (C/r) \qquad (14.1)$$

where C is the constant annual coupon, and r is the constant discount rate. So, our bond above is valued as

$$\text{Perpetual Bond Value} = (C/r) = (\$50/0.04) = \$1{,}250 \qquad (14.1\ \text{Sol.})$$

Using equation 14.1, a similar bond with a 5 percent constant discount rate would be valued at $1,000, and one with a 6 percent constant discount rate would be valued at $833.33.

TABLE 14.1

	Year 1	Year 2	Year 3	Year 4	Year 5	NPV*
Cash flow	$50	$50	$50	$50	$1,050	
Discount factor	1.04	1.08	1.12	1.17	1.22	
Present value	$48.08	$46.23	$44.45	$42.74	$863.02	$1,045

*Sum of present values

Next, take the same perpetual bond as above and add one more level of complexity: that the coupon grows at a constant annual rate of 2 percent every year into the future. For such a bond, we approximate value using a simple mathematical equivalent:

$$\text{Perpetual Bond Value} = C'/(r - g) \qquad (14.2)$$

where C′ is the coupon paid out at the end of year 1, r is the discount rate, and g is the constant perpetual growth rate. Because of the growth, C′ can be rewritten as C •(1 + g) to reflect the coupon at the end of year 1. So, we now have

$$\text{Perpetual Bond Value} = C \bullet (1 + g)/(r - g) \qquad (14.3)$$

For the bond in our example, with a coupon of \$50 growing at a constant 2 percent and discounted at a rate of 4 percent, we compute value as

$$\begin{aligned}\text{Perpetual Bond Value} &= \$50 \bullet (1.02)/(0.04 - 0.02)\\ &= \$2{,}550 \qquad (14.3\ \text{Sol.})\end{aligned}$$

In effect, when you buy a bond, you purchase a future stream of cash. In evaluating a bond, therefore, you choose to discount that stream at a rate that is appropriate given your reading of the uncertainties with regard to expected future rates of interest and the likelihood of default or downgrade.

Intrinsic Economic Worth

The same thought process applies when you evaluate stocks, but with a few notable differences. One, you have no contractual assurance about the stream of future cash. Two, as a shareholder, you are a residual claimant and get nothing until the bondholders receive what they are owed. Because of these differences, as an investor in stocks, you not only purchase protected future cash streams but mostly the ability of the company to continue constructing streams above those owed to bondholders.

In this sense, when evaluating stocks of established companies that have a long operating history, you want to evaluate the worth of their established cash flows beyond those owed to bondholders. For a new company with no history, on the other hand, you purchase their ability to construct nonexisting streams of cash so you can lay claim to those in the future. For somewhat established companies or those in transition, your evaluation must include careful consideration of stable cash flows and those the company credibly promises to construct for future delivery.

Let's now apply the process for estimating the economic worth of a perpetual bond to evaluating stocks. The commonly used dividend discount model (DDM) casts stocks as perpetual bonds:

$$\text{Intrinsic Value} = D \bullet (1 + g)/(r - g) \tag{14.4}$$

where *D* is the annual dividend per share at the beginning of the first year, r is the constant discount rate, and g is the perpetual constant growth rate of dividends per share.

For instance, as of July 2015, Walmart paid an annual dividend of $1.96 per share. Assuming a 10 percent discount rate and a perpetual growth rate of 5 percent, we approximate value as

$$\text{Intrinsic Value} = 1.96 \bullet (1.05)/(0.10 - 0.05) = \$41.16 \qquad \text{(14.4 Sol.)}$$

The key issue in this formulation is the estimation of r and g in the denominator. The discount rate (r) happens to be one of the most intractable problems in finance, and we will work through that in the pages that follow. Estimation of g is a challenge, although, for some companies at least, historical growth rates may provide a measure of guidance on future growth.

For now, let's focus on just the numerator. Is cash dividend the correct quantity to discount? The important thing to know is that the number in the numerator ought to be one that you deem your property as the shareholder—because you want to discount the stream of cash to which you are legally entitled. Current and expected future dividend is often only a part of what rightfully belongs to the shareholders. As residual owners of the company, shareholders lay claim to all earnings, after finance charges, taxes, and necessary reinvestments in the company.

The exact cash flows owed to shareholders can be subject to a good deal of debate and contention. Activist investors, for instance, often contest decisions of companies to hold cash in reserve for future opportunities. Sometimes, as in the recent case of Apple, activist investors such as Carl Icahn[2] and David Einhorn[3] engaged in a very public debate with management, insisting that they share cash with shareholders. Usually at issue are the free cash flows that the company generates, net of necessary reinvestments and payments to senior claimants such as bondholders.

For simplicity, let's assume that the company distributes all its earnings every year and all of these belong to shareholders. For Walmart, annual earnings as of January 2015 were \$5.05 per diluted share. Assuming, once again, a perpetual discount rate of 10 percent and perpetual growth of 5 percent per year, we get

$$\text{Intrinsic Value} = 5.05 \bullet (1.05)/(0.10 - 0.05) = 106.05 \qquad (14.4\ \text{Sol.})$$

This estimate of value is highly dependent, of course, on the reasonableness of assumptions. As indicated, the discount rate (r) and growth rate (g) are particularly difficult to pin down, especially since the model requires that these assumptions be constant and perpetual far into the unknown future.

Understand that the intrinsic economic value of a stock is a function of the earning power (*e*) of the company, its future prospects (g), and the rate of discount (r). Sure, this seems like a simple formulation with just three variables that we operationalize with varying degrees of confidence. But this requires that investors understand the ability of the company to generate a given level of earnings and grow them at a certain minimum rate into the long future—along with an appreciation of the key uncertainties that accompany future earnings.

The discount model computes economic value as an algebraic output. But the quality of valuation depends on the reasonableness of the estimates for the three variables—based largely on a subjective understanding of the company. So, while it may seem a simple mathematical formula, investors must understand the discount model in terms of abilities, prospects, and fundamental uncertainties about future performance.

Applying the Simple Math of Valuation

The dividend discount model (DDM) encapsulates in simple form the present value of future cash flows that are rightfully the property of the shareholders. The term "dividend" implies all cash flows that rightfully belong to shareholders, whether the company chooses to distribute those flows via dividends or share repurchase or simply retain them for business-related uses.

The discount formulation is simple but only deceptively so, as slight variations in assumptions can make very large differences in the computed value. To see this, consider as above the estimated value of Walmart as $106.05 per share—based on EPS = $5.05, r = 10 percent, and g = 5 percent.

If we change g to 4 percent, the estimated value drops 17 percent to $87.50 per share. Similarly, if we keep g at 5 percent but change the discount rate to 12 percent, the estimated value drops 29 percent to $75.75 per share.

Clearly, input assumptions impact estimates of value. It helps to have conservative assumptions, but, even then, estimates of value are highly vulnerable to mistakes. It is difficult to refute a given stock price because you can always find assumptions that justify it. Your assumptions could be corrupt if you secretly desire to prove that the price is correct. If you wanted to prove that Walmart is worth much more, simply drop the discount rate to 8.5 percent, and the formula will then compute the estimated value as $151 per share.

In order to overcome the tendency to make wrong assumptions, let's look at an alternative approach.

A Back Door to Valuation

We can approach the discount model formulation in a markedly different way: by reverse engineering the assumptions embedded in the current price. In this alternative approach, our first assumption is that liquid, well-functioning markets are correctly pricing the company in question. This sets up our null thesis as Price (P) = Value (V). That is, instead of assuming that the markets are always or mostly efficient, we set up the claim as a testable base proposition for all our analyses.[4]

Then, if we have a hunch that a particular stock is under- or overvalued, we then reevaluate the proposition of efficient markets as untrue in this particular case. That is, we formulate that P ≠ V. Further, if we think that the market may be especially undervaluing the company, then our investment thesis is that the prevailing price is sufficiently below value ($P << V$).

Aware of the insidious confirmation bias that could be corrupting our judgment, we would not try to prove the above undervaluation thesis; we instead try to refute it with good logic and doubt, applied to the important facts of the case.

If we are successful in refuting the investment thesis, then we know that our hunch was incorrect and that, in this particular case, the markets may be efficiently pricing the stock investigated. If we are unable to refute the thesis, we may be justified in our hunch that price is sufficiently below economic value. Inability to refute, in that case, helps us reach the tentative inference that an investment opportunity as expected may indeed exist.

To illustrate, let's go back to the simple algebraic manipulation of the discount model of valuation, where the future cash flows to be discounted are taken simply as the earnings per share (EPS):

$$\text{Intrinsic Value (V)} = \text{Price (P)} = \text{EPS} \bullet (1 + g)/(r - g) \quad (14.5)$$

We assume that the prevailing price (P) of the shares of a company is correctly reflecting the underlying economic worth or value (V) of future earnings flows, appropriately discounted. Rewriting the above equation, we get

$$\text{Price-to-Earnings} = (P/EPS) = (1 + g)/(r - g) \quad (14.5a)$$

Or,

$$\text{Earnings Yield (EY)} = (EPS/P) = (r - g)/(1 + g) \quad (14.5b)$$

That is, the earnings yield ($EY = EPS/P$) equates to a simple algebraic relationship between the discount rate (r) and the perpetual growth rate (g).

Now, in theory, EPS should be the earning power—or the ability of the company to continue earning at a certain level well into the future. We may sometimes estimate the earning power by looking at the historical financial record, but it may remain elusive for some companies because of a lack of historical record or a highly variable performance over the years.

As of July 15, 2015, Walmart's common stock was trading at \$73.63. For a whole host of quantitative and qualitative reasons, we suspect that the market is not recognizing several positives about the company: strong leadership, clear vision, and steady, profitable growth of operations. So, we set up the investment thesis that the stock price is sufficiently less than its intrinsic value, or, $P = \$73.63 << V$.

Then, using the above formulation, we equate valuation of future earnings with the current price:

$$EY = (5.05/73.63) = 0.069 = (r - g)/(1 + g) \quad (14.5b \text{ Sol.})$$

If we assume that the company will not grow its earnings at all ($g = 0$), then the discount rate (r) falls out as the earnings yield (6.9 percent). That is, if the company simply sustains the current level of earnings, then its stock is like a bond with a constant but perpetual coupon; the discount rate built into the current price is simply the yield, or the return on current price.

The question you must ask is whether this derived discount rate ($r = 6.9$ percent) correctly represents the scenario in which it produces constant earnings at the current rate far out into the future. Is this a reasonable approximation given the history of the company and its competitive position in the marketplace?

Alternatively, if we knew or could reasonably gauge the discount rate (r), then simple algebraic manipulation shows that we can estimate the future growth rate (g) as follows:[5]

$$g = (r - EY)/(1 + EY) \quad (14.6)$$

EY is the earnings yield (EPS/price), which in this case equals 6.9 percent. That is, we now have a theoretical estimate of future growth (g) that appears to be embedded in the price. We then try to refute the investment thesis by comparing the estimates of g with the company's historical performance and, as we will see in later chapters, in light of our subjective understanding of the company's medium- to long-term prospects.

If we assume for the time being that the discount rate is 10 percent, then we compute g as

$$g = (0.10 - 0.069)/(1 + 0.069) = 0.0294 \quad (14.6 \text{ Sol.})$$

That is, for a 10 percent discount rate, a growth rate assumption of 2.93 percent is embedded in the share price of $73.63. Another way of saying this is that at the then prevailing price of just under $74 per share, the market is assuming that the earnings will grow at a rate of just under 3 percent per year into perpetuity.

Since we chose the discount rate of 10 percent arbitrarily, let's see what happens to the implied growth rate when we do a sensitivity analysis. The implied growth rate turns out to be 1.54 percent when the discount rate is 8.5 percent, and it is 4.81 percent when the discount rate is 12 percent.

We now use the range of implied growth rates thus derived using different discount rates to try to refute the undervaluation thesis. Has the company demonstrated a growth rate of 3 percent or more in recent years? Based on the past record and qualitative factors (discussed in later chapters), is it reasonable to expect that the company will be able to grow at this rate well into the future?

It so happens that, over the preceding 10 years, Walmart's earnings per share grew at an annualized rate of about 7.28 percent; this rate over the previous five years was 3.10 percent. That is, the company's earnings happen to have grown faster than the growth rates implied in the market price of $73.63 per share, although this rate of growth seems to have slowed down considerably in more recent years. If the range of discount rates chosen is appropriate, then the expected future growth rate implied in Walmart's share price is within recent historical experience. Yet, because of a slowdown in recent years, the above computations do not quite show sufficient margin of error.

How much greater than the implied growth rate should the historical growth rate be to refute the investment thesis that price is significantly below reasonable estimates of intrinsic economic worth? The answer depends on how much confidence you have in the company continuing to deliver historical growth rates well into the future. There may be no perfect answers—it depends, as we will see going forward, on your subjective interpretations of important and observable facts.

Even so, for well-established and relatively stable companies such as Walmart, a reasonable threshold is when the historical growth rate is twice the growth rate implied in the price. Since the long-term historical growth rate for Walmart in the above illustration is more than twice the implied growth rate, it appears that the market is undervaluing the company in relation to its historical performance. But the fact of recent slowing growth warrants caution given that the current valuation reflects a future growth rate not much different from what the market appears to be expecting. So, while we cannot yet refute the thesis that Walmart is undervalued, it is important for prudent investors to remain cautious and look for other signs, as discussed later in the book.

The inability to confidently refute the thesis is grounds for some caution, but we are still far from done. That is because we used an arbitrary discount rate (10 percent) to compute the implied growth rate. The next step is to understand how to home in on a more realistic discount rate, grounded in the specifics of the company in question.

The Discount Rate

The key to correctly estimating the growth rate implied in current price is the discount rate. It is clear from the above discussion that the implied growth rate (g) varies directly with the discount rate (r), which in turn reflects the uncertainties about future performance. The greater the uncertainties that surround the company, the greater must be the expectations of future growth to justify current prices.

Textbooks typically use the capital asset pricing model (CAPM) to compute the discount rate. When so computed, the discount rate is a direct linear function of market risk (β), or the degree to which share prices vary with the overall market.[6] This reliance on market risk assumes that stock prices fully reflect the underlying value of the company. For those interested in CAPM, any standard textbook should provide a detailed explanation of it. In my view, using CAPM (or other market-based formulations such as the multifactor model) to compute discount rates is problematic for two reasons.

First, we want to evaluate the prevailing prices using markers outside the market mechanism that prices the shares. Since CAPM relies on prices or, technically, on returns from changes on those prices, it is unable to provide the independent view that we need for valuation.

Second, the discount rate we use should reflect the risks and uncertainties in the future expected earnings or cash flows. The market risk as incorporated in β focuses instead on changes in returns in relation to overall market returns. If the markets were fully efficient, then market risk could perhaps fully reflect the uncertainties in the expected earnings and cash flows; if, on the other hand, price changes do not or only loosely reflect key uncertainties about the future, using β to compute the discount rate is incorrect.

Luckily, there is a better market-based indicator of key uncertainties about future earnings: the perceived riskiness of the company's bonds.

The average yield on a company's bonds reflects the assessments of the bond market about interest rate risk and the possibility of default or downgrade. That is, both interest rates and the financial condition of the company inform the rate at which to discount all future coupons net of initial outlay. For companies whose bonds trade actively, bond yields become the baseline for the discount rate.

Whereas a borrowing company is contractually obligated to the bondholders, equity holders are residual owners—they are junior in priority and not contractually guaranteed positive returns on their investments. Accordingly, stockholders bear hazards above and beyond the interest rate and the default and downgrade risks borne by bondholders.

This leads to a structure of the discount rate for shareholders as bond yield plus equity premium. This is the same structure as that used in the CAPM formulation, but with two differences. First, we replace the risk-free rate with the yield on the company's bonds to reflect the interest rate environment along with company-specific operating uncertainties. Second, instead of relying on β to compute the equity premium, we make a qualitative assessment as to how much that premium ought to be in light of operating particulars. That is, companies with higher yield bonds and greater operating uncertainties require a higher discount rate than those with low yield bonds and stable operating histories.

Depending on the company under investigation, therefore, we can use an approximate discount rate that is two to three times the prevailing yield on the company's long-term bonds that mature in about 10 years from the date of analysis. How much higher than bond yields the discount rate ought to be is neither formulaic nor arbitrary; it must arise from subjective judgments about the uncertainties that surround the future prospects of the company.

Moreover, in setting the baseline for the discount rate, we choose bonds with 10-year maturity, as that conveys a reasonably long-term investment horizon for investing in stocks—with the assumption that stock prices are random in the short run, but respond to economic fundamentals in the longer term.

TABLE 14.2
WMT Sensitivity

r	g
6.58%	−0.26%
8.23%	1.28%
9.87%	2.82%

Let's apply this reasoning to Walmart. As of July 2015, the company had two outstanding long-term bonds that would mature in about 10 years, yielding an average of 3.29 percent. Taking three different multiples of this rate (2×, 2.5×, and 3×), we get the implied growth rates (g), as shown in table 14.2.

As expected, the implied growth rate varies with the discount rate, which, in turn, is a multiple of the long-maturity bond yield. If the company does not have outstanding bonds, then we may use bond yields of equivalent companies or the prevailing yields on suitable 10-year corporate bond composites.

In table 14.2, we see that the growth rate (g) implied in the share price of $73.63 is under the historical growth pattern of the company's earnings. But our evaluation depends on what we think is the correct rate of discount to use for this particular company at this time: if we believe that the bonds will continue to yield low to reflect low operating risk, then we will use a low discount rate and have a measure of confidence because of the low future implied growth rate (−0.26 percent) relative to the recent historical growth rate (3.10 percent). If we think that the operating uncertainties are increasing, then a higher discount rate suggests that the future growth rate implied in the price is close to what the market is expecting. In the latter case, we would have to cast doubt on the undervaluation thesis.

In order to assess which of the two possibilities is more likely, we need a good understanding of the company's history and near-term prospects. To the extent that the company in question is a well-established stalwart, the future is likely to be similar to the recent past, and we can draw inferences from the numbers above. For companies that are in a turnaround or rapid-change mode, however, the past may be a less reliable indicator of things to come. In such cases, will have to rely a great deal on qualitative analyses that we will examine later in the book.

Using multiples of bond yields as proxy for uncertainties about future performance, although not perfect, has the advantage that the yields reflect independent judgments of the bond market about the uncertainties that the company faces. In other words, this allows us to obtain a perspective from outside the stock market and gives us a semblance of objectivity in our evaluations.

So, on the one hand, the seeming mathematical precision of market β gives false confidence about knowing the risks of an investment; on the other hand, rules of thumb based on historical performance and bond yields help build subjective understanding about the future prospects of a company. Even though the latter approach is less precise, it enables a more thorough evaluation of hazards associated with particular investment candidates.

Reading the Prices

The economic worth of a company is the expected future cash flows appropriately discounted to the present. In theory, therefore, market price should summarize future prospects and the cash the company is able to deliver to investors over time. Yet, depending on the motivations of the storyteller or the mood of the moment, we can tell all varieties of stories about what the future will bring. That is, the story built into the price may or may not have anything to do with future cash flows.

We as investors are particularly interested, however, in the story of future cash flows. That is, we want to know what kinds of future cash flow the buyers and sellers are expecting, wittingly or unwittingly, when they choose to transact at prevailing prices. Do the prices reflect realistic assessments of future cash flows or a wild fantasy of people caught up in the moment? It's possible that prices tell us nothing about future cash flows but a whole lot about the mood of the moment. We need to know this.

But, we proceed as if prices truly reflect value, defined simply as expectations about future cash flows, and nothing else. Next, we try to determine the expectations that would generate the discounted future stream of cash that justifies the price. These derived expectations then become the core of our analysis, as we evaluate their veracity in light of our historical and qualitative analysis of the company.

Let's consider Walmart again. Assuming a discount rate between 6.58 percent and 9.87 percent, the growth rate implied in Walmart's share price of $73.63 varied from –0.26 percent to 2.82 percent. That is, within the given range of discount rates, a long-run annualized growth rate of 3 percent or less justified the price prevailing at the time of analysis. Yet, we also know from historical data that the company grew earnings at an average of 3.10 percent per year over the previous five years. So, the expectations of future growth in earnings built into the price were consistent with the historical reality of slowing growth in earnings.

Given this analysis, we try to understand the reasons why the market may be expecting such a slowdown in the company's future growth rate. Doing so may require evaluation not only of a slowing historical growth rate but also some digging into the company to produce fodder for additional tests to update our assessment. If it turns out that subsequent analysis reveals that earnings growth will recover to the long-term growth rate, then we may feel that the initial thesis (P << V) will hold for the time being—but subject to continuing efforts at negation.

To understand why further analysis is warranted, consider this: If Walmart grew earnings at a long-term growth rate of, say, 7.28 percent per year for the next five years, then it will have grown earnings from the current $5.05 per share to $7.17 per share five years later. If the price does not change during the period, that will give an earnings yield of over 9.7 percent (7.17/73.63). In 10 years, if the long-term historical growth rate is sustained, the company will be generating about $10.19 per share, and, at current prices, the earnings yield will be almost 13.8 percent.

That is, for a company that keeps growing its earnings at a steady rate, if the price does not change, the earnings yield will keep rising. But such a rise in earnings yield can go on only up to a point, after which prices will have to rise to bring the earnings yield down to a level that is comparable with the interest rates and corporate bond yields prevailing at that time. In this particular case, however, a recent slowdown in Walmart's growth rate means that such a possibility will require the company to get back to its long-term growth rate. Such a turnaround may or may not be possible.

In so deriving expectations of future growth built into the price, we are able to assess the extent to which prices are rational—and the investment thesis viable. But to do so, we need assurance that the future will be continuous with the past. If past earnings were wildly unstable and we cannot get a good fix on the discount rate, or if the company under question does not have much of a history, then implied growth rate has no suitable historical benchmark against which to measure up.

As such, valuations obtained by discounting expected future flows are most applicable to stable companies with long histories and a sustainable business model that will allow them to continue as going concerns. For the many companies with checkered histories or no history at all, grounding prices in credible economic fundamentals may be impossible. Cautious investors should limit their search for investment value to companies that have a sufficient and credible record of operating performance.

CHAPTER FIFTEEN

Yield—Stability—Strength

SO FAR, WE have reviewed how to think about economic worth using capitalization ratios and discounted future flows. Given the ease with which we can justify a wide range of prices using convenient assumptions, we have argued that the correct approach to estimating economic worth is to apply the principle of negation. That is, we can achieve confidence in our investment thesis when we try to refute rather than prove it. The key to using refutation, moreover, is the proper setting up of the thesis so that we may appropriately put it to clear tests; the thesis must risk rejection.

Remember, the inability to refute the undervaluation thesis for Walmart in the previous chapter means only that we have more confidence in it; we remain open to the possibility of uncovering other evidence that may help refute it. We must put the thesis to further, more rigorous, attempts at refutation. In this sense, as discussed, investing is a negative art.

In this chapter, I show how to further test the investment thesis using additional quantitative data that are widely available in the public domain. Of course, the credibility and reliability of the data are very important, and investors must learn how to evaluate the quality of the data with which they work. For the time being, we will assume simply that the available data we use in our analysis are mostly correct.

Updating the Investment Thesis

Remember that our baseline assumption when evaluating stocks is that the markets are pricing them more or less correctly. That is, we write the base expectation as No: Price = Value.

Based on our inability to refute the Walmart undervaluation thesis as in the previous chapter, our investment thesis for Walmart still stands as

T: Price << Value

So, we tentatively accept our original hunch that the stock may be an attractive opportunity and now subject our thesis to further disconfirmation analysis based on additional financial data.

Note that here we are using a nonstatistical variant of Popper's method. In the context of the hard sciences, we typically first develop a null hypothesis based on whatever theory (or belief) we may be testing and then go about trying to reject the null using carefully collated data. In investment analysis of the sort we are doing here, every situation is one-off, and we rarely, if ever, have repeat observations when evaluating a single investment. Instead of using formal statistical techniques, therefore, we use the broader principle of negation to make cautious data-driven judgments. Note also that, technically, we are supposed to try to reject the null because it embodies the belief we have about the truth in a given situation. Since the investment thesis is a hunch or emerging belief about the appropriateness of a particular stock or asset, it acquires the character of a null, and that is, therefore, what we try to refute.

In the next stage of trying to refute the investment thesis, we formalize three subtheses and evaluate those using additional batteries of empirical tests.[1] Note that we examine these subtheses *after* we have already found ourselves unable to refute the main investment thesis using the implied growth rates. If any of the tests succeed in refuting one or more subthesis, we will have cast doubt on our original hunch and will then have to carry that doubt into all subsequent analyses. If we are unable to refute any of the three subtheses, we gain greater confidence in the main thesis—and can proceed to qualitative evaluations (discussed in later chapters).

First, with the *yield tests*, we ask whether the company in question is generating sufficient earnings. We try to *refute* the notion that the immediate return we would receive from following through on the thesis is better than putting our money in the bank or in corporate or treasury bonds, or perhaps in another stock. To that end, these tests require that we compute earnings, cash flow, and dividend yields.

Second, with the *stability tests*, we try to refute the notion that the past performance of the company was stable. That is, we question the ability of the company to continue delivering the expected results through our investment time horizon. We assess stability using patterns in the historical financial and operating ratios.

Finally, with the *strength tests*, we try to refute the notion that the company is financially strong. We assess the financial strength of the company from an evaluation of its balance sheet, using a series of leverage and liquidity ratios.

1. Yield Tests

With yield tests, we question whether the immediate returns available from following through with the investment thesis measure up against the attractiveness of competing investment opportunities. In particular, we ask, "Does the stock yield a return that is comparable to fixed investments such as bonds and bills, with which there is little or no uncertainty of getting back your principal?" In other words, we try to refute the following subthesis (ST):

STa: The stock offers attractive yields.

You can invest in U.S. treasuries and get a return prevailing at a given time. Let's say that you want to invest $100,000 with a time horizon of 10 years. Suppose that the 10-year T-notes are yielding 2.367 percent, as they were as of the time of writing (July 2015). This means that if you chose to invest in these treasuries, you would get an interest payment (coupon) of $2,367 for each of the next 10 years and then get the full refund of the $100,000 you had invested originally.

The T-notes provide a good benchmark for evaluating the yields subthesis as they have no default risk, because the government of the United States stands behind these issues.

The risk that you do have when investing in the Treasuries is the interest rate risk. Suppose, for example, that while you're holding the T-notes at a 2.367 percent rate, inflation picks up and the interest rates in the economy rise to 5 percent. Now you're still getting a $2,367 payment per year, whereas if you were to invest $100,000 in T-notes in the new environment of a 5 percent rate, your payment would be

$5,000 per year. You end up holding notes that give you smaller payments than those prevalent in the higher-rate environment.

In this case, you may want to sell the low-coupon Treasuries you hold and reinvest in new Treasuries at the higher interest rate. But the market value of your old Treasuries in the new interest rate environment will be lower than what you had paid for them. Let's see how the market value of your old Treasuries will be affected by an increase in the interest rates from 2.367 percent to, say, 5 percent.

Bond Yields

What will the price of your T-notes need to be to yield the prevailing interest rate of 5 percent? We know that once you purchase the T-notes, you get a fixed coupon of $2,367 per year until maturity: 10 years in this case. Knowing this, potential buyers will demand a price that yields the same return as the prevailing interest rates at the time you choose to sell the T-notes. To yield 5 percent, the price of the T-notes you hold will have to drop in order to match the higher interest rate (e.g., by buying the new T-notes that the U.S. government is issuing at the time).

We have to solve for Price (X) in (2,367/X) = 5 percent. This gives us X as (2,367/0.05), or $47,340. That is, because of the increase in interest rates in the new environment, the value of your T-notes has dropped from $100,000 to $47,340. If you sell at this point, you will be taking a massive loss on your original investment. So, you may decide to keep the T-notes, sadly accepting a coupon of $2,367 (2.367 percent) per year and then getting back your invested principal at the time of maturity.

The T-notes, then, have no default risk, but they do expose investors to the risk of changes in the interest rates. If you are comfortable making a 10-year commitment to the Treasuries and not worrying about what happens in the interim, then the interest rate risk would not be of much concern. Just hold on to the Notes until maturity, accept the rate you got at the time of purchase, and be secure in the virtual guarantee that you will get all your money back.

It is because there is no default risk that the 10-year T-notes make a good benchmark against which to measure the attractiveness of the stock you may be considering. However, since the financial troubles post-2007, the safety (default-free) feature of Treasuries is attracting a good deal of capital, and their pricing may now be somewhat distorted, as highly risk-averse investors flock to them for the guarantee they offer.

For instance, in periods of intense fear, the Treasuries become very attractive, and demand for them rises sharply, quickly inflating their prices and lowering their yields. Similarly, during strong bull markets, risk-seeking investors abandon the safety of the Treasuries in favor of fast-rising stocks, resulting in a drop in the demand and price of Treasuries and a rapid increase in their yield. Interventions by the Federal Reserve can make this dynamic a bit more complex, but, put simply, the possibility of speculation in the Treasuries can somewhat dilute their effectiveness as a good benchmark for stock analysis.

A possibly more stable benchmark to use is the composite index of 10-year corporate bonds with a AAA or AA rating, or a very low risk of default. These bonds do not have the backing of the U.S. government but that of issuing corporations, typically among the healthiest financially. Moreover, the basket comprises bonds of not just one but several companies and, therefore, may represent the broader economy.

On July 15, 2015, about midday, the yield on a composite index of AAA-rated 10-year corporate bonds was 3.13 percent, almost a third higher than the 2.367 percent yield available on the 10-year T-notes. At the time, this yield spread of 0.76 percent (or 76 basis points) accounted for some unknown but small default or downgrade risk for a basket of high-grade corporate bonds.

Earnings Yields

When applying the bond yield benchmark to evaluate stocks, it is best where possible to use the bonds of the company itself. As of July 15, 2015, Walmart had two bonds that would mature in about 10 years. One of these, maturing in April 2024, was yielding 3.117 percent, and the other, maturing in April 2027, was yielding 3.471 percent (for an average of 3.29 percent). Both the Standard & Poor's and Fitch rating agencies classified these bonds as AA, one notch below the top rating of AAA. At the time, the yield on the 10-year composite index of AA bonds was 3.36 percent.

Even though these Walmart 10-year bonds did not get the top rating, they had a lower average yield (3.29 percent) or marginally lower default/downgrade risk than the composite of AA bonds

(3.36 percent). So, let's use this information to see if we may be able to refute our subthesis for Walmart at the given price.

As of the morning of July 15, 2015, Walmart common was trading at \$73.63 per share. For the previous full year (as of January 2015), the company had reported diluted earnings per share (EPS) of about \$5.05 per share. Assuming that the EPS correctly reflected the company's earning power, the earnings yield (EY) computes as

$$EY = (EPS/Price) = (5.05/73.63) = 0.0686 \qquad (15.1)$$

That is, for each dollar invested in the common shares of Walmart at the current price, the company generated about 6.9 cents in earnings. This is more than twice the 3.29 percent yield that the bondholders of the company were getting for the AA-rated bond maturing in about 10 years.

The difference, or the equity premium, reflects the supposition that the company's AA-rated 10-year bonds had a very low risk of default, whereas there was some irreducible uncertainty about the earnings going forward. Moreover, since companies typically do not distribute all their earnings to shareholders, earnings yields are not directly comparable to bond yields. Bondholders get their yields in cash, whereas shareholders do not, unless of course the company pays out regular dividends.

Dividend Yields

Let's compute dividend yields for the ongoing example of Walmart. In the full year reported in January 2015, Walmart paid out four quarterly dividends adding up to \$1.92 in total cash dividends per diluted share (DPS). So, we compute the trailing dividend yield (DY) as

$$DY = (DPS/Price) = (1.92/73.63) = 0.0261 \qquad (15.2)$$

At \$73.63 per share, if Walmart continued paying the annual dividend of \$1.92 per share, then for your investment of \$100,000, you will get about \$2,610 in cash every year until you sell your stake in the company. This is cash in hand and, therefore, directly comparable with the yields that the bondholders get. These dividends compare with the approximately \$3,290 that bondholders would receive in coupon payments every year for the next 10 years. Unless the company gets in trouble in the interim, the bondholders get the full principal back at maturity; shareholders have no assurance that they will get their invested principal back, and the company has the option of raising or cutting the dividends, or stopping them.

We now have bond yields to compare with earnings and dividend yields. Earnings yield is useful in assessing how much in earnings the company is able to generate from each dollar of your purchase price. Dividend yield is useful because it indicates the approximate annual cash return you can expect from your investment in the company at current prices. But what happens if the company does not issue dividends? After all, many companies do not. This brings us to cash flows.

Cash Flow Yields

By accounting convention, the \$5.05 EPS are the company's best estimate after it has deducted all expenses and taxes from the revenues. These earnings need to be translated using additional accounting conventions to see how much cash the company actually generated. Of the cash earnings, the company usually puts some back into the business in order to maintain the quality of assets and the ability to continue generating earnings.

The remaining cash earnings, or free cash flow, then rightfully belong to the shareholders even if the company decides not to distribute them. The company may use the cash it retains for other purposes such as retiring debt, repurchasing shares in the open market, or making investments in new growth opportunities. These free cash flows are theoretically the correct dividend owed to you as a shareholder and, therefore, the correct yields for analysis.

For Walmart, even though the accounting earnings were \$5.05 per share, their operating cash earnings per share (OCPS) were \$8.81 per share. So, we compute their operating cash yield (OCY) as

$$\text{OCY} = (\text{OCPS}/\text{Price}) = (8.81/73.63) = 0.1197 \qquad (15.3)$$

Of the cash generated from operations, Walmart reinvested a portion back into the company as capital expenditures of \$3.75 per share and, as a result, generated \$5.05 in free cash flow per share (FCFPS). We compute their free cash flow yield (FCFY) as

$$\text{FCFY} = (\text{FCFPS}/\text{Price}) = (5.05/73.63) = 0.0686 \qquad (15.4)$$

TABLE 15.1

10-year treasury	2.37%	Earnings yield	6.86%
10-year corporate AAA	3.13%	Dividend yield	2.61%
10-year corporate AA	3.36%	Operating cash yield	11.97%
10-year Walmart AA	3.29%	Free cash flow yield	6.86%

The yields, reported in table 15.1, show that investing in the common stock of Walmart would likely result in a much higher (more than double) free cash yield than investment in either T-notes or in a basket of AAA corporate bonds. In fact, investment in Walmart, at $73.63 per share, would yield a premium of more than twice (6.86 percent versus 3.36 percent) the company's AA-rated long-term bonds.

How much premium over the 10-year corporate AAA is acceptable remains a question, however. Unfortunately, we cannot answer this question conclusively in the abstract. Investors must understand their own risk tolerances and demand the equity premium they deem personally acceptable. For some, more than 100 percent premium over yields from good-quality bonds is sufficient; for others, their strongly risk-averse nature may demand even more equity premium, and they may choose to invest in the Treasuries instead.

For a risk-neutral stock investor, however, Walmart's equity yield premium over bond yields suggests that we still cannot refute subthesis STa. For another attempt at refutation, we next evaluate the company on the stability of its performance.

2. Stability Tests

Unable to refute the investment thesis based on implied growth rate and yield tests, the next step is to question the company's record of steady operating performance. The objective here is to look for indications that the company has sufficient earning power to continue delivering the earnings reflected in the yield tests and maintain the discrepancy between the historical and implied growth rates. We must look at the past to assess the potential for the future but, again, in the spirit of refutation. Formally, therefore, the next refutable subthesis is as follows:

STb: The company has a track record of steady performance.

There are two broad ways of assessing the steadiness of the company's historical performance. One is to redo the yields as computed in the previous section, but as earnings, dividends, and cash flows averaged over the previous several years. The other is to compute key margins and ratios so as to numerically and visually evaluate patterns for the preceding five to ten years—or, ideally, over an entire business cycle, from peak to trough back to peak again. These assessments then indicate whether we can clearly refute STb.

Average Yields

In order to examine stability using average yields, let's continue with the example of Walmart selling at $73.63 per share. Table 15.2 shows the average historical EPS, DPS, and FCFPS for Walmart.

We can make several observations from these data. For starters, the company does indeed have performance data available for at least 10 years, absent which it would be difficult to assess stability. Different investors will have different levels of comfort with the extent to which historical data are available, but brand-new companies or those with only a few years of operating history are not amenable to this analysis. The absence of historical data creates a great deal of unresolvable uncertainty and increases the chances of making Type I errors.

The data in table 15.2 show that the company steadily increased both earnings and dividends during the preceding 10 years. Free cash flows, computed as operating cash flows less capital expenditures, also

TABLE 15.2

	Average			2014
	10-Year	5-Year	3-Year	1-Year
EPS ($)	3.95	4.79	4.98	5.05
DPS ($)	1.22	1.60	1.79	1.91
FCFPS ($)	2.77	3.59	3.96	5.05
	Average			**2014**
	10-Year	**5-Year**	**3-Year**	**1-Year**
EY	5.37%	6.50%	6.76%	6.85%
DY	1.66%	2.18%	2.43%	2.59%
FCFY	3.76%	4.88%	5.38%	6.86%

increased from $2.77 in 2005 to $5.05 in 2014. This reflects increasing earnings and correspondingly larger capital expenditures each year. In addition, yields at the current price of $73.63 also show a rising trend, indicating improving performance over the previous 10 years, although at a slower rate of growth in more recent years.

Given past performance as indicated, let's assume for the moment that the earning power of the company is correctly reflected in the averages. If Walmart were to continue delivering performance as it had done on average over the previous three years, we can then use EPS = $4.98, DPS = $1.79, and FCFPS = $3.96. These correspond to yields of EY = 6.76 percent, DY = 2.43 percent, and FCFY = 5.38 percent for an investor purchasing the shares at the price of $73.63 per share.

Both three-year EY (6.76 percent) and FCFY (5.38 percent) are higher than the yield of 3.36 percent then available for a AA corporate bond composite. The three-year dividend yield of 2.43 percent is more than two-thirds (72.3 percent) of the AA bond yield (see table 15.2).

Clearly, we cannot quite refute the investment thesis for Walmart, as the stability in its operating record and financial results makes it likely that future performance would be at the current levels. Slow recent growth rates still remain a concern, however.

Patterns in Operating Data

Again using Walmart as an example, table 15.3 shows the 10-year history of operating (OpM) and net margins (NM) for the company. The company's margins show stability, indicating steady performance over the years.

Similar steadiness is evident in several financial and operating performance metrics: return on equity (ROE), return on capital (ROC), asset turnover (A T/O), and inventory turnover (Inv T/O).

The stability of historical performance suggests that the earning power of the company is robust. So we cannot quite refute subthesis STb that the company has a track record of stable performance. This means the main thesis regarding the attractiveness of Walmart stock at the then prevailing price of just under $74 survives. In fact, because of our inability to clearly refute it thus far, we have somewhat more confidence in the thesis than when we first started.

Note that the main idea here is to assess whether the company can continue delivering performance into the future and to strongly anchor

TABLE 15.3

Year	OpM	NM	ROE	ROC	A T/O	Inv T/O	Op Inc	Int Exp	Int Cov
2014	5.21%	3.38%	20.10%	13.08%	2.37	7.88	25,190	2,520	10.00
2013	5.33%	3.38%	21.01%	13.26%	2.32	7.78	25,270	2,413	10.47
2012	5.57%	3.64%	22.27%	14.44%	2.30	7.85	26,027	2,325	11.19
2011	5.53%	3.53%	22.01%	13.26%	2.30	8.03	24,622	2,382	10.34
2010	5.64%	3.90%	23.91%	14.58%	2.32	8.47	23,709	2,268	10.45
2009	5.44%	3.53%	20.26%	13.38%	2.38	8.97	22,099	2,150	10.28
2008	4.93%	3.33%	20.53%	13.42%	2.46	8.68	19,841	2,272	8.73
2007	4.92%	3.39%	19.70%	12.99%	2.30	7.97	18,467	2,253	8.20
2006	5.15%	3.26%	18.33%	12.22%	2.29	7.68	17,824	1,991	8.95
2005	5.17%	3.58%	21.12%	13.48%	2.27	7.32	16,211	1,577	10.28

such assessment in the experiences of recent history. Such anchoring is conservative, certainly, but we base it on the need to control the unbounded optimism that periodically infects investors.

The conservative nature of stability tests based in historical analysis has some costs, of course. It makes us vulnerable to missing opportunities that may come about from uncharacteristically rapid growth in the future. By insisting on stability of historical performance, we are liable to sometimes make Type II errors—letting go of opportunities that may be good but don't have a stable track record of operating performance. But we accept this trade-off to reduce the chance of making the Type I error of investing in a company that does not live up to its potentially inflated promise.

3. Strength Tests

In this section, we perform a series of tests to try to refute the thesis based on financial strength. Financially strong companies have the resources to weather economic storms and to make investments that strengthen and grow operations. Financially weak companies are vulnerable to serious setback or even collapse should internal or external business conditions turn bad; they also have limited resources to invest in future growth. So, our next subthesis is as follows:

STc: The company is financially strong.

We try to refute this subthesis using three sets of metrics: coverage, leverage, and liquidity. These tests indicate the difficulty a company may have in bearing the costs of borrowed money, the degree to which assets exceed liabilities, and the extent to which the company may lack cash funds for servicing debt obligations.

Interest Coverage

The starting point for strength tests is the interest coverage ratio, computed as follows:

$$\text{Interest Coverage Ratio} = \text{Operating Income} / \text{Interest Expense} \quad (15.5)$$

For Walmart, for the full year ending January 2015, this ratio was as follows (with all data except ratio in $mm):

$$\text{Interest Coverage Ratio} = (25{,}190/2{,}520) = 10.00 \quad (15.5\ \text{Sol.})$$

In 2014, Walmart generated $25.19 billion in operating earnings and incurred an interest expense of $2.520 billion. Table 15.3 shows the interest coverage ratios for the previous 10 years. That is, both historically and currently, the company boasts plentiful resources to cover interest expenses.

Next, we compute interest coverage more conservatively using the current-year interest expense and the average operating income from the previous three years ($25,496 million). The recomputed interest coverage ratio is as follows (with all data except ratio in $mm):

$$\text{Interest Coverage Ratio} = (25{,}495/2{,}520) = 10.12 \quad (15.5\ \text{Sol.})$$

It is apparent that Walmart can easily make the interest payments equivalent to those incurred during the year. The risk of default or downgrade is rather small, with operating income steady at over $25 billion per year.

The acceptable coverage ratio varies, of course, depending on the company. Typically, because they may be entrenched in the markets they serve, larger companies are safer than smaller companies: they have a lower rate of mortality. For a company with market capitalization over $5 billion, a coverage ratio higher than 8 means that it is in excellent financial health. The same is true for smaller companies with interest coverage upward of 10. Walmart, with a market of capitalization of well over $200 billion, had a coverage ratio of about 10.

As such, we cannot refute subthesis STc that Walmart is a financially strong company. Both the stability of operating earnings and the high coverage ratio together indicate good financial strength.

The threshold for acceptable coverage ratios also varies by industry. The ratio must be higher for companies whose revenues and earnings are volatile. Technology and fashion, for instance, are vulnerable to swift changes in fortune; well-entrenched industrial companies are relatively less vulnerable to sudden upheaval. Companies in most industries (other than utilities) become vulnerable to default when their interest coverage falls below 2.

Both high coverage ratio and stability of earnings, in combination, are important indicators of the ability of a company to weather economic storms and meet the obligations debt service. These factors are highly influential in how ratings agencies such as such as Standard & Poor's and Fitch evaluate a company's bonds, and they also influence the cost of borrowing from external sources.

Financial Leverage

The next step in trying to refute STc is to understand how much financial flexibility the company has to weather economic storms as and when they come. To do so, we evaluate annual interest payments in relation to overall debt burden.

Both high levels of debt and rapid increases in debt indicate potential problems—unless the company can easily meet the obligations thus arising. So, the first check is to view the total debt the company has in relation to its common equity—sometimes also called net assets or common shareholders' equity—which is the difference between all the assets of the company (what it owns) minus all its liabilities (what it owes):

$$\text{Debt-to-Equity} = \text{Total Debt}/\text{Common Equity} \qquad (15.6)$$

For the year ending January 2015, Walmart had a total debt of \$45,284 million and common shareholder equity of \$81,394 million. The debt-to-equity ratio was therefore (all data except ratio in \$mm)

$$\text{Debt-to-Equity} = 45{,}284/81{,}394 = 0.56 \qquad (15.6\ \text{Sol.})$$

That is, for every dollar of equity belonging to common shareholders, Walmart had 56 cents in debt. So, in addition to being able to comfortably cover annual interest payments from operating income, the company also had net assets comfortably in excess of total debt. This indicates that the company had considerable ability to borrow funds, if needed.

Assume for the moment that the company could borrow more up to the point at which its debt equals its equity. Since Walmart had \$81,394 million in equity, and its total debt was \$45,284 million, all else equal, the company had the capacity to take on an additional \$36,110 (\$81,394 – \$45,284) million in debt.

Of course, the additional debt increases the interest payments. Assuming that the interest rate on the new debt is the same as the average interest rate on the current debt, for Walmart at the end of 2014, it would be as follows (all data except ratio in \$mm):

$$\text{Interest Rate} = \text{Current Interest Expense} / \text{Total Current Debt} \qquad (15.7)$$

$$\text{Interest Rate} = 2{,}520/45{,}284 = 0.056 \qquad (15.8)$$

If the company can borrow the additional money at its current average cost of 5.6 percent, then the new \$36,110 million in debt will cost \$2,022 more in interest payments per year. This is a conservative estimate because the true cost of borrowing is much lower, as reflected in the bond yields. In any case, for the target debt-to-equity ratio of 1, the company can take on a total debt of \$81,394 million, which raises the annual interest expenses to \$4,542 million. These interest expenses must be covered by the annual operating income of \$25,190 million, resulting in a revised interest coverage ratio as follows (all data except ratio in \$mm):

$$\text{Interest Coverage Ratio} = 25{,}190/4{,}542 = 5.54 \qquad (15.9)$$

That is, if the company were to maintain earnings but increase the debt-to-equity ratio from 0.56 to 1.0, its interest coverage would drop from 10.00 to 5.54, a significant decrease but still high enough to maintain a debt rating of investment grade. In all, this shows that the company has enough remaining debt capacity to the tune of up to $36 billion.

From this analysis, we can see that we are still unable to refute subthesis STc that Walmart is a financially strong company. Let's make one more attempt at refutation.

Debt Coverage

While the capital structure provides a sense of how much of the company common shareholders own net of all liabilities, it does not fully indicate the company's ability to manage all the debt. That is because equity is simply a residual derived from subtracting all liabilities from all assets. It is not cash with which to pay off debt. Even the interest coverage ratio is simply the paper ability to pay interest expenses, not necessarily an indication that the company has cash resources to service the debts.

As such, the third set of ratios with which to evaluate financial strength indicate the strength of cash flows in relation to total debt.

Free cash flow is simply the cash from operations less the capital expenditures and other investments necessary to keep the company a going concern. As such, the ability to manage debt load is calculated as follows:

$$\text{Debt Coverage Ratio} = (\text{Total Debt}/\text{Free Cash Flow}) \qquad (15.10)$$

For Walmart, this ratio computes as follows (all data except ratio in $mm):

$$\text{Debt Coverage Ratio} = (45{,}284/16{,}390) = 2.76 \qquad (15.10\ \text{Sol.})$$

That is, Walmart generated enough free cash flow during the preceding year to be able to pay off all debt in less than three years. Once again, since a single-year performance could be an aberration, it is best to use a free cash flow average over three years and recompute the above ratio. The three-year average of free cash flow from Walmart operations was $13,075 million. As such, the recomputed debt coverage ratio for the company is as follows:

$$\text{Debt Coverage Ratio} = (45{,}284/13{,}075) = 3.46 \quad (15.10\text{ Sol.})$$

So, using the average annual free cash flows over the previous three years, we see that Walmart has the ability to pay off all interest-bearing debts in less than four years. The ability of the company to pay off all debt in less than five years is generally a good sign, but this indicates only ability, not intent. In practice, it does not actually make sense for financially strong companies to pay off their debt. In fact, as they grow their assets and equity, such companies only increase their debt capacity and take on more debt in order to fund ongoing operations and strategic activities.

In short, given that Walmart has a high interest coverage, good debt ratio, sufficient debt capacity, and strong free cash flows in relation to total debt, we remain unable to refute subthesis STc that the company is financially strong.

Net Quantitative Assessment

In spite of several formal attempts, we have thus far been unable to clearly refute the investment thesis that Walmart is a good investment prospect at about $74 per share (as of July 2015). Even so, we remain cautious because we found that the company's historical growth rate was only marginally higher than the future growth rate implied in the stock price as given. Further efforts to refute the thesis, on the basis of yield, stability, and strength tests, were unsuccessful: at about $74 per share, the company may be a good investment with the proviso that it can return to historical earnings growth rates of about 7 percent or more.

We may use the same criteria we used for Walmart on other companies as well and in other ways apply the broader principle of negation for investments other than stocks. Whatever the security, the basic principle of negation is at the heart of evaluating any investment thesis. The specific criteria for refutation depend on the context, however, and will likely vary with each company and the security under consideration.

Overall, though, we can operationalize the process for the quantitative evaluation of stocks and either cast doubt on or develop a degree of confidence in the investment thesis. Starting in the next chapter, we go beyond quantitative analysis to develop a systematic process for further trying to disconfirm the thesis using qualitative information. The ability to make sound subjective judgments about the defining narratives of the companies under scrutiny will be of particular importance.

PART FOUR

Diligence

CHAPTER SIXTEEN

Depth Analysis

THE REFUTATION ANALYSIS we've done thus far is based solely on quantitative data visible from financial statements. Additional scrutiny using the qualitative data and narrative analysis is also necessary, however. In the chapters that follow, we'll see how to highlight and evaluate information that is often dispersed through the company literature. That is, we now see how to use qualitative data to continue to try to refute the investment thesis, strengthened though it may be through our previous failed attempts to refute it using quantitative data.

Perhaps the most important and easily accessible sources of qualitative information about public companies in the United States are their reports to the Securities and Exchange Commission (SEC); companies listed on foreign exchanges have similar filing requirements in the corresponding countries. For now, to illustrate how to incorporate qualitative information into the process of refutation, let's focus on the regulatory filings of companies on the U.S. exchanges.

Of the many reports filed by the companies in the United States, perhaps the most immediately useful are the annual report (10-K), quarterly report (10-Q), current report (8-K), and proxy filing (DEF 14A). The annual report filed by foreign companies listed on U.S. stock exchanges is the 20-F. In fact, the list of filings required by the SEC is very long,[1] and any investor wanting to fully explore those will have a great deal to read.

A word of caution: The amount of information you will encounter is likely to be overwhelming. You will quickly learn that the big problem of analysis is not the lack of information but too much of it; this information is also likely to be unstructured and unorganized. It's easy to get lost in the mass of data that companies are required to report, with reporting itself sometimes becoming convoluted and confusing.

Part of the reason such complexity arises is that public companies vary in size from tens of millions in sales to hundreds of billions, and they may employ thousands of people across the world. Walmart, for instance, has over 2 million[2] employees globally, not to mention the hundreds of thousands of others indirectly connected to the company as suppliers, vendors, and contractors.

Public companies are complex entities, and the mandatory reporting is meant to ensure that they take the time to explain how they're doing to investors and other interested parties. But the regulatory requirements can be so cumbersome that even simple facts can become befuddling and opaque to the uninitiated.

Perhaps the best way to navigate through these filings, therefore, is to be clear about what you're looking for in the vast amounts of reported information and go straight to the specific qualitative data with which to try to refute the investment thesis. Not all information in the filings is equally important; the key to being a wise investor is to have or develop the skills to quickly locate important facts that are relevant for the analysis at hand and then to make analytical judgments about the key uncertainties that characterize the investment thesis.

Just as we have tried to refute the investment thesis on the basis of implied growth, yield, stability, and strength, we are now ready to dive deep inside the company to look for hidden traps and pitfalls. These potential vulnerabilities are mostly qualitative and, although we may use some quantitative markers, evaluating them requires considerable subjective judgment. As is true with most professions that rely on a body of experiential knowledge, only with experience will an investor be able to make such judgments with confidence. But the basic elements of qualitative inquiry can be learned fairly quickly.

The principle of negation with which to approach the deep dive is the same as the one we have been using thus far, with one major difference. Instead of quantitatively refuting a clearly articulated investment thesis, we are looking for qualitative or narrative data that may help disconfirm the investment thesis. Because the judgments made in doing so are based on personal interpretations of qualitative data, you may not be able to clearly "hard" refute the thesis. The intent here is still to cast doubt to such an extent that disconfirmation is all but obvious.

That is, our approach still is to interpret conservatively and to try to disconfirm the emerging beliefs based (by this time) on the previously executed but unsuccessful quantitative tests designed to refute the investment thesis. The skills necessary for the next stage of analysis favor journalists over mathematicians, poets over quants. The objective of the qualitative analysis is to try to cast doubt on the defining narratives of the company. We will try to do so on three broad fronts.

First, if we have thus far been unable to refute the thesis on financial strength, we now want to use the quantitative data reported in the footnotes to the financial statements (as opposed to those in the tables) to disconfirm that the company has few or no obligations other than interest-bearing debt that is visible in the balance sheet. We must also evaluate such data to make a qualitative inference about the operations of the company. We want to check that not just debt but the overall financial burdens of the company are manageable and that its assets are in good order.

Second, if we have thus far been unable to clearly refute the thesis using the stability tests, we now want to try to disconfirm the ability of the company to continue on its historical trajectory. As such, we try to discredit the business model of the company and question its ability to deliver consistent performance and growth in the near future.

Finally, if we have thus far been unable to refute the company using the yield tests, we now want to disconfirm the proposition that the company is in an opportunity-rich environment and that it has suitable leadership in place to sustain the business and navigate through the uncertainties that inevitably lie ahead.

Let's take each in turn.

CHAPTER SEVENTEEN

Dive for Strength

WHEN INVESTING IN a company, the hidden problems can be the most dangerous, the ones that aren't immediately obvious but which could quickly surface and destroy your investment. While there are any number of hidden problems that could be plaguing a company, it is advisable to at least watch out for the most notable ones.

Often, the best place to start the search for potential trouble spots is the balance sheet. Even though the investment thesis may be credible by now, having survived a series of quantitative tests, we need to look deeper for potential liabilities and suspect assets that make the investment vulnerable.

We need to do such diligence because companies can stay within the reporting rules and still be able to hide obligations or faux assets within the thicket of their mandatory SEC filings. Regulators often play catch-up with companies, some of which find clever ways to navigate their troubles around complicated reporting requirements; sometimes those clever ways are benign, but, on occasion, they hide important weaknesses.

In this chapter, I discuss in particular the following items often buried in regulatory filings: (1) operating leases; (2) pension and post-retirement obligations; (3) litigation and lawsuits; (4) off-balance-sheet liabilities; and (5) quality of assets.

Operating Leases

If a retail clothing company wants to open another store, it has a couple of options for doing so. It can purchase space in a desired location, in which case it will have to put the full cost of the assets on the balance sheet and take depreciation charges as periodic expenses. If it uses debt to finance the purchase, then debt will be recorded as liability corresponding to the new assets on the balance sheet. If it is a cash purchase, then the cash account would be depleted, and the fixed asset account would rise by the same amount.

Alternatively, the company could simply lease the new space from another party that owns the property. In this case, the space does not show up at all on either side of the balance sheet, and the company reports lease payments as periodic operating expenses on the income statement.

Even though a company does not report operating leases on the balance sheet, those are in fact contractual obligations. The company must service such obligations and, if it so chooses, break the contract only after paying a substantial penalty for doing so. As such, operating leases are equivalent to interest payment on debt the company would have taken if it had bought properties rather than leased them. By leasing property, its keeps those assets and associated liabilities off the balance sheet, giving the impression of better financial health than may be justified because the usual debt ratios do not take them into account.

While operating leases are in fact reported in the notes to financial statements, no explicit mention of them is currently made in the balance sheet. The practice of keeping leases off the statements has been considered controversial for quite some time, as it seems to hide the true extent of financial obligations. So, after a long period of discussions and public comment, the Financial Accounting Standards Board (FASB), recently agreed in principle to change the way companies account for operating leases, to require them to explicitly report them as liability—operating-lease obligation—with corresponding assets, on the balance sheet.[1] According to a news report, showing leases on the balance sheet would increase reported debt by as much as $2 trillion in the aggregate across companies in the United States.[2] For individual companies such as CVS, if the rule were already in place, total operating lease commitments of $27.3 billion as of the end of 2014 would be added to about $18.3 billion in total debt. Other companies, such as those in the airline industry, are even heavier users of operating leases and will see their balance sheets expand considerably.

This proposed change has invited criticism from opponents who claim that an increase in reported financial obligations might in some cases lead to violations of existing debt covenants. Such issues will need to be resolved over time, but, on the whole, this is a good fix for investors. Even so, changes in lease accounting will not take effect for another couple of years as administrative and technical issues are sorted out. In the meantime, investors must look out for financial obligations arising from operating leases.

Let's take Walmart again to illustrate the effect of operating leases on leverage ratios. At the end of 2014, the company reported owning only 52 of the 1,564 distribution facilities tied to their international operations. Third parties owned and operated 34, whereas the company leased and operated an additional 70 distribution facilities. In its domestic operations, the company owned 104 of 134 distribution facilities. Of the 24 distribution facilities tied to its subsidiary Sam's Club, the company owned only six. Additionally, a substantial proportion of domestic stores (815 of 5,321, or about 15 percent) and international properties (5,130 of 11,767, or 44 percent) were also leased. In all, leasing was an important and significant part of the company's operations.

As of the end of 2014 fiscal year, the company reported almost \$18 billion in noncancellable operating leases, representing average annual rental payments of about \$1.5 billion over the next five years.

As such, the interest expense of \$2.5 billion was not the only periodic obligation of the company; it had an additional annual payment of \$1.5 billion in operating leases. This \$4 billion is then the correct figure with which to recompute the coverage ratio, which now drops to 6.30:

$$\text{Fixed Charge Coverage} = \text{Operating Income} / \text{Fixed Charges} \tag{17.1}$$

$$\text{Fixed Charge Coverage} = (25{,}250/4{,}000) = 6.30 \tag{17.1 Sol.}$$

Moreover, the \$1.5 billion or so in annual operating lease payments, if assumed to persist well into the future and discounted with a rate of, say, 5 percent, yields a debt equivalent of \$30 billion, which is not visible on the balance sheet. That is, if the company were to actually own the leased assets, it would have to somehow finance roughly \$30 billion. So, by adding this amount the company's debt, the equivalent obligations of the company go up from \$45,284 million as shown on the books at the end of 2014 to just over \$75 billion. This recomputation raises the debt ratio from 56 percent to 92 percent.

How does this new analysis update your judgment about the company as a potentially good investment? Can you now refute the investment thesis?

From the revised debt ratio now incorporating operating leases, Walmart still seems like a financially healthy company, although somewhat less so than it appeared before we accounted for its operating leases. If we capitalize all operating leases and assume that the company's target debt levels equal common equity, it appears to be nearing that objective and have much less debt capacity than previously computed. We still cannot refute the subthesis about financial strength, but we should now be cautious about the debt levels going forward.

Operating leases are one kind of hidden problem. So long as the company does well operationally and each location generates enough cash to comfortably meet lease obligations, there's no problem. But if and when the company begins to get into financial trouble from, say, a sharp decrease in revenues, the burden of contractual lease payments can add to the company's woes. This analysis, you might note, leads to a more cautious evaluation of the company as an investment opportunity than a similar analysis I conducted in the previous edition of this book. Note, therefore, that you should periodically evaluate the investments in your portfolio, as a thesis that is viable in one set of conditions may not remain so when conditions change.

For many companies, such as some airlines or retailers or manufacturers who rely heavily on leases so that they don't have to own the corresponding assets, incorporating operating leases into the analysis can change the evaluations of financial strength. This just turned out be the case for Walmart, raising some flags about their underlying financial strength.

Pension and Post-Retirement Obligations

Many companies manage their pension plans so as to be able to provide for employees once they retire. This is a moral and legal obligation, contractually obligating the company to make future payments in return for service the employees provide while they are working.

Two types of plans are common among companies in the United States: defined benefit plans (DBPs) and defined contribution plans (DCPs). The essential difference between the two is that the former can create significant liabilities for the company, whereas the latter limits or eliminates the financial obligations to retirees. Under DCPs, both the company and the employee are responsible for savings for the employee's retirement fund. As such, given that pension fund liability is one less thing to guard against, DCPs are generally better news for investors.

Many companies, such as Walmart, Google, and Microsoft, offer only DCPs and are off the hook for managing the pension assets of their employees and retirees. As such, we cannot refute the investment thesis for Walmart on financial obligations from pension fund deficits.

The trend for several years now has been for companies to limit their exposure by eliminating benefit plans and encouraging employees to take control of their own savings by offering such things as company matches. Even so, many long-enduring companies sometimes have significant pension fund obligations that expose them to risks that arise from managing billions of dollars in retirement plans.

For those interested in more detail, accounting textbooks or public websites are a good place to start. Refer in particular to the Pension Benefit Guaranty Corporation, a U.S. government agency tasked with providing oversight and assistance to private-sector pension plans. Here, I can only briefly discuss the financial impacts of defined benefit plans.

In DBPs, a company contributes to a pool of pension funds, which it manages by conservatively investing in a mix of asset classes such as stocks, bonds, real estate, and so on. These invested funds, or assets of the pension plan, the company draws on as necessary to pay its retirees in accordance with some formula based on factors such as age and salary at retirement and number of years of service. How well the company invests and manages these pension assets influences how secure they are and how fast they'll grow to cover future contractual obligations to the retirees.

In managing the pool of pension assets, the company assumes the liability for any current and future deficits. If it invests its funds poorly or incurs significant investment losses, the pension plan will show a large deficit, creating what are called unfunded pension liabilities for the company.

By law, the company must cover unfunded liabilities periodically, forcing them to put up cash to reduce or eliminate the deficit in a reasonable amount of time. Naturally, this obligation creates a problem, since the cash for pension plan deficit reduction (to fund the unfunded liabilities) takes money away from operating or financing activities necessary for conducting business; they also threaten dividends and share repurchases. For investors, therefore, the key is to understand how much the company has by way of pension assets and obligations.

To gain traction on the impact of pension obligations, let's take the example of ConAgra Foods (CAG). For the year 2010, the company reported a shortfall in its pension plan in part because of the downturn in the equity markets. As such, the company contributed $123 million to the pension plans and another $55 million to cover postretirement healthcare obligations. In all, in order to make up for the shortfall, the company took a charge of $178 million that year. In the previous year, 2009, the company took a charge of $319 million because of similar shortfalls from a downturn in the equity markets. The pension- and retirement-related charges amounted to 33 percent and 25 percent, respectively, of reported net earnings of $978 million and $726 million in 2009 and 2010.

It is clear, therefore, that pension and post-retirement obligations can create substantial risks and liabilities for investors of companies that manage their defined benefit plans. A quick check on those obligations is an important part of the process for trying to refute the investment thesis.

A particularly careful investor will dig deeper to see how a company estimates pension assets and obligations. The fair value of plan assets is relatively easy to pin down as companies report these in their annual (10-K) filings. Start with the fair value of plan assets at the beginning of the year, and then make additions and subtractions of things like returns on those assets, contributions by employees and employer, payments to retirees, and sundry items. These adjustments yield the fair value of plan assets at the end of the reported year.

Estimates of plan liabilities, also called projected benefit obligations (PBOs), require actuarial assumptions. Again, start with the PBO at the beginning of the year, make adjustments as necessary to accommodate changes during the year, and come up with a revised PBO at year end.

The difference between the end-of-year plan assets and obligations indicates whether the pension fund has a surplus or deficit. A deficit in the fund at the end of a fiscal year creates unfunded liabilities that the company is obligated to fund in short order.

Note in particular that the estimates of PBOs are subject to error or manipulation. Unjustifiably rosy assumptions can lead to low estimates of future obligations, implying that the company is financially healthier than it actually may be. If the obligations turn out to be much higher than anticipated and plan assets do not generate the expected returns, the company will be on the hook to plug the deficit. Investors must pay attention, therefore, to what assumptions the company is using in making estimates of fund assets and liabilities.

Unfunded pension liabilities are long-term liabilities in the balance sheet, but the assumptions embedded in the estimates of obligations and assets are not quite visible there. Investors must unearth the assumptions and actual historical performance of plan assets from the company's 10-K filing. In this sense, unfunded pensions are an invisible, but potentially significant, cost for shareholders.

Litigation and Lawsuits

For most publicly traded companies, lawsuits are usually part of doing business. Often they settle these lawsuits out of court because of the very high costs of litigation and uncertainty about outcomes. Such routine lawsuits are usually of little concern, as their costs are part of running the business.

Investors should look more closely at lawsuits that have the potential to put the company under or perhaps cost several years' worth of cash flows. Issues such as conflict with other parties regarding key patents or large-scale fraud can be quite costly, as the resulting losses divert massive amounts of cash away from operations and shareholder-friendly activities. Such large, and sometimes potentially fatal, lawsuits also distract management from the business of running the company.

Take, for example, Armstrong World Industries back in the late 1990s. This was a profitable blue chip company with sales of about $3 billion and a history going back to the late nineteenth century. Well entrenched in the building products industry, the company made floor and ceiling systems as well as cabinets and sold into the residential and commercial markets.

Yet, on December 6, 2000, Armstrong World Industries filed for bankruptcy protection. It had been under pressure from lawsuits related to asbestos in their products at one time. For those historical wrongs, the claims against the company had built up, and it had set up reserves against those claims. But the weight of the lawsuits became unbearable, and in 2000, the company reported facing 173,000 personal injury claims to the tune of $1 billion over the next several years.

For investors, the challenge is to know when the lawsuits are significant in terms of cost and when they are routine. This takes some digging around, of course, but one sign to look for is a company setting reserves aside; from there, it is key to make an educated estimate about the total potential cost of a lawsuit in relation to the size and strength of the company's annual cash flows.

It is possible that the market will sometimes punish a company for lawsuits even when the potential costs are a small fraction of the company's annual free cash flows. Careful digging may reveal that, even in the worst-case scenario, the potential cost of a lawsuit is not a threat to the company in any meaningful way. Excessive fear about minor issues may in some situations offer attractive opportunities.

Off-Balance-Sheet Liabilities

Liabilities not disclosed in the balance sheet are akin to hidden bombs that can destroy a company and your investment in it. This problem is perhaps best illustrated by the infamous case of Enron, which had set up special-purpose entities (SPEs) so as to control assets without owning up to the debt necessary to finance the purchase of those assets. In essence, a typical transaction involved selling assets to a newly set-up SPE or having it buy assets from third parties, co-signing a bank loan to the SPE to finance the purchase of those assets, and then guaranteeing those loans with the company's own stock or some other company assets.

Because of limitations in the accounting rules at the time SPEs were set up, the loan guarantees were not visible in Enron's balance sheet. In recent years, abuses have led regulators to tighten the reporting standards for SPEs, and investors can now find related information in mandatory filings. But at the time of Enron, the debt ratios monitored by the rating agencies, banks, and investors appeared to remain within proscribed limits—allowing the company to continue doing business without undue scrutiny.

It turned out that nonconsolidation of some of the SPEs was not legal, and Enron had to bring them back on their books. This resulted in a massive decrease in reported income for 1999 and 2000 and a substantial increase in reported debt. Thus began the rapid unwinding of the SPEs and the demise of Enron. Investors who did not understand the hidden obligations and hung on to the stock too long ended up suffering massive losses.

Even as Enron was collapsing under the weight of the SPEs and related fraud, another kind of off-balance-sheet chicanery was taking off.

As far back as 1988, Citigroup invented and others quickly followed with what came to be called structured investment vehicles (SIVs). An SIV is an operating finance company, usually set up by a large bank as a separate entity that functions in many ways like a traditional bank but with some major differences. Taking advantage of the (usually) upward-sloping yield curve, the SIV borrowed short- to medium-term money at low interest rates by issuing commercial paper and medium-term notes. It then used the proceeds to make higher-yielding long-term investments. The spread between the interest earned on long-term investments and the cost of short-term borrowed funds created the profits for the principals. This is no different, in principle, from your local bank taking demand deposits from you in exchange for very low interest rates and then turning around to make higher-interest loans for cars and mortgages.

The advantage for sponsoring banks was that the SIVs were not on their books and, for the most part, fell outside the purview of bank regulation. As such, through SIVs, banks could benefit without having to raise additional monies to bulk up their capital base. Without the SIVs, such financing and lending activity would show in the balance sheet, and banks would have to raise more equity capital to meet the reserve requirements. The SIVs allowed banks to obviate that. The success of this new asset class was that, by the summer of 2007, 36 SIVs had assets of more than $400 billion under management.[3]

The trouble for the SIVs and for their sponsors was in their very design. First, unlike traditional banks, where the government guarantees demand deposits, the commercial paper issued by the SIVs had no such guarantees. Safety for those who bought the commercial paper from an SIV was in the backing of the parent banks. At the time, if the parent bank appeared to be of high quality, an SIV was able to issue commercial paper and medium-term notes at very attractive (low) rates.

Second, the long-term assets in which the SIVs invested were usually investment-grade corporate bonds and asset-backed securities of long maturity, those built by securitizing such things as student loans, car loans, and, of course, commercial and residential mortgages. The supposed high quality of long-term investments was also a signal of the safety of the short-term money borrowed by the SIVs.

The financial crisis of 2007–2008 changed all that. Many of the mortgage-backed securities (MBSs) that the SIVs had bought for high-interest yields dropped sharply in value because of increasing homeowner defaults, forcing significant write-downs. This created a panic, of course, among those who had loaned short-term money to the SIVs by buying their low-interest, short-maturity commercial paper with the assumption that they were lending, in essence, to parent banks with strong balance sheets.

The market for MBSs had already begun to dry up because of troubles in the wider economy, and the fear that the SIVs were now too risky was adding fuel to the fire. With their assets shrinking and unable to borrow freely in the commercial paper market any more, the SIVs tried to sell the assets, partly to pay back the commercial paper coming due and partly to get what they could for sharply revalued long-term investments on the books. With everyone trying to unload those similar assets in a panic, prices were depressed even further.

Since the long-term assets were collateral for short-term debt the SIVs had borrowed to finance those same long-term assets, their troubles escalated very quickly. It became difficult to refinance commercial paper, the short-maturity debt, as it became due. A shrinking pool of monies with which to finance long-term investments pressured the SIVs even further to sell those assets in their loan portfolios. But with so many SIVs rushing to sell their long-maturity assets in a fast-falling market, prices went into a downward spiral, and a full-blown panic quickly set in.

Soon enough, unable to sell the assets to generate liquidity, the SIVs started defaulting on their commercial paper. Such defaults set the panic even deeper. In just a few months, for instance, Victoria Finance, a $6 billion SIV managed by Ceres Capital Partners, had their credit rating slashed from AAA to below investment grade. Ceres Capital defaulted later in the year. Many other SIVs on both sides of the Atlantic began winding down or going out of business.

Under pressure from the U.S. Treasury, large banks, such as Bank of America, Citigroup, JPMorgan Chase, and HSBC, started rescuing their own SIVs and, as a result, had to absorb very large losses. On October 2, 2008, the *Financial Times* reported that Sigma Finance, the last surviving and the oldest of the SIVs, dissolved when JPMorgan pulled funding from it.[4] By the summer of 2009, according to a news report, 95 percent of the peak assets in the SIV sector had been written down.[5]

The SIV story is instructive for many reasons. The idea of borrowing for less and lending for more has been around for a very long time; SIVs were playing a version that allowed them to do so outside the purview of banking regulations. It was a good idea so long as it worked; it could have continued working if the rating agencies had been up to correctly evaluating the complex securities that the SIVs were putting on their balance sheets. But the SIVs relied too much on the rating agencies and appear not to have done their own due diligence on the long-term assets in which they were massively investing; they were investing on blind faith.

More important, the lesson to be learned from both SPEs and SIVs is that companies feel a great deal of pressure to do things off the balance sheet. The demand for consistently high returns on invested capital and the incentives used to reward managers are such that opportunities to generate new business are hard to pass up. Smart people induced by career advancement opportunities and by the chance to make more money come up with interesting and creative ideas that look good on the face of it, but which may be full of hidden risks that invisible to the uninitiated. Often, as John Kenneth Galbraith once noted, these innovations are creative ways of taking on more debt, where the returns are visibly attractive and immediate but risks and uncertainties remain invisible for the most part.[6]

To discover these hidden risks, we must look closely at the fine print in mandatory filings. Look especially for complex financial arrangements that create significant liabilities for the company. If many of these arrangements exist, they may be grounds for disconfirming the investment thesis.

Quality of Assets

Liabilities are only one side of the equation, however. The other important consideration when trying to disconfirm an investment thesis is the quality of assets. After all, what you as an investor own is not only future cash flows but the very assets that enable a company to deliver those future flows. Common equity is calculated as follows:

$$\text{Common Equity} = \text{Total Assets} - \text{Total Liabilities} \qquad (17.2)$$

We know that common equity is the residual (also called book value), or assets net of all liabilities. If the liabilities turn out to be different from what you see in the balance sheet, your ownership stake reduces accordingly. Similarly, for a given level of liabilities, errors on the asset side of the balance sheet carry over to the equity account. If assets are inflated or shown to be much larger than they actually are or have a great amount of risk built into them, then the equity account reflects that inflation, misleading investors into thinking that they own more in net assets than they actually do.

Perhaps the most common problems on the asset side of the balance sheet are errors in measurement. It is not easy for companies to count each line item on their books; some physical assets, such as inventories and property, are spread all over the globe or are otherwise unavailable for an easy in-person count. As such, each line item on the asset side is an aggregation of estimates that accountants make using appropriate estimation procedures; they are subject to errors.

The likelihood of measurement errors increases for certain kinds of assets, such as plant and property, which are usually recorded at historical cost or, when acquired in a merger, at estimated fair value at the time of the transaction. In some cases, the estimates can be so out of line with the actual market value of the assets that the measurement errors become quite severe.

Imagine, for instance, that a building shows up as a line item of, say, \$50 million on a company's books on a historical-cost basis; suppose also that the market value at prevailing prices is \$100 million. The difference of \$50 million is then an undervaluation that deflates common equity by the same amount.

Assume for a moment that the asset in question is not a building but a portfolio of high-risk subprime bonds worth \$100 million. Rules require that these and other financial assets be recorded or marked to whatever value at which they are traded at about the time the books close at end of quarter. A sudden drop in the market or trading value of the bonds reduces their asset side of the equation and translates into lower equity. In fact, many banks had subprime mortgage–backed securities on their books just before the housing market crash in 2007; as those securities traded at plummeting prices during the crisis, the asset base of these banks shrunk and wiped out the minimal equity on the books.

Banks and financial institutions often have loans and complex financial instruments on the asset side of their balance sheet. If investors do not correctly assess the quality of loans and the risks embedded in financial products, such assets pose serious risks to them. Investing in financial-sector companies is often hazardous, therefore, for most investors who do not have the expertise and the resources to make a thorough evaluation of the asset or loan portfolio.

In fact, the risks embedded in the assets sometimes become so great that some managers, under pressure to deliver on expectations, may begin to contort data and use deceptions that are virtually impossible for an average investor to catch.

Consider, for example, the case of Lehman Brothers and its accounting gimmick, now known notoriously as Repo 105. It appears that as the financial crisis of 2007–2008 picked up steam, Lehman, like many others, had a strong urge to unload some of its risky assets (bonds) and pay down its massive debt. But the markets were already seizing up, and bond prices were plummeting. In such an environment, selling its own inventory of bonds boded massive immediate losses. So, with the bonds on the balance sheet virtually illiquid (unless sold at massive loss), the company devised an imaginative scheme.

According to the Chapter 11 bankruptcy examiner,[7] just before Lehman closed its books for a quarter, it went to the repo market for overnight lending and swapped some of their risky bonds for cash (thus moving bonds off the balance sheet). It then used the cash from those bond sales to pay down its debt and report a healthy-looking balance sheet at the close of the quarter. Then, as soon as the quarter closed, Lehman borrowed back the money and bought back the bonds swapped earlier. The examiner suspected that Lehman did not really sell the bonds but, in fact, used them as collateral to borrow money for the short term, with the understanding that the company would buy them back (at cost plus interest) shortly thereafter. Yet, the company classified the swaps as sale so that it could get the risky bonds off its balance sheet.

The trick came to be known as Repo 105 because Lehman swapped $105 worth of bonds in order to borrow $100 in cash, giving the impression that it had sold the risky assets at a discount. According to the examiner's report, the company moved tens of billions of dollars off the balance sheet using this trick and $50 billion in just the second quarter of 2008. Moreover, the company did not disclose these transactions in its filings or even to its own board, so no one was the wiser until after the company had collapsed under the weight of large quantities of highly toxic bonds on its balance sheet.

For all but the most sophisticated and well-resourced investors, manipulations like Repo 105 are difficult to catch. Many variations to the theme exist, and smart professionals think up new ways of pushing at the edges to find creative solutions to difficult problems. Repo 105 appears to be a case of creativity applied to a highly suspect cause. It shows that investors must look out for toxic assets on the balance sheet, both as cause and consequence of risky behaviors that sometimes cross the line to become fraud.

To recap: For investors practicing the fine art of investing wisely, a careful scrutiny of the balance sheet and associated risks is an indispensable part of due diligence.

CHAPTER EIGHTEEN

Define Good Business

FOR THE INVESTMENT thesis that still stands after all the previous attempts to refute it, the next step is to make judgments about the manner in which the business creates economic worth. A business blessed with good economics, when purchased at a good price, improves the likelihood of good to great returns over time. Shares of companies in businesses with poor economics may sometimes offer good opportunities when prices are especially depressed, but they do so at considerable hazards and limited upside potential. As investors, then, our task is to try to uncover and disconfirm the narrative that the investment under scrutiny has sound economics intrinsic to it—or that the company underlying the stock is fundamentally a "good" business.

From the viewpoint of investors, perhaps the simplest way to define a good business is one that, on average and over time, consumes a dollar to produce a stream of cash that, when appropriately discounted, amounts to something more than a dollar. In evaluating how much to pay for such streams of cash, investors remain fundamentally interested in the ability of a business to make more from less.

Business Economics

Measuring the performance and potential of a business is a complex endeavor; the metrics used to do so depend on who is measuring what. For instance, if we define performance as the degree to which a company dominates the markets it serves, then we must clearly define those markets; yet, as constructs, markets defy objective definition. If we think of performance as corporate social responsibility, then we must be clear about what social responsibility means and which specific measures best proxy that aspect of performance. If we focus on financial performance, then we must decide which specific measures we ought to use and why. Do we measure returns to shareholders, returns on the capital deployed, or cash flows? Market returns or accounting measures?

As if finding good measures is not complex enough, determining the time horizon over which to measure performance is not straightforward either. The quarter and year are arbitrary periods commonly used because of convenience and convention. In reality, some businesses (e.g., day trading) may require daily measures of trading performance, whereas some others (e.g., large-scale construction projects) may need evaluation over the life of its project or across a business cycle.

Moreover, any one dimension of performance may not be sufficient given the different stakeholders often associated with an organization. Different types of equity holders, different classes of bondholders, the executive team, midlevel managers, the rank and file, suppliers, customers, and others all bring different perspectives to the table and demand that the company use measures that best reflect their particular interests.

Sometimes, because of power differentials among the parties involved, one stakeholder may dominate the debate and force a single perspective—on financial, social, or market power measures. For instance, during bankruptcy proceedings, the creditors of a company have a disproportionate say in how to distribute the residual assets. When a company is about to go public, institutions and large equity investors have a great deal more say than do the other parties, including the founders of the company. But even in cases where one stakeholder dominates the debate, the other perspectives don't necessarily go away—they just recede into the shadows for the time being, biding their time to reassert themselves as conditions change and opportunities arise.

Much of the conflict in and around organizations arises, in fact, because of differences in opinion about what to measure and how to measure it. A classic case is that of conflict between shareholders and bondholders, as the two categories of capital have different objectives. Bondholders typically want preservation of capital and an assured coupon through maturity. Shareholders, on the other hand, want to leverage the limited liability bestowed upon them; they want managers to take on more risk, even if the greater risk may endanger the survival of the company and jeopardize payments to bondholders. Conflicts can also arise among bondholders themselves when different maturities and different levels of seniority put their interests at odds.

It is important, therefore, for investors to understand the political dynamics inside the company and make judgments regarding the degree to which the metrics used to measure performance support their interests. As we will see in chapter 19, some managers will clearly articulate their shareholder friendliness and follow through with actions such as share repurchases and dividends. Others may argue that different aspects of performance are more important because of the multiple stakeholders they must satisfy, or because long-run performance is possible only when noneconomic considerations remain at the forefront. Ultimately, however, economic performance is the same as future cash flows discounted to the present and the ability of the company to deliver such on a consistent basis.

Equity investors should, therefore, cut through the complexities that surround performance measurement and keep their focus on economic performance—on cash flows and the efficiency with which managers deploy the capital entrusted to them. They must, however, evaluate the efficiency with which the company uses not only equity capital, but also the efficiency with which the company deploys all capital at its disposal, including debt capital.

As we move through the illustrations that follow, remember that measuring performance is not as straightforward as it may seem. Even so, I show relatively simple ways to achieve a first-cut grasp of the effectiveness with which managers deploy the equity and debt capital entrusted to them.

Capital Efficiency

A handful of simple ratios and the key factors that drive them can give a quick sense of how efficiently a company deploys capital. These are

1. Return on equity (ROE)
2. Return on assets (ROA)
3. Return on capital (ROC)

That is, we operationalize economic performance as the efficient use of (1) equity capital (ROE); (2) total assets (ROA); and (3) total capital deployed (ROC).

Return on equity (ROE) provides a great deal of insight when broken down using the so-called DuPont formula. Let's use some simple algebraic manipulations to see how this goes. By definition, ROE is the ratio of net income (NI) to common shareholders' equity (CEQ):

$$\text{ROE} = \text{NI}/\text{CEQ} \tag{18.1}$$

We can rewrite equation 18.1 as

$$\text{ROE} = (\text{NI}/\text{TA}) \bullet (\text{TA}/\text{CEQ}) \tag{18.2}$$

Since total assets (TA) is in both the numerator and denominator, equation 18.2 is mathematically equivalent to equation 18.1. Therefore, since NI/TA is ROA and TA/CEQ is financial leverage (Lev), we can rewrite equation 18.2 as

$$\text{ROE} = \text{ROA} \bullet \text{Lev} \tag{18.2a}$$

So, ROE is the product of (1) efficiency, with which the company uses its total assets to produce profits (ROA); and (2) financial leverage (Lev), defined as the dollar value of total assets for each dollar of common equity. In this sense, ROE is leverage-adjusted ROA. Since total assets are usually more than common equity, ROE is usually also greater than ROA.

We can further rewrite equation 18.1 by also incorporating total revenues (TR):

$$\text{ROE} = (\text{NI}/\text{TR}) \bullet (\text{TR}/\text{TA}) \bullet (\text{TA}/\text{CEQ}) \tag{18.3}$$

Again, since total revenues (TR) and total assets (TA) are in both the numerator and denominator, they cancel out to yield equation 18.1. Furthermore, because NI/TR is simply return on sales (ROS), (TR/TA) is asset efficiency (AE), and (TA/CEQ) is financial leverage, we have

$$\text{ROE} = \text{ROS} \bullet \text{AE} \bullet \text{Lev} \tag{18.3b}$$

Note that ROS reflects the amount that flows to the bottom line for every dollar of sales; AE is the dollar amount of sales that the company generates for every dollar in total assets; and Lev is the dollar value of total assets for each dollar of common equity. So, return on equity is mathematically equivalent to the product of profitability, asset efficiency, and financial leverage.

Furthermore, from equation 18.3, we see that

$$\text{ROA} = (\text{NI}/\text{TR}) \bullet (\text{TR}/\text{TA}) \tag{18.4}$$

$$\text{ROA} = \text{ROS} \bullet \text{AE} \tag{18.4a}$$

As such, ROA is simply a product of profitability and asset efficiency.

Using the same logic, we can also determine return on capital (ROC). If TC is total capital deployed in a company, or total equity (TE) plus total interest-bearing debt (TD), then

$$\text{TC} = \text{TE} + \text{TD} \tag{18.5}$$

$$\text{ROC} = \text{NI}/\text{TC} \tag{18.6}$$

We can disaggregate equation 18.6 to yield ROC as a product of return on assets (ROA) and total capital leverage (CapLev):

$$\text{ROC} = (\text{NI}/\text{TA}) \bullet (\text{TA}/\text{TC}) \tag{18.7}$$

$$\text{ROC} = \text{ROA} \bullet \text{CapLev} \tag{18.7a}$$

Note that CapLev is similar to Lev except that it indicates the full financial leverage, incorporating debt capital along with total equity capital, which comprises both common and preferred shareholders' equity. As in equation 18.3, we can write ROC as

$$\text{ROC} = \text{ROS} \bullet \text{AE} \bullet \text{CapLev} \tag{18.8}$$

Return on capital, which indicates the efficiency with which a company deploys capital is, again, simply a product of profitability, asset efficiency, and full financial leverage.

The three capital efficiency ratios—ROE, ROA, and ROC—together reflect the operating and financial performance of a company. The higher these ratios, the more efficient is the company's use of the financial resources (equity, debt, and assets) available to it; this is good

TABLE 18.1
Three-Year Averages Ending Fiscal Year 2012

	WMT	TGT	COH	MSFT	CAT
ROE	21.63%	17.86%	51.86%	35.59%	31.87%
ROA	8.36%	6.18%	32.23%	19.03%	5.54%
ROC	13.27%	9.08%	51.33%	30.52%	10.22%
ROS	3.59%	4.11%	21.12%	28.72%	7.72%
AE	2.33	1.50	1.52	0.66	0.71
Lev	2.59	2.89	1.61	1.87	5.78
CapLev	1.59	1.47	1.59	1.60	1.84

economics and efficient operations. The ratios rise with financial leverage, however, so investors should check that higher capital efficiency is not simply derived through from financial engineering but grounded in well-run operations.

Table 18.1 shows three-year averages of the variables just discussed for five well-known companies: Walmart (WMT), Target (TGT), Coach (COH), Microsoft (MSFT), and Caterpillar (CAT).

Note that, for the three years ending in the 2012 fiscal year, Walmart had used its capital more efficiently than had Target. For instance, compare Walmart's 21.63 percent ROE with Target's 17.86 percent. Note also how the two companies accomplished those numbers. With ROS at 4.11 percent, Target was 14.5 percent more profitable than Walmart (ROS = 3.59 percent). Target also had higher financial leverage than had Walmart (2.89 versus 2.59).

Even so, Walmart more than made up for the deficiencies in these two areas by delivering a much higher asset efficiency. The company generated, on average, $2.33 in sales for every dollar of assets, versus only $1.50 for Target. That is, the efficiency with which Walmart utilized assets rewarded shareholders with better utilization of equity capital.

Note also that ROC (WMT 13.27 percent; TGT 9.08 percent) was much lower than ROE—indicating that both companies had substantial debt. This reliance on debt is also visible in a much lower full financial leverage (CapLev) than the equity-based financial leverage (Lev): 1.59 versus 2.59 for Walmart and 1.47 versus 2.89 for Target.

Table 18.1 also shows that both Coach and Microsoft had strong average ROE, even though Coach was by far a much stronger performer. Again, a closer look shows that Microsoft had a three-year average

ROS of 28.72 percent compared to 21.12 percent for Coach. Microsoft also had a somewhat higher financial leverage at 1.87 versus 1.61 for Coach. But, Coach far outperformed on asset efficiency with 1.52 versus 0.66 for Microsoft. This difference in asset efficiency produced a much higher ROE of 51.86 percent for Coach, as compared with 35.59 percent for Microsoft.

A closer look reveals that Microsoft had lower asset efficiency in part because, at the end of fiscal year 2012, the company had more than $60 billion in cash and investments, or more than 60 percent of its total assets. Coach, in contrast, had under $1 billion in cash and investments, which made up 28.2 percent of its total assets. Computing three-year average asset efficiency net of cash, Microsoft's number changes from 0.66 to 1.53, and the asset efficiency of Coach increases from 1.52 to 2.12. As a result, the noncash ROE for Microsoft and Coach recompute as 82 percent and 72.24 percent, respectively. In essence, both companies made highly efficient use of equity capital, and this was in large part because they were both highly profitable. In a way, large cash balance was a drag on ROE.

Furthermore, both companies delivered high ROE in spite of very little debt. As such, ROC for both companies (COH 51.33 percent; MSFT 30.52 percent) was close to ROE.

Finally, in table 18.1, note that Caterpillar had a three-year average ROE of 31.87 percent. But look at how it accomplished its high ROE in spite of modest profitability. At 7.72 percent, its three-year profitability (ROS) was about twice that of Walmart or Target, but it was much lower than that of Coach or Microsoft. At 0.71 percent, Caterpillar's asset efficiency was very low. But, the financial leverage of Caterpillar was very high at 5.78, and that is what drove its ROE north of 30 percent. Substantially lower ROC and ROA betray the high amount of interest-bearing debt on the company's books.

Clearly, companies can legitimately increase ROE by taking on a great deal of debt. But at some point, debt can create substantial obligations that may endanger the financial health of the company. Therefore, as discussed in chapter 15, investors should not take ROE at face value but examine closely how it is accomplished and what it might imply about profitability, operating efficiency, and especially debt burden. Hence, even if the investment thesis cannot be refuted based on the company's overall capital efficiency, it may be possible to refute on the basis of strength tests as discussed in the case of Caterpillar.

Efficient use of equity capital (ROE) is particularly important for stockholders because it relates directly to the intrinsic valuation of the company.[1] In fact, following the discount flow model, discussed in chapter 14, we can show that the intrinsic value (IV) of a company relates directly to ROE, along with book value (BV), growth rate (g), and discount rate (r), as follows:

$$IV = [ROE \bullet BV \bullet (1 + g)/(r - g)] \tag{18.9}$$

That is, the higher the ROE, the more likely it is that the intrinsic valuation of the company will be higher, provided we hold constant the other terms in the equation. Understanding ROE is, in other words, imperative for investors to invest wisely.

Cash Economics

The above discussion about ROE presumes innocence about the many meaningful differences between accrual and cash accounting. Usually, we have to make assessments about the economics of a company from afar and mostly through its financial statements and other mandatory filings. It is necessary, therefore, to understand the many thorny issues that surround the reporting of performance through company filings. Reading the company literature is itself a bit of a skill, in fact, as the various rules and vast discretion that managers and accountants apply in preparing filings can sometimes distort and mislead rather than clarify and reveal.

Financial statements are difficult to understand because they are prepared under the guidance of complex rules encoded in the Generally Accepted Accounting Principles (GAAP); such rules give managers and accountants wide discretion in how they report financial information. Sometimes the accounting is so complex, in fact, that it can be difficult for an average investor to ascertain the true economics of a company. This is especially true with regard to the income statement and balance sheet because these follow the complex rules of accrual accounting. The measures of capital efficiency that we have used so far are constructed using variables from the income statement and the balance sheet, and, therefore, they are subject to quite a bit of managerial discretion and possible distortion.

One way to overcome this problem is to penetrate the statement of cash flows, which uses cash accounting and is sometimes (although not always) a better representation of a company's true economics. Moreover, understanding how cash flows in and out of a business provides important insights into its enduring power to produce cash. Hence, in order to be able to disconfirm an investment thesis on the criteria of good economics, we must also examine how the company gets the cash to finance its operations, how much cash those operations generate, and what the company chooses to do with the cash so generated.

In the remainder of this chapter, therefore, we go beyond capital efficiency issues to outline concepts for understanding the overall financial picture of the company in terms of sources and uses of cash.

Financial Statements in Brief

When evaluating companies, investors have three financial statements to interpret. The statement of financial condition (SFC), or balance sheet, presents the overall financial health of a company as a snapshot of the assets and liabilities at a point in time.

The statement of income (SOI), or income statement, presents revenues the company has generated and in broad strokes outlines the expenses and taxes incurred during a given period (quarter or year). The income account provides basic insights into how the revenues flow through the expense structure.

The statement of cash flows (SCF), or cash flow statement, reports the sources and uses of cash from the operating, investing, and financing activities of the company. The SCF provides an overview of how much cash the company generates from operations and how management chooses to allocate cash to various purposes.

A fourth filing, the statement of shareholders' equity (SSE), reports changes in the ownership structure of the company. Although very important at times, we will not discuss SSE here so that we can focus on the operations and financial condition of the company.

In combination, the three financial statements—the SFC, SOI, and SCF—describe the overall operating and financial condition of the company. In order to be able to challenge an investment thesis on fundamental economics, investors must understand each statement in interaction with the others.

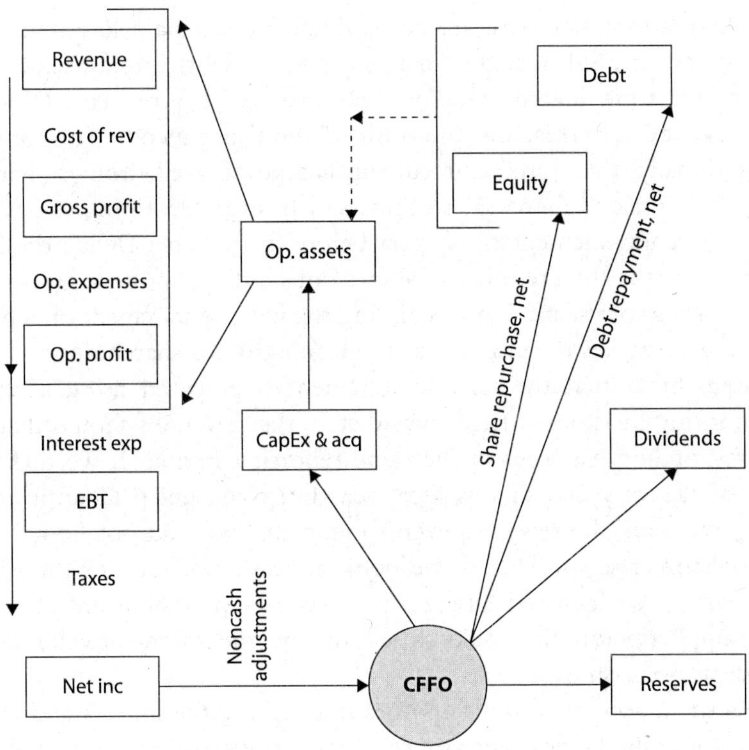

Figure 18.1 Financials at a glance: the accrual and cash flow economics of a hypothetical business

The schematic in figure 18.1 provides such an overview. Take particular note of the cash flows from operations (CFFO) at the bottom of the figure. We can often learn a great deal about the economic character of a company, in fact, by understanding how much cash a company generates on an ongoing basis and to what specific purposes it allocates its cash resources.

As shown in figure 18.1, the income statement reflects the basic economics of the company based on accrual accounting methods. The starting point is usually an examination of revenues from the sale of products and services; sometimes a more thorough analysis reveals the breakdown of revenues from different segments or lines of business. Revenues filter down through the cost structure to produce operating income (earnings) from operations. Preliminary insights into the company's cost structure are also evident in the main line items in the statement. Subtract the financing cost of debt (interest expense) from operating income, and we get earnings before taxes (EBT). Pay the various taxes, and the bottom line is net income (earnings). Occasionally, there are nonrecurring charges as well, from activities such as a loss or gain on sales of assets or from restructuring of operations. Usually, such charges appear before the tax line. Divide the net income by the total number of shares outstanding, and that gives you net earnings per share. Understanding the income statement on a per-share basis makes the analysis more meaningful for shareholders.

Remember that the income statement is prepared using accrual accounting methods, where rules dictate that revenues should match corresponding expenses in the same reporting period. If we make a sale at the very end of this fiscal year but don't get paid until next year, we book the revenues even though the cash did not flow from the customer to us. That is, we book noncash revenues for the year. Similarly, if we incurred expenses purchasing supplies but did not pay the supplier before the books closed, the income statement will reflect those as noncash expenses.

As such, accrual accounting does not capture the inflows and outflows of cash. Hence, analysis of the statement of cash flows must always accompany income statement analysis. That is, adjustments for noncash revenues and noncash expenses allow us to see how cash flows in and out of the company.

The first item in the statement of cash flows is net income, followed by adjustments such as adding back all noncash expenses and subtracting all noncash revenues. The biggest add-back is usually the depreciation and amortization expense. Next up are any changes to the working capital, which shed light on the efficiency of operations. Changes in accounts receivable, accounts payable, and inventories are the chief working capital adjustments. These values show how much cash the key operating activities and transactions generate and consume.

Noncash adjustments convert accrual net income into cash flow from operations (CFFO) or, simply, operating cash flow. This is the crucial number. For a company in steady state, the CFFO is usually the primary source of cash, and it strongly influences what opportunities the company can pursue without having to raise external financing. Companies with strong economics usually generate strong operating cash flows, usually much more than those needed for routine maintenance and growth; weak companies need to supplement operating cash flows with external sources of financing.

What does the company do with operating cash? Skillful uses of operating cash can make a company strong over time; poor uses of this cash can break a good company in short order.

From the CFFO circle in figure 18.1, follow the flows of cash to its various uses. Foremost, the company must put money back into operations so that it can sustain itself by replacing depreciating assets. That is, it must refresh its assets and strengthen its operating capabilities. Next, the company must invest in future growth opportunities, as most healthy companies want to grow even if the goal is simply to keep up with inflation in their cost structure. So capital expenditures, or the monies reinvested in operations, are especially important to ensure future operating cash flows.

Depending on their strategic objectives, companies can also legitimately use operating cash to make acquisitions or asset purchases. Either way, capital expenditures and acquisitions together reflect reinvestments in the company to ensure future financial health. These reinvestments become part of the company's asset base necessary for ongoing operations and continued competitiveness. In this manner, some of the operating cash flows into the fixed assets to refresh or expand operations.

The remaining cash after subtracting capital expenditures (CapEx) and routine acquisitions from CFFO is the free cash flow (FCF), with which the company can satisfy other, perhaps discretionary, uses for its cash. For instance, part of the free cash flow goes toward paying dividends to shareholders. Most companies with a long record of paying dividends have strong incentives to continue doing so. For such dividend-paying companies, discretionary cash flow is actually the surplus free cash flow after paying dividends.

The discretionary cash flows are the enablers of a variety of other purposes, such as share buybacks and debt repayments. Many American companies producing surplus cash buy back their shares periodically. This is partly a way to reward shareholders by increasing their share of future earnings, but sometimes companies buy back shares to manage per-share metrics.

The discretionary cash flows out to repay outstanding debt, in part to reduce the debt burden and in part to create debt capacity for future financing needs. Then there may be other minor uses of cash, but the remainder, if any, usually goes into the reserves and shows up as cash on the balance sheet.

Note that a lack of sufficient operating cash jeopardizes the various operating and financing activities that depend on it. In such cases, external financing becomes unavoidable, and the company has to go to the debt and/or equity markets to raise money. Both such endeavors are costly, as borrowing increases the debt burden, and issuing additional equity dilutes the ownership of existing shareholders.

However, even financially healthy companies often go to the debt markets opportunistically when interest rates are low—and use those funds to repurchase shares or, occasionally, to pay special dividends. As such, operating cash flows are key not only as a measure of past financial successes but also for future operating health.

So, we cannot quite refute a thesis to invest in a company based on an analysis of economics alone, especially if the company generates strong cash flows. A thesis for a company that has trouble producing cash from operations may, in contrast, be refuted based on poor future prospects. To put all this in perspective, let's again evaluate Walmart (figure 18.2).

In the fiscal year ending January 2015, Walmart had revenues of $483 billion and reported $16.4 billion in net income. Upon making noncash adjustments, the company showed $28.6 billion in operating cash flow. Note that operating cash was 74 percent more than reported net income. CFFO is usually more than net income because most companies add back the noncash depreciation expense to net income during the process of converting from accrual to cash accounting. Efficiency in the use of working capital also generates cash. In the last reported year, Walmart added back $9.2 billion in noncash depreciation expense and squeezed out more than $2 billion from working capital, mostly by increasing accounts payables and increasing accrued liabilities.

Of the $28.6 billion CFFO, the company reinvested $12.2 billion (43 percent) back into operations through capital expenditures (CapEx). Note that CapEx is higher than the $9.2 billion depreciation expense during the year. The difference between CapEx and the depreciation charge is usually a sign that the company may be investing more than just to keep up with deterioration of its asset base; CapEx greater than depreciation suggests that the company may be expanding its its asset base, perhaps to pursue growth opportunities. Walmart did not report cash outflows for acquisitions during the year.

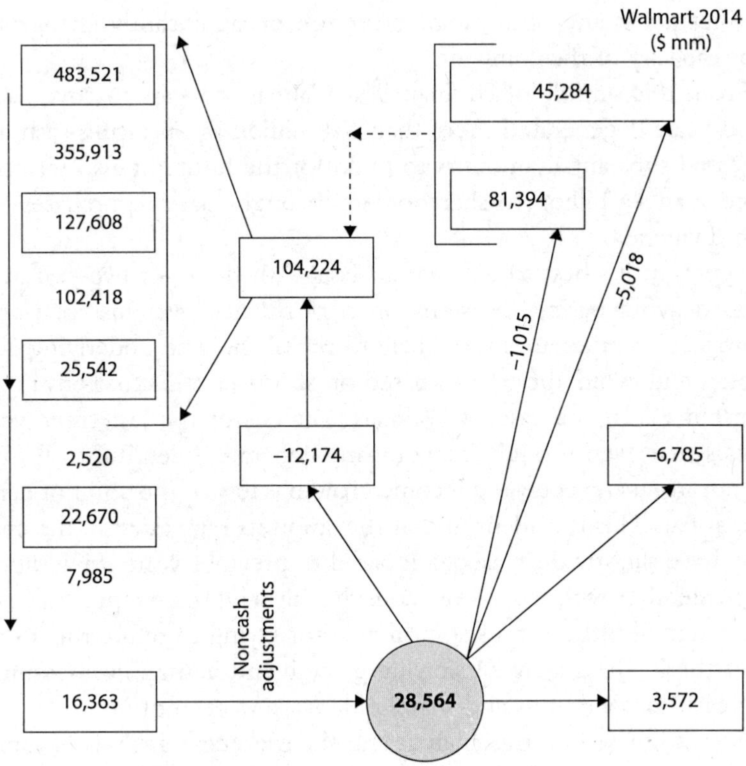

Figure 18.2 Financials at a glance: the economics and cash flows of Walmart for fiscal year 2011

The next item of note is the dividend payment of \$6.8 billion, or 24 percent of the operating cash flows. Since Walmart has a long record of paying dividends, both CapEx and dividends figure in computing the discretionary cash flows as \$9.6 billion.

The company also bought back just over \$1 billion of its own shares and paid back a net of over \$5 billion in short- and long-term debt. This left about \$3.6 billion for other activities, such as purchasing non-controlling interests in other companies and building up cash reserves for pursuing other strategic opportunities.

Note that the new debt issue changed the capital base of the company: the net repayment of debt lowered the debt level, and share repurchase marginally reduced the equity account. These financing activities were small relative to Walmart's size, and they did not significantly change the capital structure or significantly change the debt capacity of the company.

From this outline of its financials, Walmart appears to have had a good year. It generated more than $28 billion in operating cash and allocated substantial amounts to build for the future; it also returned more than $7 billion to shareholders through share repurchases and cash dividends.

Typically, it's best to do such analysis with three- or five-year averages to avoid basing decisions on performance over just one year. Multiyear averages are more likely to reveal the true underlying economics and avoid aberrations based on short-term fluctuations in circumstances. In the case of Walmart, analysis of the last three years reveals that even though the company generated plentiful cash from operations, its revenue and income growth is low to the point of being almost flat. This is evident in that the amounts reinvested in the company have slightly decreased compared to previous years. In addition, its dividend growth has slowed considerably, and share repurchasing is down significantly. For a skeptical investor trying to refute the investment thesis, these signs of slowing growth and hesitation in committing cash to operations and shareholders are worth noting.

Even so, based on this analysis and the preceding analysis of capital efficiency, we are unable to refute the subthesis that Walmart has good economics. Our original investment thesis stands as is, therefore—although, going forward, we must incorporate into our thinking signs of slowdown.

In the next chapter, we check on the people in charge of the company.

CHAPTER NINETEEN

Watch the Game

A GOOD BUSINESS produces strong financial performance over time, but such performance takes considerable work to accomplish. To that end, a well-defined business model, competently executed, is essential for consistently strong operating performance and cash flows, both of which are essential for creating economic worth. As part of due diligence, therefore, investors must assess the quality of the company's business model and the ability of managers to monetize it.

A business model articulates the mechanisms through which the company delivers products and services to make money. It clarifies one or more value propositions that the company aims to deliver to customers and the operating model to deliver those propositions in an economically efficient manner.

To be effective, value propositions must have two essential features embedded in the products or services being offered: desirability and distinctiveness. That is, the company's core products must offer clear use or functionality that is desired by specific groups of customers. Absent such desire, the company faces apathetic customers and an uphill battle generating sales. Even if there is general desire, however, it does little good unless the company's products are distinctive enough from those offered by others. Distinctiveness turns general desire into demand and sales for the company's products over those of others. In practical terms, value propositions are operationalized by correct positioning of products such that their desirability and distinctiveness are obvious to customers in the target markets.

Delivering value propositions requires a proper structuring of necessary assets and activities that enable the competent execution of operating models. Without execution, value propositions remain unrealized and the company unable to generate economic returns. Yet, without a clear sense of desire for and distinctiveness of its products in the minds of target customers, a company's operating model remains rudderless and, ultimately, economically ineffective. Hence, successful business models result from tight integration of well-honed operating models with clear value propositions.

In order to be able to disconfirm the investment thesis, investors must try to understand and make judgments about the robustness of the business model—both the value propositions and operating infrastructure. Of course, also important in this evaluation are assessments of the architects of the business model (entrepreneurs and leaders) and the ability of the operators (managers) to realize the promise of the business model through proper execution. This is because models don't execute themselves; people build and run them, refine and improve them. So, the purely analytical aspects of business models must be understood in combination with what we discuss in the next chapter, "Meet the Managers." In all, it is important to understand that if the model is unclear, or is clear but analysis reveals fundamental weaknesses in the ability of managers to execute and monetize it, then investors must disconfirm the investment thesis.

The Best Buy Business Model

Consider Best Buy, for instance. The company got its start in 1966 when Richard Schulze opened a single-store audio specialty retailer, Sound of Music. Best Buy came into existence as a name change in the early 1980s. By the early 1990s, the company had grown to be a significant player in electronics retail. Part of the reason for its rapid growth and economic success was that the company had shrewdly committed to the emerging big-box store format. By the end of the 1990, Best Buy was the largest specialty electronics retailer in the country. It competed with Circuit City (which filed for bankruptcy in 2008), Fry's Electronics on the West Coast, Indiana's Gregg Appliances, and general retailers such as Walmart and Target. Electronics retail was the game; Best Buy played it by aggressively rolling out big-box specialty stores.

The power of big-box stores like Best Buy derives from their ability to attract and build traffic flows. Traffic depends on the range and mix of products in the store. So, the challenge for retailers comes in the form of a dilemma: If they don't have in-demand products to display, customers won't show up; if they don't have enough shoppers coming in the door, they cannot access the volume discounts that manufacturers reserve for big retailers.

In response to this challenge, many retailers choose to integrate manufacturing into their operations. Branded clothing companies, such as Gap, American Eagle, and Ann Taylor, manage stores that carry only their own products. Company-owned and -operated retail stores enable close contact with customers, and well-developed networks of contract manufacturers help control production costs. Logistics and operations remain subservient to the brand, with manufacturing tightly integrated with the stores to ensure that brand management remains the top priority.

However, retailers that carry many different lines of products usually cannot integrate backward into manufacturing. They don't own the brands they stock, and the many owners of the many brands they carry can harden terms if traffic withers and business starts lagging. To make matters more challenging, customers are notoriously quick to go elsewhere for better deals or sharply curtail spending during tough economic times. A typical retailer is, therefore, strategically vulnerable, experiencing a consistent squeeze from both ends but having limited options for relieving those pressures.

One way some retailers have traditionally addressed this fundamental vulnerability is by building big stores that carry a wide assortment of products in vast quantities—in essence bringing their entire inventory to shelves in the storefront. The availability of a full range of products helps build traffic in individual stores; a large number of stores dispersed geographically helps control costs by enabling scale economies in advertising, vendor contracts, infrastructure spending, and administrative overhead. Large volumes of sales absorb fixed costs, allowing them to lower prices and instigate the virtuous cycle of high traffic—higher sales—better supplier terms—lower costs—high traffic. That is, big-box stores were a key element of the operating model that allowed retailers to deliver their value proposition—selection and price—better than small-format stores. Pioneered by companies such as Walmart and Kmart in the early 1960s, this model became a dominant form of retail in the United States in less than three decades.

Best Buy was among the first specialty big-box stores (along with Home Depot, Staples, Toys "R" Us, and Sports Authority). The company built up a network of big-box stores across the country, filled those stores with a wide array of electronics products, and kept prices competitive by successfully taking advantage of scale economies to build relationships with manufacturers. The company soon built one of the strongest retail brands in the country.

With a sharp value proposition—selection and price—firmly in place, Best Buy turned its attention to executing a well-conceived operating model. Capabilities in logistics and distribution were critically important to keeping inventory under control and costs down, and heavy promotion and in-store service were necessary to keep the traffic flowing. Over time, as Best Buy fine-tuned the execution of its operating model and reliably delivered their value proposition, customers responded.

On the strength of a sharply defined value proposition and an increasingly well-honed operating model, Best Buy's revenues rose 46-fold, from $665 million at the 1990 fiscal year end to over $30 billion at the end of fiscal 2005; during the same period, market value of the company's common equity rose 376-fold, from $69 million to over $26 billion.

Investors who understood the big-box-enabled operating model and recognized early the rapidly developing operating ability of the company to efficiently deliver selection and price benefited handsomely for their insight. Ten thousand dollars invested in the common equity of the company at the beginning of fiscal year 1990, if held for the duration, would have grown to more than $3.4 million by the end of fiscal year 2005.

A Changing Context

Certain key assumptions undergird the value propositions that define successful business models: they must evolve as a changing world makes those assumptions invalid. The essential premise of the big-box store model is that consumers want selection and low prices, and they will drive great distances for those. The economic success of big-box stores is predicated on the assumptions that (1) a wide selection of competitively priced products will attract shoppers in large numbers; and (2) high traffic will create enough sales to justify the high costs of running such stores. With the coming of the Internet and online shopping, however, changes taking place in the larger landscape of the retail industry were about to seriously challenge these assumptions.

A fundamental challenge for Best Buy was that retail businesses have low gross margins and big-box stores have high fixed costs because their operations require large recurring expenses for such necessities as rent, utilities, insurance, and staffing. To be profitable, the high fixed costs of big-box stores and the low gross margins of electronics retail made Best Buy highly dependent on volume of sales. Falling sales could create havoc on the economics of the company. If store traffic dropped because of an economic downturn or changes in consumption patterns, inventory would quickly become stale, and the stores would suffer heavy losses from trying to lure customers with aggressive promotion and markdowns.

Since its business model had been a spectacular success for more than a decade, and perhaps because of this, Best Buy was slow to respond to an emerging threat that would greatly undermine the logic of big-box stores. The emergence of Amazon and other online retailers offered customers a viable, and in some ways superior, alternative for shopping for electronic goods. Selection and low prices, while still desirable, were no longer a source of distinctiveness for Best Buy. Since it sold the same branded goods that were widely available on the Internet, customers could simply turn to better deals from the comfort of their laptops and, increasingly, from their smartphones.

Internet retailers, moreover, had no need for expensive real estate or floor inventory in multiple locations; they could operate with the much more competitive cost structure of large distribution centers from which they shipped products directly to customers. Ironically, therefore, what were once the strengths of the big-box model—floor space and wide selection—became a liability because of the high relative costs associated with them.

To add insult to injury, instead of shopping at the Best Buy stores, customers began to use them as showrooms, using service staff on the floor to educate themselves and make purchase decisions and then going to the Internet for the best deals. The stores continued attracting traffic, but it was traffic without sales.

A new breed of competitor was challenging the company with its quickly evolving Internet-enabled business model. Even though Best Buy looked good in terms of historical growth rates and performance record, alert investors paid heed to emerging headwinds and the seeming lack of strong response to defend or quickly evolve the big-box store format. It became increasingly clear that its original value proposition was no longer distinctive, as customers now could easily search the Internet to locate products and then compare prices across websites. The weakened value proposition would eventually lead to a slowdown in sales, which, in turn, would undermine the operating model, the efficiency of which depended crucially on the volume-driven economics of big-box stores. All this made Best Buy questionable as an investment.

The company did belatedly respond with Best Buy Online, but the tide had already turned, and masses of customers were ditching the brick-and-mortar stores to go shopping online. Perhaps impressed with its past successes, Best Buy was slow to see that the fading of their value propositions was threatening the core of its business model. Incredibly, even as online commerce was gaining momentum and threatening its foundations, the company continued to emphasize the traditional model and moved aggressively into other countries, such as Canada, China, and England.

When it did finally recognize the inevitable, Best Buy tried to integrate the physical stores with the Internet by offering free store pickup for products purchased at Best Buy Online. This was too little, too late, however. Online commerce had continued unabated in the meantime, and Internet retailers had sharpened their own models as well.

Missed opportunities, a failing business model, and dimmed future prospects for the company were visible in its market valuation. While the annual revenues climbed to more than $50 billion in fiscal 2011, the market value of the company had shrunk two-thirds from its peak of over $28 billion in 2006 to well under $10 billion in 2012.[1]

The same year, Best Buy announced that it was closing 50 of its 1,400 domestic big-box stores. The company began an overhaul of its business model, lowering the number of big-box stores and reconfiguring the remaining stores with an emerging concept—the store within a store. As of the first writing of this text in 2012, the company had begun to implement specialized display centers for increasingly competitive device manufacturers such as Apple, Samsung, and Microsoft. Over the next several years, the company managed a slow turnaround on a smaller store base with fewer employees; sales per store recovered, and the company again became profitable, although at lower gross margins. But competitors such as Amazon continued to gain in strength, and new online pure-plays such as Newegg.com and ThinkGeek.com emerged as viable options for consumers shopping for electronics. The online trend was obvious by then, and, as evidence of things to come, RadioShack—a competing in-store model—declared bankruptcy. It seemed that the glory days were gone as the new context was no longer friendly to the old logic of big-box stores.

Lessons from Best Buy

The struggles of Best Buy illustrate the importance of understanding the business models of the companies in which you invest. Good investment prospects are not just about profit and loss in the short run: strong investment performance comes from businesses that home in on the fundamental problems they must solve for paying customers and then assemble, align, and concentrate resources to address those problems in a systematic way. That is, companies create economic value when they consistently deliver well-articulated value propositions through well-executed operating models. Durable and meaningful rewards for investors come from selectively investing in companies that solve significant problems at a sufficiently large scale to make the efforts economically meaningful.

Business models are, in fact, a crucial due diligence check for investing wisely. They can help sort out companies that are genuinely good investment bets from those that are value traps—companies that suffer low market valuations because of truly dim prospects. That is, a clear understanding of the business model of a company can help refute an investment thesis even if the price looks attractive in quantitative tests.

Clearly, historical successes are no guarantee that a business model will continue being successful in the future. In fact, as we see in the history of Best Buy, past successes may make necessary changes difficult, even when the changing external context undermines the value propositions on which those successes were based. For companies to continue being successful and attractive as investment opportunities, their business models must evolve to keep their products relevant in new environments.

Yet, unless investors periodically monitor a company for major disruptions to its business model, the need for reassessing the investment thesis may not be become evident until it's too late. Although clear in hindsight, it was not easy for casual investors to comprehend the huge impact that the Internet would have on Best Buy. Changes at the margin, such as Best Buy Online, were not adequate to thwart the challenge posed by the purely Internet-based models to the company's value proposition that their network of big-box stores was delivering. Unfortunately for the company, the Internet induced an accelerating pace of change in consumption patterns—and changed the shopping behaviors of millions of people who had previously shopped and found contentment at Best Buy.

Changing a once successful business model is difficult, as it is painful to undo the assets, routines, and practices associated with past successes. In addition, managers resist the disruptions that any overhaul requires, in part because it's hard to let go of the familiar and in part because new directions bring new uncertainties. It is perhaps for this reason that companies often continue with ways of doing things long after their erstwhile successful business models are no longer effective. Investors must watch out.

Mechanisms of Wealth Creation

What made Best Buy successful between 1990 and 2005 is very different from how Dell changed the personal computing industry in the 1980s and 1990s. Why Home Depot succeeded differed a great deal from why Monster Beverage achieved stunning success as a leading energy drink company. Panera Bread had a different model than Starbucks or McDonald's. Priceline.com and Expedia, although in the same general business, go about attaining success in very different ways. Similarly, Nike and Under Armour do things very differently even though they both compete in footwear and athletic apparel.

Business models come in many different stripes, in other words, both within and across industries. More so these days, new models are emerging frequently as entrepreneurs leverage emerging technologies and changing consumption patterns to exploit new opportunities. The ability of investors to grasp the details of a particular business model depends at least to a degree on prior knowledge and experiences.

Given the particulars of skills and knowledge investors bring to an evaluation, it may be possible to clearly understand certain business models and pick up on nuances about how particular companies function. Other business models may be opaque to some investors because of their lack of familiarity with the industry or its inherent complexities.

In some cases, particular investors may understand a business model clearly but also see enough instability and risk to keep them away from the company in question. In other cases, value propositions may be clearly articulated by management, but there is no clear evidence that the company can successfully and profitably execute to deliver on those propositions.

For instance, some investors may find the value proposition and operating model of Expedia too complex because of their lack of familiarity with the travel industry. But, they may have just the skills to read much into how energy drink company Monster Beverage, online jeweler Blue Nile, or entertainment company Netflix go about delivering on well-specified value propositions to generate revenues and profits. Understanding a company's business model allows investors to set up their investment thesis for disconfirmation and, therefore, improves the quality of their investment choices.

It follows, then, that investors would be well served by limiting themselves to those companies whose business models they can understand and evaluate. By narrowing the focus of inquiry, investors can be well prepared to refute theses for companies on the grounds that they are too complex, opaque, risky, defenseless, or poorly suited to changing competitive conditions. Limiting the investment program to such zones of comfort is essential for investing wisely.

Business Model Essentials

A business model is best understood as the mechanism—value propositions plus combinations of assets, activities, and routines—that consumes resources to produce cash flows greater than the original investment. From the cash flows thus produced, the operators of the model—the managers—reinvest a portion to sustain, evolve, and strengthen the mechanism, with the rest either returned to investors or placed in reserve for future investments.

At least in hindsight, therefore, the strength of a business model is evident from the average historical returns on invested capital. Such future returns depend on the resilience of the model to sustain or shift its core elements in response to changing circumstances.

Essential to a business model are (1) the value proposition of products in the particular markets where they are sold; and (2) the resiliency of the operating capabilities necessary for creating, marketing, and distributing those products. To the extent that a company has a sharply defined and well-executed business model in an opportunity-rich environment, it is likely to generate high cash return on capital and create substantial economic worth for investors.

The model schematic in figure 19.1 outlines one such mechanism for generating cash flows. It outlines the logic for how a company produces and sells in order to deliver profits, in the face of competitors that serve the same consumers or end users. When fleshed out, the model helps assess how big the product markets are and the various channels used to get products to those markets. The model also clarifies the arrangement of production assets and the ability of the company to innovate and control costs in the procurement, manufacturing, distribution, and sales processes.

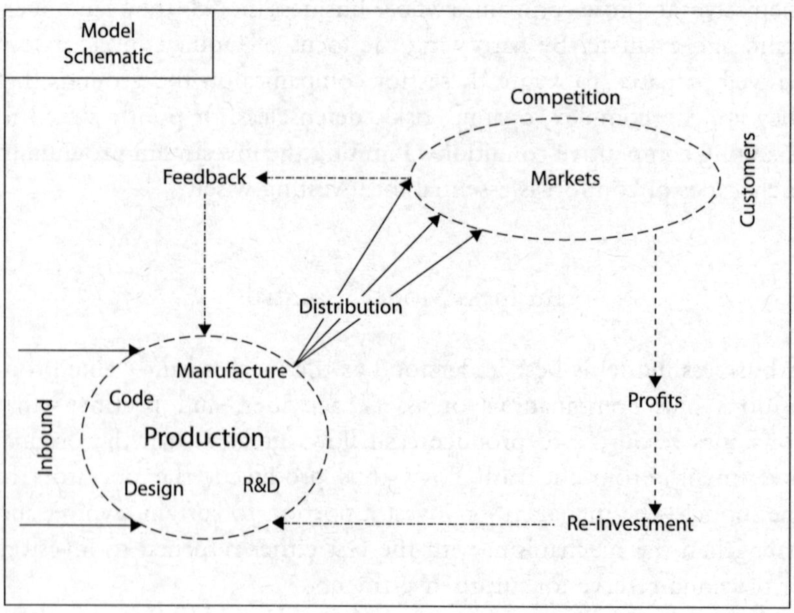

Figure 19.1 Full-view business schematic of a hypothetical manufacturing company

To illustrate, let's consider Coach, the maker of accessories and gifts targeted at female shoppers. The company's value proposition is "affordable luxury," embodied in stylish and well-constructed handbags but at a price much below higher-end foreign competitors. As of 2012, the company's operating model was anchored by outsourced manufacturing with strong quality control, continuous market research with rapid product development to support a strong brand, and a network of company-owned stores that increasingly included outlet stores for price-conscious customers. The key elements of the company's business model were as follows:

1. Coach sold as an affordable mid-range luxury, with designer handbags mostly under $300 and occasionally going to price points above $1,000. Price points were above mass-market handbags that sold for as little as $50 but well below European luxury brands, such as Gucci, Hermès, and Prada, which sold designer bags for thousands or tens of thousands of dollars.
2. The value proposition was to provide great design and robust construction with all the trappings of a well-established brand. This proposition targeted style-conscious young women looking for affordable options for accessories.
3. Coach served three broad geographical markets. Nearly 70 percent of sales came from the United States, about 18 percent from Japan, and the rest from other parts of the world, with China the new growth target.
4. A strong design team actively incorporated feedback from customers via ongoing surveys and research studies. This facilitated fine-tuned product development and positioning.
5. The company did not own manufacturing plants; it outsourced production to a network of qualified and closely monitored contractors. Coach tightly controlled the supply chain from design through manufacturing and distribution.
6. Coach brought products to customers through company-owned stores, select department stores and specialty stores that were consistent with their brand positioning, and its company website. The proportion of factory outlet stores in the mix was growing rapidly. As compared with full-price stores, outlet stores sold products from 10 percent to 50 percent discount and broadened the market to include price-sensitive customers.

7. During the period between 2009 and 2011, Coach reinvested about $470 million, or about 17 percent of operating cash flows, back into the business. Of this amount, $375 million was to refresh assets, and the remaining was intended for future growth.

Over time, Coach had fine-tuned a highly efficient operating model that supported a clear value proposition (high-end luxury within reach), which it had operationalized through correct product positioning (great product, good price, well-known brand, widely accessible through company-owned stores and affiliated third parties). A successful business model and competent execution were evident in the company's enviable financial performance: its revenues grew at a compounded annual rate of 20 percent, from $616 million in 2001 to $4.8 billion 2012. During the same period, its average return on capital was 41.5 percent; in 2012, the return on capital was just over 52 percent. Market value of the company's equity followed suit, rising 13-fold, from $1.7 billion in 2001 to a high of $22.7 billion in 2012.

As we saw in the case of Best Buy, however, even successful business models remain vulnerable because changes in the external environment are forever threatening the tight fit between a well-defined value proposition and its corresponding operating model. While the performance of Coach up until 2012 had been strong, therefore, alert investors would have wanted to understand how its model was evolving in response to the changing competitive landscape—and be particularly sensitive to an emerging lack of coherence between value propositions and the logic of its operating model.

Starting in about 2010, Coach markedly slowed down the growth of their full-price stores in North America and substantially increased the growth rate of factory outlet stores. In 2009, for instance, the company had 330 full-price stores and 111 factory outlet stores, which represented about 35 percent of total retail square footage. By the end of 2014, the full-price store count was 332, whereas the count of outlet stores had increased to 207, which now represented over 55 percent of total square footage. The company was planning to close about 70 more full-price stores in fiscal year 2015.

It appeared that Coach was drastically altering their business model in the United States, catering more and more to what it called value-oriented customers. The shift in emphasis from full-price stores to outlet stores that sold discontinued and discounted products suggests that the value proposition of affordable luxury was undergoing some sort of modification, pehaps toward a greater emphasis on affordability and less on luxury and exclusiveness. It was not clear whether this shift was reactive in response to or proactive in anticipation of trends toward bargain hunting among their core shoppers, or whether it was instigated by increasing competition from similar brands such as Michael Kors and Kate Spade. It's also possible that the company had determined that the high-margin business had run its course, and it was time now to commit a shift toward a low-margin–high-volume economic model. Whatever the case, even as the company continued to expand internationally (especially aggressively in China), it was shifting the value proposition in its domestic market.

At the same time that it increased the number of outlet stores in the United States, Coach also broadened its offering to include shoes and apparel, raised the average price of handbags, and promised to strengthen their luxury brand positioning. There was clearly an emerging disconnect between the continued emphasis on luxury branding and the operating model moving toward factory stores and discounted pricing. That is, at first glance at least, the company's business model was no longer as coherent as the one that had led to its phenomenal success until 2012.

Coincidentally, the emerging incoherence between its value proposition and operating model was beginning to show up in Coach's financial performance. For 2014, Coach reported its first ever drop in revenues, its lowest gross and operating margins in 10 years, and a net margin of only 16.3 percent compared with an average of about 22 percent over the previous five years. Its return on capital for the year dropped to 32 percent from an average of 47 percent over the preceding five years. For those invested in Coach, inconsistency between the value proposition and the operating model turned out to be very costly. The company's market value dropped by almost two-thirds, from a high of $22.7 billion in 2012 to below $8.5 billion as of July 2015.

There are many nuances to any business, of course, but the key for investors is to try to cast doubt on the dominant narrative of how it makes money—either from logical holes in the business model or by discovering problems in the ability of the mechanisms so revealed to make profits and produce cash flows.

The Walmart Business Model

Walmart has its origins in rural 1960s Arkansas, when Sam Walton discovered a way to serve the needs of people living far away from shopping centers. The initial value proposition of the company was access to discounted packaged goods in the rural south, and the company delivered on this through opportunistic buying and shrewd merchandising. As the company grew rapidly from Arkansas to the rest of the south and then the southeast, quickly filling the unserved niches of rural America, its increasing scale made it possible to offer a clarified value proposition of consistently low prices, enabled by an operating model that incentivized hard bargaining with suppliers and that, with the help of a strong top-down culture, kept costs obsessively under control.

Low prices attracted a great deal of foot traffic, and in-store help greatly improved the shopping experiences of customers bewildered by the plethora of products suddenly within easy reach. The company set off on an explosive growth trajectory, with annual revenues rising from $44 million in 1970 to $1.6 billion in 1980 and to $8.5 billion in 1985.

As Walmart grew in size, it invested heavily in information technology and logistics capabilities, in part to contain the complexity of its growing operations but also to ensure that its value proposition would not be undermined by empty shelves. These investments further strengthened its operating model and set the company apart from competitors with the ability to offer a broad assortment of merchandise at low prices. Soon, confident of its organizational capabilities, the company instituted a formal everyday low price (EDLP) strategy and deeply entrenched itself in the world of discount retail. By the time Sam Walton died in 1993, Walmart had become the largest retailer in the country. The same year, the company also formed its international division, starting a rapid expansion into South America, Europe, and (through the acquisition of Asda) the United Kingdom.

Even as Walmart grew in size and scope, it leveraged formidable distribution and logistics capabilities to innovate new retail formats. Having started as a typical discount retailer carrying mostly general merchandise, the company rapidly entered the grocery business in the United States—by the end of fiscal year 2015, groceries comprised more than half of the total U.S. revenues.

TABLE 19.1

Store Format	2015	2010	2000	Business Focus
Discount	460	803	1,801	General merchandise
Supercenter	3,431	2,747	721	General merchandise, grocery
Neighborhood market	644	158	7	Grocery
Grocery as % of revenue	56%	53%	18%	

Source: Company website. (Data for U.S. operations only)

As shown in table 19.1, in early 2000, Walmart operated over 1,800 discount stores, 721 supercenters, and seven small-format neighborhood stores in the United States. As of 2015, the mix of formats had changed dramatically. The company now operates 460 discount stores, 3,431 supercenters, and 644 neighborhood stores. The trend toward both supercenters and much smaller formats continues, and the original discount stores seem to be on the way out. The company also continues to innovate new formats, such as a fast-growing category of 2,500-square-foot stores on college campuses.

Also between 2000 and 2015, Walmart made a significant shift toward the grocery business: whereas grocery accounted for only 18 percent of total U.S. revenues at the beginning of 2000, by the beginning of 2015, grocery accounted for 56 percent of total revenues. Even as grocery becomes more important for the company, it continues to innovate store formats on the strength of its logistics capabilities—with the objective of bringing point of purchase physically near where customers live.

The move toward grocery was accompanied by heavy investment in new distribution centers. Whereas the company had 45 distribution centers in 2000, by the beginning of 2015, that number had increased to 134, about the same increase (198 percent) as growth in total revenues during the period, from $166 billion to $483 billion (192 percent). Yet, much of the recent growth in distribution centers has come from the company leasing rather than owning them. In 2008, for instance, the company owned 106 of its 121 distribution centers; in early 2015, the company owned only 102 of the 134 distribution centers that supported its operations, suggesting that it had increasingly shifted this key asset from asset/debt in the balance sheet to operating lease in the income statement.

With grocery now making up more than half the company's sales, it's remarkable that Walmart has maintained its operating margins above 5 percent and its net margins at about 3.5 percent. These are considerably higher than those of large-chain grocer Kroger, whose operating and net margins over the last five years have averaged 2.7 percent and 1.3 percent, respectively. That is, Walmart's business mix is going increasingly toward the lower-margin grocery business; although it has thus far been able to sustain good margins, perhaps because of scale, better efficiencies, and merchandise sales, it's unclear how long it can continue generating so much better performance than a well-run specialist like Kroger.[2] Grocery remains a low-margin, dynamically competitive business, characterized by bankruptcies (e.g., A&P, Fresh & Easy) and new entries by low-cost competitors (e.g., ALDI, Lidl).

The lower margins of its growing grocery business will likely continue putting pressure on the operating margins of Walmart's domestic retail business, which comprises about 60 percent of the total company-wide revenues and accounts for just about 79 percent of operating profits. The international segment, comprising 28 percent of company-wide revenues, makes up 23 percent of operating profits, but its operating margins are lower (4.5 percent versus 7.4 percent for domestic retail; Sam's Club makes up 12 percent of total revenues, but with an operating margin of only 3.4 percent).

The company's domestic merchandise business is under significant pressure as well. Even though the company has had much success in traditional retail formats, Walmart seems to have missed much of the growth in online retail, which directly threatens the merchandise business. Although company leadership had begun to articulate the need to follow the rise of the web as far back as 1999, the company has been slow to respond and has largely yielded online shopping to such innovators as Amazon and eBay.

Fast-improving technologies have enabled increasingly tech-savvy shoppers to search for, compare, order, and receive goods without having to get in their cars, drive, and stand in checkout lines. While still valid, low prices and a wide assortment of goods are no longer sufficient to get the current generation of shoppers to visit stores. Along with selection and price, many shoppers also want to save time and avoid the inconvenience of having to go to a store. Recognizing this, online retailers are quick to redefine and deliver on an expanded value proposition: search, compare, and select on the web; then click and wait for home delivery. Moreover, these retailers continue to develop the infrastructure to compress delivery times.

For a fast-growing segment of shoppers, online shopping dulls the value proposition of low price and wide assortment in physical stores because the web allows for price comparison and offers an almost infinite assortment of goods. Many online retailers have established themselves with an emphasis on shopping efficiency, and they have built their operating models specifically to deliver the value proposition that low prices and wide assortment can be had along with the convenience of not having to go to a store.

Consider, for instance, a key asset in retail: the distribution center. For a company such as Walmart, distribution centers serve to supply retail stores and are, therefore, designed to move goods in bulk, crates at a time, loaded onto trucks and shipped out on well-defined delivery routes. An online retailer such as Amazon, on the other hand, organizes its distribution centers to be able to pick a single unit of an item at a time and pull together a small box to be shipped to customers' home addresses. These differences indicate the fundamental differences in the business models of the two companies, and to the extent that customer preference may be shifting toward online shopping, give considerable operating advantage to the likes of Amazon.

Clearly, online shopping is just one more way for people to acquire the goods they want; it coexists with traditional modes of shopping by offering a value proposition that is different from those delivered by physical stores. It is plausible that online shopping is expanding commerce rather than simply replacing in-store shopping. But, as technology evolves and Internet retailers further sharpen their models, buying online is likely to become deeply ingrained in the shopping behaviors and consumption patterns of ever increasing numbers of people. Brick-and-mortar retailers will have to evolve their business models by uncovering new value propositions and modifying their operating models for new realities. Surely, traditional retailers are trying to develop hybrid models, where customers can order online and pick up at the store or where retailers use stores as distribution centers for shipping out online orders. It's not quite clear, however, if these are cost-effective operating models to deliver the emergent value proposition of online shopping.

Walmart has only recently begun to deliver on customer preferences for shopping efficiency and time savings. For 2014, the company reported $12.2 billion in revenues from global e-commerce, up 22 percent from the previous year but still only a fraction of the more than $480 billion company-wide revenues for the year. Moreover, likely hampered by an operating focus on brick-and-mortar stores, it remains far behind Amazon—which continues to sharpen and strengthen its online operating model, as evident from its 2014 revenues of $89 billion, up 46 percent from 2012.

The strategic challenge for Walmart is to create a robust presence in online shopping without undermining the vast infrastructure built over the years to serve what is still a very large brick-and-mortar retail business. The key remains the company's ability to expand its value propositions and evolve its operating model to meet the new realities of retail. Company leaders have begun to articulate several experiments and initiatives that they claim will integrate their logistics capabilities and network of stores with e-commerce. But it remains to be seen how well it will flesh out those new models and then execute them to shift its center of gravity from old retail to the new world of cyber shopping. In this endeavor, Walmart is up against entrenched and formidable competitors who continue to sharpen the operating models they have built ground up specifically for the very environment they have helped create.

As we saw in the case of Best Buy, online retail is a considerable challenge for brick-and-mortar stores selling undifferentiated products. Given the imperatives of their current store-heavy operating model, Walmart faces strong inertia in the face of headwinds that seem only to be getting stronger. So, it is important to try to assess the extent to which the new retail environment is having an impact on the company. Below I illustrate one way to do so.

Table 19.2 shows five-year data for same-store sales growth for Walmart (WMT) stores in the United States and those for Kroger (KR). The first column shows annual inflation (based on the consumer price index [CPI]); the second and third columns present same-store sales growth for the two companies. Clearly, Walmart's same-store sales growth was significantly lower than inflation, whereas Kroger's same-store sales grew at a much faster rate.

We know that more than half of Walmart store sales are from groceries. If we assume that the company's per-store grocery sales grew at about the same rate as Kroger's same-store sales growth, it is likely that a lower overall rate of same-store sales growth for Walmart would

TABLE 19.2

	CPI	WMT	KR	WMT Merchandise
2014	1.62%	0.50%	5.20%	–2.10%
2013	1.46%	–0.60%	3.60%	–2.40%
2012	2.07%	1.80%	3.50%	0.05%
2011	3.16%	0.20%	4.90%	–2.25%
2010	1.64%	–1.60%	2.80%	–3.00%

Source: Data from www.bls.gov and company websites.

imply that, as estimated in the last column of table 19.2, the company's merchandise business had experienced sharp sales declines over the last five years. Indeed, since nonperishable packaged products are the most vulnerable to online shopping and shipping, it is plausible that Walmart's discount business is under a great deal of pressure. This is a rough analysis, of course, but the implication is consistent with the company's actions: rapidly converting big-box discount stores into supercenters to reduce reliance on merchandise and grow its grocery business.

Unless the company turns around its merchandise business and grows its e-commerce at breakneck pace, the above analysis suggests that shifts in customer preferences will continue to create significant challenges for Walmart. Fast-evolving technologies and rapidly shifting customer preferences—from the instant gratification of buying in store to the convenience of online shopping and from low prices to less time to shop—do create significant challenges for Walmart going forward. These require a massive transformation of its operating model to align with the forces sweeping through the retail landscape; given the company's investments and commitments in the existing infrastructure of brick-and-mortar stores plus its distribution centers, such a transformation seems difficult. If merchandise revenues continue to fall, the high fixed cost of operating these stores will put pressure on margins and, eventually, make them unprofitable. Then, the large number of operating leases will become increasingly burdensome.

Investors evaluating the Walmart investment thesis must take note of these facts. Even though quantitative analysis was not able to refute the thesis, qualitative analysis reveals an increased amount of debt in the balance sheet and a liberal (perhaps excessive) use of operating leases. Qualitative analysis also reveals the importance of headwinds from online retail and the inertia of the company's current operating model. All these factors cast serious doubt on, and perhaps even disconfirm, the thesis that, at about $74 per share, Walmart is an attractive investment.

It may be that the company can successfully leverage their supply chain capabilities, long history of innovation, strong culture of cost control, and laser focus on low prices to discover new value propositions. But it may also be that the iceberg has met global warming and is now melting. While Walmart is clearly a strongly entrenched company, changes in the retail landscape present challenges that prudent investors cannot ignore.

CHAPTER TWENTY

Meet the Managers

IN THE MODERN corporation, small or large, power is highly centralized in the hands of a few people who make most if not all key decisions. These people, the top management team (TMT), exercise considerable discretion as to what gets priority, who gets the money, and what gets done. If not also the architects of the business model, they are its operators, ultimately responsible for the performance and financial health of the company and, therefore, for the safety of your investment in it.

Because of the power they have, good managers can create tremendous value for shareholders. Steve Jobs, to take a well-known example, transformed the music industry by imagining what he could do with an external hard drive, a commodity widely available in the civilized world. Upon recognizing the potential in the hard drive, he boldly allocated company resources to build a global business that changed the way we listen to music. Moreover, even as he built the iPod, Jobs developed a powerful platform for innovations that has given us the iPhone and the iPad. One good insight from one good manager created billions of dollars in value for Apple shareholders.

There are many other examples of good managers creating economic value by building new companies and by transforming existing ones. Sam Walton built Walmart, Ray Kroc built McDonald's, Thomas Watson, Jr. revived International Business Machines, Jack Welch transformed General Electric (GE), Larry Ellison built Oracle, Phil Knight built Nike, Louis Gerstner revived International Business Machines yet again, Bill Gates built Microsoft, Jeff Bezos built Amazon, Howard Schultz built up Starbucks, Reed Hastings built Netflix; the list goes on.

The performance of a company and of your investment in it depends largely on the skill with which leaders seek opportunities and allocate capital to construct new or solidify existing streams of cash. Good managers are, in essence, good stewards of the resources entrusted to them by suppliers of capital at risk: the shareholders. They concentrate on delivering strong operating performance that, over time, has the potential to create a great deal of wealth for shareholders.

But there is another side to this story.

Many managers are not keen on anyone's interests but their own. For shareholders, usually widely dispersed and often owning too small a part of the company to have much say in its affairs, not having managers who look after their interests bodes trouble.[1] Because they control the resources of the company, managers have all the power and, as history teaches us, with power comes the potential for corruption in its many forms: hubris, entrenchment, nepotism, negligence, incompetence, and downright fraud.

In many instances, top managers have systematically looted the wealth that was at their disposal, using company resources as if they were monies in a personal account. For shareholders, there is perhaps no more important an issue than the competence, integrity, and character of the managers in control of the companies in which they have invested.

With the likes of Ken Lay and Jeffrey Skilling of Enron, Bernie Ebbers of WorldCom, Dennis Kozlowski of Tyco, John Rigas of Adelphia Communications, Conrad Black of Hollinger International, and, of course, the one and only Bernie Madoff, we are reminded that capitalism produces its share of misfits and crooks in high places, and that unwitting shareholders are easily duped.

The many high-profile cases notwithstanding, investors can lose even when executives do not engage in criminal action or outright fraud. Managers can enrich themselves in any number of ways, for the simple reason that they are in control of the resources and close to the action; they have a great deal of discretion as to what goes on and what gets reported.

While most managers do their jobs honestly, and well-run companies usually have considerable internal controls to prevent misdeeds, investors trying to disconfirm their investment theses must keep a lookout for what may be amiss in the character of the people who run the companies in which they invest. Investors must learn to make judgments about the competence and trustworthiness of the managers running the company, and to assess the degree to which their words and actions demonstrate respect for the rights of the shareholders.

Evaluating managers can be difficult, especially if you don't have direct contact with them. Information about the managers is often spotty, and business issues can be complicated; you may also have insufficient access or resources with which to uncover major fraud, especially when those committing the fraud actively camouflage their actions. Big investors and institutions with large amounts of capital at stake may be able to hire specialists, such as forensic accountants and private investigators, to evaluate the background and character of top managers. For small investors, however, digging deep into every company out there is simply impractical.

As such, for both small and large investors, a quick run-through of some of the basics can be useful, especially to the extent that knowing how to investigate the quality of a company's managers will help keep your money out of the hands of at least the most egregious offenders.

In order to make preliminary judgments about the quality of managers, therefore, let's review three broad areas: (1) demographics—to understand the people and the dynamics is in the executive suites; (2) track record—to evaluate past accomplishments by way of tangible results; and (3) oversight—to comprehend the incentives and monitoring mechanisms in place. Significant doubts about managers arising from such scrutiny may be grounds for disconfirming the investment thesis.

Demographics

The first set of issues in the evaluation of managers concerns the demographic profile of the team at the top of the organization. Here we are concerned with (1) the background and tenure of the top managers; (2) the dynamics and stability of the top management team; and (3) turnover and succession in the top ranks.

Background and Tenure

Investors must understand where the key managers have cut their teeth. Inevitably, managers bring their past into current assignments, so it is useful to know their breadth and depth of experiences. We cannot know for sure the competence and integrity of the person from simply his or her background, but background data can nevertheless be useful for gaining insights into the quality of those in charge.

Also useful for such insights are the age and tenure of key people on the top team. Are they young, say, in their 40s and 50s, building careers and wealth, or are they older, more experienced people looking to sew together an institution to which they may have devoted their careers? How long have they been with the company? Such questions provide no clear answers, but they give helpful clues to the motivations that may be driving the actions of managers.

Investors must try to understand how the stewards of their capital think, to see the constraints and possibilities as the managers do, and to understand their game plan for creating economic value.

More than demographic information, the quality of thinking of the managers is the key to understanding how good they are likely to be as stewards of your capital. A peek into the thinking of managers is usually available from what they say in interviews, in letters to shareholders, and in earnings calls with analysts. Although not quantifiable, particularly important is the clarity with which the managers articulate what strategic objectives they're trying to accomplish, why those objectives are important for creating economic value, and how they are going about accomplishing their objectives.

Evaluating managers in this way takes some maturity and experience, of course, but doing so is essential for closely monitoring your investment in the company. So, in combination with quantitative markers, such as past performance, you must make subjective judgments about the quality of the people leading an organization. If your judgment casts doubt on the integrity or quality of the people at the top of a company, then it may be wise to reject the investment thesis even if other, more objective, criteria do not provide grounds for you to refute it.

Team Dynamics and Stability

Typically, while all members of the top team in a well-run company are professionally at the top of their game, the chief executive officer (CEO) and chief financial officer (CFO) usually drive key decisions: one has the overall responsibility and sets the tone; the other keeps an eye on the money. One cannot do his or her job well without the full cooperation of and in full coordination with the other. Sometimes, other functions, such as design, merchandising, logistics, or information technology, are key for long-term success. Even so, the CEO and CFO are usually the people to watch closely.

Beyond the top two executives, a good sense of the whole team is important as well, because running a business is essentially a team sport. Many minds check on each other, and many hands make it possible to execute the game plan. As such, investors must try to understand how much the CEO dominates the team and how stable the team is.

The CEO dominating the team is not necessarily a bad thing. It is quite common for strong chiefs to drive good companies. Jack Welch at GE, Bill Gates at Microsoft, Steve Jobs at Apple, Larry Ellison at Oracle, Howard Schultz at Starbucks; the list of strong individuals who built wonderful companies and rewarded their shareholders incredibly well is very long. Strong CEOs are desirable, in fact, as long as they have a consistent record of delivering strong operating performance over time. They are the ones who have figured out how to hit the sweet spots, and it's okay to let the company be under their watchful eye.

The trouble comes when dominant CEOs become entrenched in spite of persistent anemic performance. It is, in fact, very difficult to displace a poorly performing but powerful CEO, and it takes Herculean effort on the part of shareholders to do so. Investors should watch out for entrenched CEOs in poorly performing companies.

The other extreme of entrenched CEO is, of course, a revolving door to the corner office. Companies that cannot retain a chief and need frequently look for a new one are likely to suffer from the lack of stable leadership. Until the company hired Meg Whitman, Hewlett Packard had a revolving door in the corner office, and, given the instability at the top, its shareholders suffered immensely. Yahoo! fared similarly until the company hired Marissa Mayer. A happy medium for CEO tenure is somewhere around 10 years: long enough to take control of the company and shape it but not so long that it makes the company stale or stifles the ambitions of talented professionals in the waiting.

As it goes with the CEOs, so it goes with the rest of the management team. While the entrenchment of loyalists is a concern in poorly performing companies, team stability is important for good companies to continue delivering performance. It takes time for people to develop good working relations with each other, to work as a cohesive team; it does little good if the company is unable to retain skilled executives. Revolving doors not just in but also around the corner office can be highly unsettling by getting in the way of good team dynamics that are essential to developing and executing good game plans.

Turnover and Succession

Even good CEOs must eventually retire. When they do, the transition to new leadership can be disruptive unless the company has a succession plan. Such a plan is especially helpful if the CEO departs suddenly, as was the case when, in August 2010, Hewlett Packard forced out the talented CEO Mark Hurd because of a scandal. Death, illness, or allure of better opportunities can be among the many reasons why a CEO may suddenly leave.

Succession planning is not natural to most companies, as the current CEOs don't often want to think about the end of their own careers. Talk of succession may also raise personnel issues inside the company, such as power struggles and other unsettling dynamics among internal candidates. Perhaps for these reasons, many charismatic CEOs hold the top spot long beyond their productive years.

Still, leadership succession is an important issue, and some large companies, such as Walmart, GE, Johnson & Johnson, and Intel, do a good job of it. These companies have the luxury of size, of course, as their many divisions are the breeding and testing grounds of future leaders. Some of these companies are, in fact, leadership factories of sorts, as their alumni often go on to lead other companies.

For smaller companies with fewer resources, planning for future leadership is more difficult. Even so, depth of executive talent and clear succession planning are important investor considerations.

In this regard, too, we are unable to challenge the investment thesis for Walmart. The company has a long history of stability at the top and smooth leadership transitions about every 10 years or so. Leadership transitions appear to be well planned, and those filling the top executive roles bring a great deal of energy and extensive operating experiences to the job.

Track Record

Of primary importance in the evaluation of managers is their ability to deliver results in the form of (1) financial performance in the recent past; (2) the quality of the financial statements through which they present their accomplishments; and (3) tangible evidence of their shareholder friendliness.

Financial Performance

Clearly, investors would like the management team to have delivered satisfactory operating performance over time. If you have been unable to refute the investment thesis of a company on valuation, yield, stability, strength, or liquidity, and the deep dive into the company literature has not yet revealed any fatal flaws, then the chances are that you will find past performance to reveal competent management.

The key here is to understand how efficiently the current managers have run the company. Usual operating ratios, such as inventory turnover, asset turnover, operating cycle, and cash management, are particularly important. These show the guts of the operation and help you to assess the competence and operating capabilities of managers.

As we saw in chapter 18, also important to evaluate over time is the efficiency with which the managers have deployed capital in the past; return on equity (ROE) and return on capital (ROC) are both useful indicators. High and steady returns, when compared with those of direct competitors or similar companies, usually mean that the managers are making good use of the resources entrusted to them.

It is important to note that sustained financial performance results from consistently good execution of the operating model, which, in turn, must be fine-tuned to deliver on the strategic objectives of the company. Hence, a good track record reflects an advanced ability to integrate the many different elements of the business, entailing both analytical and people skills. Such skills are difficult to judge, but alert investors can get a measure of managers by closely following their public statements and visible strategic initiatives. Specifically evaluating managers' words for clarity of thinking and coherence of articulated strategy can go a long way toward being able to put meaning to financial performance.

Let's return to the ongoing example of Walmart. As of the end of 2014, the company showed good operating performance over the preceding decade—with steady margins and strong cash flows. Its growth rate has slowed in recent years, however; as discussed in chapter 19, seismic changes in the retail environment have created significant strategic challenges for the company. Given the slowness with which Walmart responded to those changes, a case can be made that the leadership culture has been perhaps somewhat insular or misdirected at best. Even though the company has delivered acceptable financial performance, its neglect of online retail, despite quickly gaining ground in this area, suggests that it underperformed on the important role of adapting its operating model to evolving customer preferences. The company has responded strongly in recent years, but the decade-long slowness with which it did so resulted in industry leadership passing to emergent competitors such as Amazon. As such, cautious investors would be best to withhold judgment on the competence of the top management team; the investment thesis is, in other words, is weakened based on this criterion.

Accounting with Honesty

We can also obtain insights into the temperament and trustworthiness of the management team from the quality of the company's financial statements. This is because managers and outside accountants (auditors) have a good deal of discretion in how they report the economic activities of the company. Ultimately, accountants can do little by way of shading the numbers if managers are not complicit in doing so. Hence, the quality of the financial statements reflects the integrity of the management team.

When they sense significant irregularities, accountants can either resign or give a qualified opinion—a signal that the managers were unhelpful in resolving material issues in the financial statements. Sometimes, however, accountants can enable managers in reporting that hides big troubles in the operations or in the economic structure of the enterprise. This is because even the rulebooks leave considerable leeway in how to interpret data and what assumptions to use to make the various estimates that go into pulling together the many line items in financial statements. That is, with the help of their accountants, managers can stay within the rules and still be able to stretch the truth to paint a picture that is rosier than it ought to be.

Aggressive accounting practices reflect the eagerness of managers to meet and deliver the expectations often already built into stock prices. Especially in fast-growing companies where expectations of future growth are very high, pressure on managers to deliver the numbers is intense; some managers may respond to such pressure by insisting on or facilitating aggressive choices in reporting. Moreover, once managers cross the line and get fancy with their reporting, it is likely that they will do so again; eventually, the seemingly innocuous evasions or exaggerations turn into shades of falsehoods and then outright lies.

Managers can accomplish aggressive accounting in any number of ways, so at least a passing acquaintance with some of the most common forms of stretching the truth is important for investors to have. Many books exist on the subject, and investors can acquire a working knowledge of the most common forms of deceptions. It is not possible to cover the full range of accounting shenanigans here, so we will consider just a brief framework to understand the kinds of tricks that distort the true economics and financial condition of a company.

Investors must scrutinize financial statements for problems with revenues, expenses, assets, and liabilities. Misstating these gives distorted impressions of how well the company is performing and how strong it is financially.

In particular, investors must find out how often and how significantly the company restates revenues and/or earnings. To the extent that managers cut corners in reporting over time, seemingly minor choices can add up to substantial pressure in the reporting regime and, eventually, a forced restatement.

Similarly, large restructuring charges every few years could be a reflection of aggressive reporting over the years followed by what professionals call "big bath" accounting. Hence, paying attention to the reporting history of a company is a useful way to monitor accounting practices and the quality of the management.

Particularly dangerous for investors is when a company alters the top line, misrepresenting how well their products are selling. Computer Associates, for example, misstated over $3 billion in revenues during the late 1990s, largely to meet analyst expectations and, arguably, to keep the stock price at high levels to benefit top executives who had stock options and bonuses tied to delivering performance.

The executives appeared to have recorded revenues prematurely by keeping the reporting quarter open for several days beyond the official closing date in order to incorporate new contracts as sales. The falsehood became too difficult to continue after a few years, however, and the company finally reported earnings below expectations in the first quarter of 2001. The CEO went to jail for conspiring to file materially false financial statements and for obstructing justice by lying during the investigation. Investors paid dearly for this subterfuge.

More brazenly, Qwest Communications recorded fictitious revenues when it did asset swaps with other companies and then posted their side of the swap as revenues. The company fraudulently booked over $3 billion between 1999 and 2002. According to the charges filed by the Securities and Exchange Commission (SEC), the company also understated expenses by $231 million over the same period. Again, investors paid dearly for accounting shenanigans by managers.

In short, as is evident from the cases of Computer Associates and Qwest Communications, it is especially important for investors to understand the revenue line. Strong revenue growth can sometimes overcome reporting problems on the expense side, but misstating actual sales can be devastating for investors, potentially destroying their entire investment.

Accounting shenanigans also often involve shifting items between the income statement and the balance sheet. For instance, a company may meet aggressive sales targets by incentivizing customers to build up their inventories or sign multiyear contracts before the end of the reporting period. These noncash revenues, booked aggressively on the income statement, show up as inflated accounts receivables in the balance sheet.

Similarly, companies may defer current-period expenses to future periods and thereby inflate current operating earnings. Those expenses then appear on the balance sheet as inflated current liabilities, only to be brought back on the income statement another year or during a "big bath." Then, companies may pre-pay future expenses and hold them in current assets, only to bring them back as expenses on the income statement in some future period when operating performance turns out to be healthier than expected.

Because the Generally Accepted Accounting Principles (GAAP) that govern financial reporting provide only broad guidance, managers and their accountants can stay within the rules and still make choices that overstate revenues and understate expenses in any given period. The integrity and honesty of managers is crucial in how they make reporting choices; how conservative they are in making those choices may be a proxy for how trustworthy they are.

Managers who repeatedly inflate reported performance can be trouble for investors. Keeping an eye out for aggressive accounting can go a long way toward avoiding potentially debilitating losses; aggressive accounting is a usually a negative signal about those at the top.

Coming back to Walmart, a review of the financial statements does not reveal obvious shenanigans. The company's revenues appear to be robust, as they are essentially cash payments by customers for the goods bought in stores. Consistency of margins and operating ratios suggest that it is unlikely to be swapping expenses between the income statement and the balance sheet. Operating cash flows have consistently been above net income, indicating robustness of accrual accounting numbers. The company also does not seem to have any major restatements of financial statements. Based on these criteria of accounting honesty, in other words, we are unable to cast serious doubt on the Walmart investment thesis.

A Shareholder-Friendly Orientation

Since equity owners hold the residual risk and stand to lose a great deal if the company performance collapses, the shareholder friendliness of managers is an important concern. Managers must be good stewards of their capital, not only in word but more so in deed, as reflected in dividends payments and share repurchase programs.[2] These are two tangible ways of rewarding shareholders for risking their capital: dividends put cash in their hands, and repurchases support the market for the company's shares and give equity owners marginally greater ownership.

Although tangible returns to shareholders, dividends are not easy to reduce or eliminate once initiated; they commit the companies to future cash outflows. Investors often buy into companies for the promise of future cash dividends and expect such cash inflows to be steady, predictable, and to grow over time. Frequently raising and then cutting dividends and raising them again sends mixed signals and is generally a bad practice that most good companies try to avoid.

Even so, it is common for companies to declare special dividends now and then. In the summer of 2004, for instance, Microsoft declared a one-time special dividend of $3 per share, putting to good use $36 billion of the $56 billion cash hoard it had piled up over the years. Similarly, clothing retailer Buckle paid a special divided of about $2 per share for three years starting in 2009. It so happens that in both cases, a few insiders were also very large shareholders who benefitted handsomely from the windfall. Whatever the motivation, sharing the wealth with shareholders is the right thing for companies to do, provided, of course, that they can afford both current and future cash outlays. Investors should beware and ensure that, in order to pay dividends, the company does not dip into the funds needed for necessary business expenditures or future growth.

Share buybacks are more of an indirect benefit, as they reduce the number of shares outstanding, thereby increasing the proportion of earnings and ownership for remaining shareholders. Over time, this increased ownership can yield significant rewards. Share buybacks also allow for a good deal of flexibility as companies can be opportunistic and regulate purchases depending on conditions.

Investors should know, however, that share buyback programs are also beneficial if the company is not simultaneously issuing significant numbers of shares through stock options and warrants. Many companies make liberal use of stock options in their compensation packages, for instance, and dilute the ownership share of outside equity investors. When they repurchase shares, these companies in effect buy back those additional shares exercised by options and warrants holders, severely diluting gains to the other shareholders. This is sometimes a way for managers to enrich themselves while giving the impression that they are returning money to shareholders, which they are not actually doing to the extent that the share buyback may imply.

At the end of fiscal 2010, for instance, Procter & Gamble had about 2,843,500,000 common shares outstanding, but the average diluted share count during the year was 8.82 percent higher at about 3,099,300,000. The overhang of diluted shares was in large part from payment used in the company's 2005 acquisition of Gillette.

During the first three quarters of fiscal 2011, the company spent more than $4.5 billion buying back shares. With an average share price during the period of about $61, this amounted to about 74,361,000 shares bought back. Yet, the actual share count decreased by only 52,207,000 to 2,791,293,000 at the end of the third quarter. This implies that the company bought 22,154,000 of the diluted shares and spent over $1.35 billion to do so.

In effect, Procter & Gamble actually bought back a lot more shares than was reflected in the reduction in basic share count. Of the

$4.5 billion spent in the buyback, more than $1.35 billion provided no net benefit to the existing shareholders. By implication, if share buybacks are a roundabout way of benefitting managers, they can be costly for shareholders, and investors must keep a close eye.

Unfortunately, share dilution appears to be a common practice across corporate America, and it is particularly rampant in some areas of the economy, such as the technology sector and fast-growing start-ups. Investors must watch out for companies that issue a great deal of options to executives and then buy back those shares at possibly inflated market prices. Such subterfuge can severely undermine wealth gains for shareholders.

Share buybacks are also not helpful if managers use them simply to manage per-share metrics. If total earnings are flat or declining, a company can buy back shares to show growth in earnings per share and, ironically, take resources away from projects that may in fact help renew top-line growth.

Such actions are especially hurtful if companies purchase overvalued shares, as they are then not only poorly using resources but also making bad investment decisions. In 2011, for example, Netflix spent nearly $200 million buying shares when prices were rising fast. Soon after the buybacks, the company's market valuations dropped sharply, and, within months, the share price was under 30 percent of what it had been at the time of the purchases.

In fact, it is surprisingly common for companies to overpay for their own shares and then not to buy them when low market prices make their shares more attractive. According to a *Wall Street Journal* report,[3] U.S. companies in the aggregate bought close to $600 billion worth of their own shares at the peak of the market in 2007; in 2009, when prices were historically low after the crash, companies in the aggregate spent less than $100 billion on share buybacks.

Then there are companies that will simply not pay dividends or participate in repurchase programs at all, arguing that they need the monies to reinvest in and grow the business. This argument for not paying dividends or repurchasing shares has merit when the company has a history of attaining far above normal returns and a well-articulated, rich set of opportunities for future growth. This holds true for fast-growing companies that clearly need the resources to continue growing and/or establish market positions.

Many companies also preserve cash as a cushion against unexpected liquidity crunches or for investing opportunistically. Apple, for instance, has rarely bought back shares over the last decade, and, in fact, its share count steadily went up from 710 million in 2002 to 909 million at the end of fiscal year 2010. Share dilution as of the end of 2010 was at 1.32 percent. The 10-year average return on capital for Apple stood at just under 19 percent as of the end of fiscal 2010. In recent years, after considerable pressure from investors, the company started issuing a small dividend and, in 2014, bought back a substantial number of shares outstanding.

For most steadily growing established companies, it is reasonable for investors to expect a share of the spoils. In the case of companies that generate sufficient cash but do not issue dividends or repurchase shares, two things are possible: Either they are holding on to cash and generating poor or risky returns on it, or they will do something questionable with it. If they're hoarding too much cash, it is important to try to understand why they may be doing so.

It is sometimes possible that managers are skilled and have a history of using cash wisely. Berkshire Hathaway, for instance, does not issue dividends, nor does it buy back its shares; the company instead uses its operating cash for acquisitions and investments that have historically produced good returns for shareholders.

The other possibility for hoarded cash is that the managers will misuse it, either spending on nonproductive things, such as lavish corporate offices, or frittering it away on hubris-driven, empire-building acquisitions. The better course of action from the point of view of investors is that a company not keep any unproductive cash on the balance sheet for long but, instead, raise monies as needed for out-of-the-ordinary acquisitions and strategic initiatives. Piles of cash can do little good and much harm.

Prudently sharing the spoils of genuinely good performance reflects a healthy shareholder orientation; it should be welcome. As shown in the previous chapter, Walmart demonstrated shareholder friendliness by avoiding dilution, consistently buying back its own shares, and steadily growing cash dividends. Although top-line growth has slowed in recent years, and both share buybacks and dividend growth were low in the past year, we cannot refute the investment thesis for Walmart based on their friendly orientation toward shareholders.

Oversight

A third set of issues in the evaluation of managers concerns the incentives they have for delivering performance and the extent to which they are answerable to shareholders through the board of directors. Investors must be concerned with the compensation structure and the relationships managers have with the people who are supposed to monitor them.

Executive Compensation

How much should executives make? This has been a controversial issue in recent years, and strong voices argue both sides of it. Some say executive pay is too much, whereas others say they deserve as much as they're paid. Both arguments are valid to a small or large extent. Irrespective of how much an executives make, compensation packages can be good or bad depending on how they motivate and incentivize desirable behaviors—both in terms of encouraging good operating and in terms of encouraging shareholder-friendly actions.

Compensation data on publicly traded American companies are available in the proxy (DEF 14A) reports that companies file with the SEC in preparation for the shareholder meeting every year. Investors can access broad compensation data for the top earners who meet certain criteria as required by regulation. The report also discloses the different components making up the total compensation package.

In its April 2011 proxy filing, for instance, Walmart reported compensation data for six named executive officers (NEOs). Several things are evident from those data: The total compensation for all six NEOs for 2011 was just over $62 million, or 0.38 percent of the total net income that year of over $16 billion.

The ratio of compensation to income, or the compensation ratio, is a useful metric to see executive pay in relation to total company profits. This ratio varies by size of company, of course, but it can suggest how reasonable the compensation is in relation to net profits generated, ultimately, for shareholders.

As shown in the second column of table 20.1, Walmart's compensation ratio of 0.38 percent is in line with those of other large companies.[4] For ExxonMobil, the compensation ratio for 2011 was

0.24 percent, for Johnson & Johnson 0.44 percent, for Procter & Gamble 0.30 percent, and for Coca-Cola 0.47 percent. It appears that the total compensation for Walmart's top earners was in line with what other large companies were paying in relation to annual net income. Among large technology companies, Intel had a compensation ratio of 0.37 percent, Microsoft 0.18 percent, and Apple 1.06 percent. It is clear that high ratio by itself means little, for Apple has since continued to grow both revenues and profits.

Typically, the compensation ratio increases as the size of the company decreases. Target, which is about one-sixth the size of Walmart, had a compensation ratio of 1.24 percent for the year ending January 2011. Costco, larger than Target, had a compensation ratio of 1.42 percent.

The ratio gets troubling for smaller companies, however, as compensation in relation to net earnings can be quite large. Abercrombie & Fitch, for instance, had a compensation ratio of 25.29 percent, with 61 percent of the reported NEO compensation going to its chief, Michael Jeffries. This number is obviously unusual and ought to be of concern to shareholders, especially when compared with competitors such as American Eagle (15.85 percent) and Aéropostale (7.59 percent).

TABLE 20.1

Company	CompRat*	Salary Comp†
Walmart	0.38%	8.72%
Johnson & Johnson	0.44%	8.68%
Exxon Mobil	0.24%	8.43%
Microsoft	0.18%	10.26%
Target	1.24%	12.28%
Procter & Gamble	0.30%	15.10%
Abercrombie & Fitch	25.29%	13.29%
American Eagle	15.85%	21.94%
Aéropostale	7.59%	22.64%
Costco	1.42%	19.74%
Intel	0.37%	7.39%
Coca-Cola	0.47%	6.88%
Apple	1.06%	1.92%

*CompRat is total compensation as a percentage of total net income.

†SalaryComp is salary as a percentage of total compensation.

All else equal, unjustifiably high compensation must raise questions, especially when a few top managers make a large proportion of the total earnings of the company during the year.

While keeping an eye on total pay is helpful, even more important is the compensation structure. For public companies, as shown in the third column of table 20.1, fixed salary is usually a small proportion of total compensation; the rest is variably tied to measures of performance.

For the year ending January 2011, for instance, Walmart NEO salary was 8.72 percent of total compensation.[5] Salary as a proportion of total compensation is similarly low for other large companies: Johnson & Johnson 8.68 percent, Exxon Mobil 8.43 percent, and Microsoft 10.26 percent. Others weighted salary somewhat higher: Target 12.28 percent, Abercrombie & Fitch 13.29 percent, Procter & Gamble 15.1 percent, American Eagle 21.94 percent, Aéropostale 22.64 percent, and Costco 19.74 percent. Still others weighted salary substantially lower: Intel 7.39 percent, Coca-Cola 6.88 percent, and Apple 1.92 percent. A low proportion of fixed salary in relation to total compensation is usually a plus for investors, as it indicates reward for performance.

Moreover, the structure of variable compensation indicates whether managers are oriented toward the short term or the long term, whether they are oriented toward strengthening core operations or maximizing short-term performance in the stock market.

Investors must, therefore, try to understand the nature of the incentives built into variable compensation: What behaviors do compensation packages encourage among top managers?

In a way, ideal compensation structures have a healthy mix of all the elements we've discussed but which favor actions that steadily build the core operating strength of the firm. To this end, compensation structures should (1) orient managers toward the long term; and, at the same time, (2) encourage them to strengthen operations to deliver sustained high returns on invested capital.

Returning to our example, on these criteria, the judgment of potential Walmart investors must remain mixed. Although it is a shareholder-friendly company, its financial performance has been robust historically, and its leadership team are good operators of the business, the leadership teams at Walmart was very slow to respond to seismic changes in the retail industry. As of this writing, they are clearly taking strong action to make up for lost time, but it's not quite clear how much irreparable damage such slowness may have caused.

Board of Directors

Last but not least, shareholders elect members of the board to safeguard their interests against possible misdirection or misappropriation of funds by managers. In most companies, governance structures are such that managers make day-to-day decisions; the board weighs in on important decisions, such as the hiring of a CEO and big strategic initiatives; and the shareholders have a direct say in major decisions, such as mergers and acquisitions. In theory, the board provides the oversight to ensure that managers act in the interests of the shareholders—who are usually dispersed and, in many cases, do not have the skills or access to monitor the goings-on of the company. Top executives report directly to the board, which has the authority to recruit, incentivize, and monitor managers and to authorize important actions, such as mergers and acquisitions.

In practice, it does not always work that way. In many companies, managers have a great deal of say in who gets on the board of directors. In some cases, strong CEOs fill the board with people they like and those who are favorably inclined toward them. In a well-known story from some years ago, the board of Walt Disney was stacked with managers, outside professionals doing business with the company, and close associates of very long-time CEO Michael Eisner. News media reported that Eisner refused to discuss succession even after nearly 20 years at the helm. It was only after Roy Disney, the company founder's nephew, resigned from the board and started a long and costly campaign that the CEO was finally persuaded to step down.

Even when the CEO and top management team are not entrenched, the board is not as free as theory would have us believe. Members of the board do not have the same immersion in day-to-day operations as do the managers running the company, and they don't have access to information other than what is channeled to them. Their term lasts only a few years, and, a particular board membership being only one of many commitments, they are usually unable to devote fully to the job. As such, the role of a typical board member is advisory and their oversight cursory.

Moreover, board members don't usually rock the boat too much lest the managers don't support their election. Asking too many difficult questions and putting managers on the defensive is a socially difficult thing to do anyway, but board members often have to tread cautiously partly because they don't know much and partly because a miffed CEO can withdraw support. This is usually a meaningful threat because not only is it prestigious to be on a board, but remuneration can run into several hundred thousand dollars per year. The prospect of losing money and privileges can undermine the independence of board members and hinder the proper oversight of managers.

In practice, the board of directors can be the instrument of strong-willed managers; occasionally, directors do serve to safeguard the interests of shareholders.

Governance regulations require boards to have audit committees and compensation committees for formal oversight on specific issues. These committees do useful routine work, but rarely do they take an activist position, especially if the CEO and managers are deeply entrenched and powerful. Members of the board only have so much time, after all, to devote to what is essentially a part-time sinecure. In fact, board members are the social elites who serve on the boards of multiple companies at the same time, and, therefore, may have even less devotion than what a single part-time job would demand.

Where the boards often do play an active and useful role is when the company has large shareholders, such as active investors and family trusts. Such strong interests on the board can resist the power of managers and exert the right kind of pressure needed for good oversight.

Boards play a useful role in critical periods, such as the hiring of a new CEO, and the evaluation of potentially transformative events, such as mergers or acquisitions. They also get into action in times of crisis, such as the discovery of fraud or outright violations of clearly articulated codes of conduct. Moments of crisis allow board members to overcome trepidations about crossing the managers, partly because of the clear justness of their actions but also because of the social support they may get from each other.

Although mostly deferential to CEO Conrad Black, for example, the star-studded board of Hollinger did eventually come together to force him out in response to an emerging scandal about the misuse of company funds. Similarly, upon discovering that its CEO was engaged in inappropriate conduct, Best Buy's board reacted quickly to oust him. Later, upon learning that the founder of the company had known about the conduct but had not disclosed it, the board ousted him as well.

Such instances of a board playing a proactive role, while not uncommon, are few and far between; they come rather late to do much good for shareholders, who have by then already suffered for too long.

In all, there is no substitute for investors to do their own due diligence and rely on personal judgments about the competence, character, and integrity of top management teams. Good managers are worth their weight in gold; bad managers can be a whole lot of trouble. Boards of directors are limited in their ability to control bad behavior by managers.

Long term Walmart investors must come to terms with the fact that, as of April 2015, the company is controlled by the Walton family, who own more than 50 percent of outstanding shares. Founder Sam Walton's son S. Robson Walton was chairman of the board for many years, and that role recently passed to another family member, Gregory Penner. Family control by itself is not a direct concern to shareholders, as closely held companies often represent significant current and future wealth potential for generations of family members. In many cases, incentives for the family members can be strongly aligned with those of shareholders. Yet, such close control also has the potential to distort incentives, and family dynamics can create significant challenges to the competent management of operations. This is especially so when the board is stacked with family-friendly outsiders and is thus unable to provide sound counsel to managers and protect the interests of minority shareholders. Also, family members several generations removed from the founder can become insulated with the business and other shareholders, which in some cases can lead to abuses that are difficult to monitor or control. For this reason, long-term shareholders of Walmart must closely monitor the actions of the family members engaged in the oversight and management of the company.

Ultimately, evaluation of the top management team is a crucial part of investment analysis. Based on a range of quantitative and qualitative information, as discussed above, investors should make judgments about the competence and integrity of the company's managers. If it turns out that your analysis reveals grave doubts about the managers or their oversight, then you must disconfirm the investment thesis.

PART FIVE

Policy

CHAPTER TWENTY-ONE

Diversification

CONSIDER TWO LIKELY events, X and Y, that you think can happen with probabilities p(X) and p(Y), respectively. What is the probability that both events will happen at the same time?

Assume first that the two events are independent of each other. Say that X represents heavy rain in Seattle on a particular day, and Y represents a train accident in New York on the same day. The two are far apart in distance and in their nature, so we can assume they are unrelated and independent of each other. Hence, the probability that both occur is the product of individual probabilities, or $p(X\&Y) = p(X)\,p(Y)$.

If $p(X) = 20$ percent, and $p(Y) = 1$ percent, then $p(X\&Y) = 0.2$ percent. The chances of the two incidents happening at the same time is much smaller than the chances of either happening individually.

If another event, Z, were to represent flooding in Seattle on the same day as heavy rain occurred, then we know the chances of Z increase with X. In this case, we have $p(X\&Z) = p(X)\,p(Z|X)$. That is, the probability that both X and Z will happen is the probability of rain multiplied by the probability of flooding conditional upon the probability of rain.[1]

So, if $p(X) = 20$ percent, and $p(Z|X) = 50$ percent, then $p(X\&Z) = 10$ percent. Even though the two events are related, the chances of them happening together remain small. But the higher the conditional probability of Z given X, or $p(Z|X)$, the higher is their joint probability. The limiting cases are (1) $p(Z|X) = 1$, always flooding when heavy rain; and (2) $p(Z|X) = 0$, never flooding when heavy rain.

This, in essence, is the foundation of modern portfolio theory. The greater the independence between the returns of two stocks, or the smaller the conditional probabilities of the two, the lower is the likelihood that the returns of the two stocks will move together in the same direction. The theory is that if you hold a diversified portfolio of, say, two unrelated stocks, the probability is small that both stocks will go bust at the same time.

"Modern" Portfolio Theory

Around 1950, before Markowitz, intuition about the benefits of diversification was well established. That this was common knowledge is evident, for instance, in the well-known 1924 book *Common Stocks as Long Term Investments* by Edgar Lawrence Smith. But no objective measures of risk existed at the time, especially for the joint risk of a bundle of investments. So, Markowitz took up this problem as a topic for his doctoral dissertation in economics and, using concepts from the statistics texts of the time, formalized the concept of portfolio risk. In particular, he defined the risk of a stock as the standard deviation of its returns and then formulated portfolio, or joint, risk using conditional probabilities, or covariances of returns of all stocks in the portfolio.[2]

Of special note in Markowitz's equation was the correlation between the stocks in the portfolio.[3] If the returns correlate perfectly, then portfolio risk computes relatively simply and is for the most part uninteresting, as investors would instinctively know to try to avoid having two such stocks in their portfolio.. That is simple enough. But what excited Markowitz was that most stocks did not move in perfect unison. Subject to the same systemic factors, such as the economy and political environment, correlation between stocks was usually partial but almost never zero. It was such imperfect correlations that made the practical implications noteworthy.

In order to reduce portfolio risk so defined, investors now had to solve the problem of finding stocks that had minimal or even negative correlations. But Markowitz went a step further: he defined efficient portfolios as those groupings in which the proportion of each stock is such that the portfolio risk is minimal for a given expected return of the portfolio.

As the number of stocks in the portfolio increased, the number of terms in the Markowitz equation multiplied fast; calculating portfolio variance and risk became computationally intense. But, with increasing computational power, such math became less and less of a problem. In essence, Markowitz's genius was in showing how to lower investment risk, mathematically and specifically, by grouping unrelated stocks into a portfolio.

An implication of this formulation was that investors ought to be thinking of risk not in terms of single stocks but in terms of portfolios of stocks. Particularly fascinating was the corollary that the risk (or valuation) of a single stock by itself should mean very little in large, well-diversified portfolios. The number of covariance terms increases as the size of the portfolio increases, and they overshadow the effect of the weighted variance of any one stock.

When you add a single stock to an existing portfolio of 30 stocks, for example, the new stock adds its own weighted variance term but also 30 covariance terms—the covariance of the new stock with each of the already existing stocks. These 30 additional covariance terms influence the change in portfolio risk much more than the risk of one new stock by itself.

Two implications are usually derived from the math of computing portfolio variance: (1) the risk of a single stock does not matter that much; and (2) each buy or sell decision must be made in light of whatever stocks you already have in the portfolio. As we will see later, the second implication is certainly very helpful, but the first implication that the risk of any one stock does not matter is patently misleading.

At the time, though, this was breakthrough thinking, and Markowitz earned a Nobel Prize for conceiving portfolio risk and especially for delivering the math to make it possible. This way of thinking about investing revolutionized finance and is now deeply entrenched in investment education. One of the early extensions to Markowitz's work was by William Sharpe, with his idea that the risk of a single stock ought to be evaluated in relation to the overall market risk. Think of a fully diversified investor who owns a basket filled with all the stocks in the market. To that market basket you want to add another stock; the issue is the degree to which that additional stock will increase or decrease the risk of the market portfolio.

This concept, beta (β), is simply a mathematical formulation that normalizes covariance between the stock and the market basket (index)—usually approximated by the S&P 500 Index. This formulation made it possible for each stock to have a number, β, that captured its covariance with the overall market.

Other modifications followed, but the core ideas that took hold were that we can approximate the risk of a stock with a simple statistic (standard deviation) and that we can compute portfolio risk using returns data for each stock in the portfolio.

The Trouble with Portfolio Theory

Markowitz formalized the long-standing intuition about investors needing to spread their bets; his important contribution was elevating the concept of risk from individual stocks to the portfolio and then deriving a mathematical formulation for computing the latter using the former. While his mathematical formulation remains conceptually appealing and theoretically sound, its operationalization remains deeply problematic. And that is because Markowitz illustrated the model using variance and standard deviation of returns as a proxy for risk. He seemed to be showing how to compute portfolio risk if the risk of each of the component securities was known with some confidence.

To his credit, Markowitz understood that the statistic for volatility is not risk. Having read Graham and Dodd, he was well aware that risk was a complex construct and needed to be assessed using security analysis to carefully evaluate the many complexities inherent in the business being evaluated. Effective security analysis is labor intensive, however, and it requires subjective judgments based on careful study of the facts of the case, one company at a time. Such subjective evaluation is difficult to standardize and for that reason terribly inconvenient for large-scale portfolio construction. Perhaps because of this, Markowitz's caveat was, and remains, largely ignored.

Using a statistic for risk certainly makes the math possible, but it stretches credulity to say that the way prices moved in the past is a perfect, or even good, indicator of the uncertainties of future cash flows associated with the company in question. This statistical formulation of risk does not say much about the many operating, technological, and competitive challenges or uncertainties a company may face, nor does it acknowledge that the price paid may be significantly different from any reasonable estimates of economic worth. In order to get past these difficulties, portfolio theory assumes that markets are efficient and perfectly price all stocks and that prices fully reflect all information about a company.

In practice, not having a good fix on individual company risk makes the modern portfolio theory formulation not only of little practical use but downright dangerous—incorrect estimates of the risk of a single security in, say, a 50-security portfolio compounds the error when computing portfolio risk because the risk of that one security must be multiplied and added many times over.[4] Even if the distributions were Gaussian and standard deviation were the correct proxy for security risk, we know now that those statistics are not stable but can change over time, sometimes with great rapidity; correlations and covariances, too, are unstable. Thus, it is very difficult to find robust and durable estimates of portfolio risk.

To continue using modern portfolio theory to form portfolios requires one to ignore its substantive problems that arise from defining risk as a simple statistic. I submit that the conceptualization of as central a theoretical concept as risk should not be limited in this way. Unfortunately, for over 60 years, we have continued to erroneously define risk as the standard deviation of returns and gone deeper into reductionism via other statistics such as skewness and kurtosis.

Portfolio optimization and mathematical fine-tuning remain at the core of investment research, teaching, and practice. This way of thinking has become stronger with time, even as concerns about core assumptions have remained. The past few decades have seen many efforts to better define risk, but in finance research these have mostly been mathematical in orientation. Researchers continue to use past returns data by necessity, and, for the most part, they continue to ignore the fundamental business and management issues that are key to understanding the true hazards of investing.

As I have shown, value investing differs from modern portfolio theory in its focus on subjectively but deeply understanding the wealth-creating mechanisms of businesses, and the difficulties and uncertainties that managers face as they construct and operate such mechanisms. It is this focus on the business that was the intent of Graham and Dodd and, I'd argue, has been the basis for the long-term success of many professional investors, including Warren Buffett. All these investors clearly recognize that, as Edgar Lawrence Smith had intuitively practiced and Graham had repeatedly argued, investing is a group operation; spreading the bets intelligently across companies in a portfolio is sound practice. Markowitz tried to formalize this idea and got it mostly right in theoretical terms, but the field of finance has not quite followed through with a credible and robust way to proxy for the theoretical chance that investors might lose their invested principal. I submit that the arms-length mathematical approach simply cannot adequately capture the complex of factors that comprise true risk. We need to understand the wealth-creating machinery by getting up close with the businesses in which we invest.

CHAPTER TWENTY-TWO

Another Way to Portfolio

CLEARLY, THE CORE idea of building diversified portfolios to temper the hazards of investing is sound, and it can be developed further—but we must first shed the pretense of objectivity and challenge the notion that risk can be measured using a simple statistic. Instead, we must acknowledge that risk is a complex construct that needs to be carefully assessed, and we must understand the importance of incorporating subjective probabilities into our thinking about how to construct diversified portfolios. Only then, as Markowitz had originally intended, can we harness the power of portfolio-level thinking. By understanding risk as uncertainties that surround an investment thesis, we can justify conducting deep business analysis so as to identify a handful or more suitable but unrelated companies that can be grouped into a well-conceived portfolio.

A good understanding of a company's history and its business model, management team, and valuation in relation to price can provide a broader sense of the hazards to invested principal. From such a broader view, we may assess, if subjectively, the chances that the investment thesis will deteriorate or worsen drastically. That is, rather than relying upon the variability of past returns, we rely instead on well-informed judgments about the key sources of uncertainties and the hazards that the thesis may face.

Let's, therefore, reconceptualize risk as the probability of loss. Although not as precise as the standard deviation of past returns, we can assess the subjective probability of loss from the quantitative and qualitative techniques of analysis we have thus far examined. That is, we will emphasize the need for understanding future prospects and especially the chances of meaningful deterioration in cash flows from the company under evaluation.

Take again two companies equally weighted in a portfolio. Assume that we have carefully examined these companies through quantitative refutation and qualitative disconfirmation exercises and believe they offer potentially attractive investment opportunities. Let's suppose that we come to the subjective judgment that there is a one-in-four chance of near-term problems with the companies. The problems could arise from internal issues or because of the macro environment, which the companies cannot control. Let's also say that you assess a 25 percent chance that the performance of either company could drop by 20 percent in the next year.

Instead of focusing on what price the market is attaching to a company at a given time, you're trying to understand the key uncertainties about the ability of the company to deliver strong cash flows. Let's also assume that the companies are very different, their future prospects mostly independent of each other. Say one is a retail company in India and the other a defense company in the United States. That is, assume for the time being that the economic performance of the two companies is unrelated.

Making the assumption of independence greatly simplifies the math and allows us to see the risk implications of pulling the two companies into one portfolio. Lack of independence complicates the math, but the basic message about the benefits of diversification doesn't really change.

Based on our assumptions, the subjective probability that the performance of this two-company portfolio will drop 20 percent is as follows:

$$p(\text{Portfolio} - 20 \text{ percent}) = 0.25 \bullet 0.25 = 6.25 \text{ percent} \quad (22.1)$$

The math works the same as in Markowitz's calculation except that instead of deriving risk from the variance of past returns, the emphasis now is on assessments on potential problems with the underlying companies. By working diligently through the process of refutation and disconfirmation, and by selecting companies to reduce the chance of poor performance down to one in four, we have reduced the chances of the portfolio dropping by 20 percent in the near term to only 6.25 percent.

TABLE 22.1
Portfolio Size and Probability of Loss

Company	P (−20%)
1	25.00%
2	6.25%
3	1.56%
4	0.39%
5	0.10%

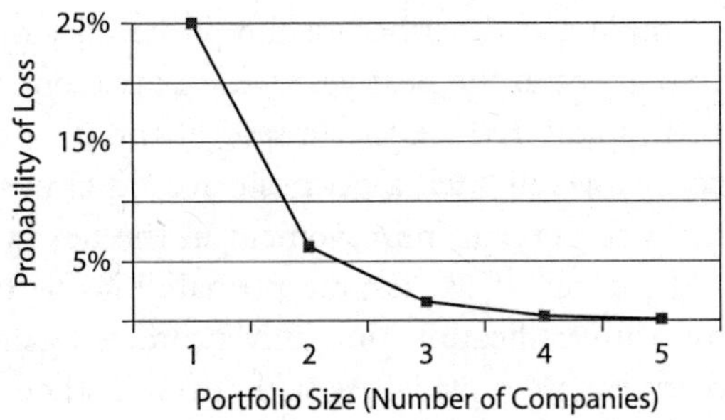

Figure 22.1 Another way to portfolio

Similar results are obtained when you expand the portfolio with additional companies with a similar risk profile, subjectively evaluated. As evident from table 22.1, the chances of the overall portfolio performance dropping 20 percent over the next year decrease rapidly from 25 percent in one company, to 6.25 percent in a two-company portfolio, to 0.1 percent in a five-company portfolio. Moreover, as in figure 22.1, how sharply the probability of loss drops depends on the initial probability of loss that, in this case, we assumed to be 25 percent. This initial probability is the crux of the issue; the formal process of disconfirmation analysis influences it a great deal.

Clearly, diversification substantially reduces the chances of loss. This illustration shows that we need only a handful of well-selected companies with little or no correlation in their economic fundamentals. This result may seem surprising, but several formal studies, including a seminal paper from half a century ago, show that well-constructed portfolios eliminate the bulk of company-specific risk with as few as 10 securities.[1] Contrary to conventional wisdom, it does not make economic sense to build overly diversified portfolios, especially in situations where you can subjectively assess hazards to your thesis with a great degree of confidence.

The Downside of Diversification

Conventional wisdom is that diversification helps protect the downside of negative portfolio performance, yet diversification also dampens the prospects of good performance. To take the mirror image of the example just described, if the probability of each company improving 20 percent in the next year were 25 percent, then the same logic would also rapidly reduce the upside of the portfolio. Just five independent companies in such a portfolio would almost ensure that you will not get a 20 percent improvement in the next year.

In effect, if we assume probabilities to be symmetrical, then portfolio diversification not only protects against the downside but also dampens the upside. As such, even in theory, diversification enables a defensive posture by severely limiting upside potential.

Furthermore, in times of crises, such as the recession following the technology-driven company market boom of the late 1990s or the deep recession following the financial market meltdown of 2008, the economic performances of even relatively unrelated companies become highly correlated because they are all subject to the same systemic issues. A receding tide lowers all boats.

As such, when you need protection during a systemic downturn, high correlations undo the protective effects of diversification. As correlations among companies increase due to systemic factors such as recessions or panics, joint probabilities increase, and portfolio performance suffers. On the other hand, during economic recoveries or growth phases, whatever independence remains among the companies in the portfolio undermines the overall portfolio performance and growth.

Ironically, then, diversification is not helpful when you most need it during systemic downturns, and it hinders performance when you least need it during systemic upturns.

Moreover, not only does broad diversification limit upside potential, relying on modern portfolio theory requires the kind of statistical analysis that diverts attention away from the particulars of the companies in the portfolio—and makes it impossible to conduct a thorough company-centered disconfirmation analysis.

Valuation in the Mix

Conventional wisdom has it that diversification ought not to be within one class of securities, such as domestic companies, but across asset classes and across geographies—stocks, bonds, commodities, currencies, real estate, domestic, international, and so on.

Yet, nowhere in the conventional theory is the valuation of the component securities in the portfolio mentioned. Nor is there much guidance about how to determine the probabilities of future returns. Instead, the usual tools for portfolio construction rely on measuring correlations and covariances of past returns and take on faith that the markets are efficient and price everything correctly at all times.

The reliance solely on past returns data to estimate expectations of future returns is problematic especially in the absence of a clear understanding of how well a particular security is priced in relation to reasonable estimates of economic worth.

In practice, to know or even confidently estimate the probability that the price of a particular company will go up or down is virtually impossible, let alone the magnitude of that change or the time horizon over which such a change will occur. Absent knowledge of such probabilities, the variance of a portfolio is indeterminate: In spite of vast quantities of data and the elegant math invoked to compute statistics, we cannot assess the risk of a portfolio with any precision.

For this reason, we have been discussing companies rather than stocks; our focus is on economic performance so we can evaluate the ability of a company to generate cash flows well into the future. We rely on subjective probabilities based on good judgments that come in part from a thorough use of the process of disconfirmation. The fundamental question that investors should persist in asking is simply this: Is the price attractive in relation to reasonable estimates of value?

To this end, we must evaluate each company on its own merits and select it into the portfolio if the prevailing price is attractive in relation to reasonable estimates of underlying worth. Considerations of the overall impact on the existing portfolio risk remain important but secondary to those of the intrinsic worth or valuation of each company in the portfolio.

In essence, protection for investors comes not from overly broad diversification but from good valuation in relation to prevailing prices. Well-constructed portfolios need not be larger than only a handful of well-selected companies with robust prospects. Valuation remains by far the single most important criterion in company selection and portfolio construction.

Concentrated portfolios do have a downside, however. They are usually quite volatile, and novice investors can have trouble staying the course in the face of sudden and massive fluctuations. For those with rightfully earned confidence in their valuations, however, fluctuations in prices are not necessarily a bad thing, as they can provide opportunities for accumulating a position. But for those not yet confident in their own analysis, concentration can be difficult to manage.

The confidence with which you construct a valuation-centered portfolio depends, therefore, on the confidence in your analysis. The greater the confidence, the more concentrated the portfolio can be: portfolio size increases with decreasing confidence in your abilities. In essence, a company must not be included in the portfolio just because the standard deviation of returns or the beta (β) is low. Whatever the past returns of a stock may be, the lack of a thorough effort to disconfirm the investment thesis for a company makes the investment speculative and raises hazards for the investor.

As an illustration, consider again a portfolio of companies in which the expected future performance of each is largely independent of those of all the others. Assume, then, that you have selected each company with care and that the probability of a 20 percent decline in economic performance in the near term is now reduced from 25 percent to, say, 10 percent.

That is, you now have a sufficient margin of safety to feel that the chance of a significant decline is only about 1 in 10. In such a scenario, you will see a sharp reduction in the number of companies required for the risk of the entire portfolio to decline by 20 percent. Just three companies will reduce the risk to 0.10 percent, and five independent companies will provide almost full diversification.

Based on the mathematical logic of grouping stocks, diversification is relatively straightforward. The key to proper diversification is to realistically assess the probability of loss on individual commitments. Yet, in order to estimate such probabilities properly, you need confident insights into the underlying valuation, or economic worth, of each company in the portfolio. Provided you can make realistic assessments of the odds, as we will examine in the next chapter, once you have confident estimates of value at hand, portfolios grounded in mathematical expectations can readily help produce strong upside with limited downside.

CHAPTER TWENTY-THREE

Core Holdings

REMEMBER THAT TRADITIONAL diversification dampens both the downside as well as the upside in portfolio performance. With the good of protection during the downswing comes the bad of hindrance on the upswing. That's the math.

In this chapter, I discuss how to build valuation-driven portfolios with asymmetric payoff structure—or portfolios that limit the downside while still preserving much of the upside potential. I show that portfolios constructed one company at a time, using the process of disconfirmation, can do just that and should, therefore, be at the core of investment programs.

The disconfirmation approach seeks to ensure that the price paid for a security is sufficiently below reasonable estimates of economic value, so that the chance of negative surprises is small. The valuation-centric process of disconfirmation, which includes evaluation based on both quantitative and qualitative criteria, truncates the distribution of future returns such that losses are limited, whereas the upside is not.

Continuing the example from the last chapter, suppose that the process of disconfirmation has yielded companies for which the probability of a 20 percent drop in valuation is down to 10 percent, but the probability of 20 percent appreciation for each company is 50 percent. Assume also that the remaining 40 percent probability is for no change in valuation. Let's also assume economic independence among companies. That is, you have found companies that have asymmetric payoffs strongly in your favor: each company has a greater probability of gain than loss.

TABLE 23.1
Value Portfolio with Asymmetric Payoff

	10% Chance of –20% Return	50% Chance of +20% Return
Number of Stocks	P (–20%)	P (+20%)
1	10.00%	50.00%
2	1.00%	25.00%
3	0.10%	12.50%
4	0.01%	6.25%
5	0.00%	0.10%

As is evident from table 23.1, if you had just three companies in the final portfolio, the probability of a –20 percent portfolio performance is only 0.1 percent (1 in 1,000), whereas the upside chance of a +20 percent portfolio return is 12.5 percent (1 in 8). That is, disconfirmation analysis helps construct portfolios in which you create a favorable asymmetry of future potential returns. Comprising only a handful of unrelated companies, such portfolios are relatively easy to monitor and update.

Portfolio Theory and Investor Behavior

For investors not well versed in statistical analysis, applying modern portfolio theory is difficult. Computing standard deviations, variances, and covariances requires a good deal of historical data, and, with thousands of companies to sort through, data crunching can easily get out of hand.

Furthermore, the theory is not much help with finer issues, such as portfolio size, the historical time period over which analysis should be done, or what the time horizon ought to be for measuring performance. Nor is there any way to know if past data are meaningful for future performance. Not only is modern portfolio theory difficult to enact, grave doubts persist about the very usefulness of the kind of statistical analysis it requires.

Modern portfolio theory may actually encourage investors to engage in self-defeating behaviors. By defining risk mathematically as the standard deviation of returns and insisting that markets are efficient, the theory encourages investors to ignore thorough company analysis.

Instead, it emphasizes assembling a group of lightly correlated companies with little consideration of valuation or business fundamentals. That is, instead of encouraging diligence on particulars and valuation based on realities that businesses face, the theory entices investors into overly broad diversification and indexes.

Indexes exacerbate the problem of overdiversification. Because they comprise many companies that together broadly represent a particular sector or the economy at large, indexes focus attention on aggregate metrics for the whole group of companies but hide from view the particulars of any one. That is, the criteria for inclusion in the index is typically representativeness rather than the valuation or wealth-creating potential of the companies. Index investing is predicated on the belief that investors cannot sort good companies from bad ones and that buying a whole basket of companies somehow solves the problem of sorting correctly. But this logic has several flaws.

First, the performance of an index is a direct function of the weight assigned to each component company. Different weights can lead to vastly different results. An index overweighted on companies with poor prospects will, for instance, provide much weaker returns than one overweighted with appropriately priced companies with excellent economics. So, an index is not a singular group but one of many possible combinations of any given set of companies.

Moreover, indexes typically include many companies—the Dow Jones Industrial Average (DJIA) comprises 30 companies, the S&P 500 Index comprises 500 companies, the Russell 3000 comprises 3,000 companies, and so on. Because indexes comprise so many companies, it's difficult to analyze each company within an index for quality and prospects. As such, indexing enables a type of blindness that disables investors from seeing the particulars and diverts attention, instead, on aggregate statistical measures. Almost by definition, indexing inherits all the shortcomings of diversification: it's useful when you don't need it and not much good when you do.

For those skeptical about indexing and wanting to make their own robust portfolio, the theory has no good advice. As a result, not quite knowing what to do, many investors interested in individual companies end up trading excessively and chasing performance that remains elusive for the most part.

Often driven to action by hype and hope of a quick gain, and with no credible theory as a guide, investors buy more on a whim than after thorough analysis. They buy and sell too often to have the time to understand the fundamental drivers of wealth creation, with no regard for reliable estimates of intrinsic economic worth.

At the same time, skeptical of modern portfolio theory, investors ignore its most valuable insight: that the returns and hazards of investing should be portfolio-level concerns. In spite of the fact that investment theory has strongly suggested the benefits of group-level analysis, investors appear to pay little or no heed to the benefits of systematically grouping well-chosen companies.

The Core Portfolio

A sensible way to think about investing is in terms of core portfolios comprising between five and ten companies. As discussed in the previous chapter, we can realize the benefits of diversification through the valuation-based selection of only a handful of unrelated companies. The limited number of companies allows for easy monitoring and an in-depth understanding that together facilitate good investment decisions.

Investors must be careful when buying each of the five or ten companies in a core portfolio. The chief emphasis in selecting companies for such a portfolio is on disconfirmation and defensive valuation; focus must remain on the fundamental strength of operations that enables good economic performance (cash flows) delivered over time.

With such efforts to limit the downside of each company in the portfolio, investors must also spread selections across different sectors. By so limiting yet spreading the bets, the core portfolio contains the information demands placed on investors; this, in turn, enables deep understanding and close monitoring of each selected company.

Unlike modern portfolio theory, which emphasizes portfolio-level risk to the virtual neglect of the many uncertainties that inevitably surround individual companies, the emphasis here is on minimizing the initial probability of loss. As discussed previously, this initial probability is critical, as it directly influences the rate of decline in the overall probability of loss as the size of the portfolio increases.

In this view, the extent of optimal diversification varies depending on the relative valuation of companies in the portfolio. If it turns out that valuations are particularly attractive for several companies in one sector, then the concern over diversification must not get in the way of sensible investment decisions. Investors can rarely go wrong buying great companies at good prices.

Once we define investing as solving the problem of making valuation-driven core portfolios, we must align our behavior to this way of thinking. No longer do we need to search for variances and covariances across the entire spectrum of companies listed on the various company exchanges. No longer must we constantly adjust the portfolio to keep up with the changing covariances. No longer do we need to trade excessively, or buy and sell companies that we don't understand beyond the short-term statistical characteristics of their past prices and returns. No longer must we broadly and blindly diversify the portfolio, filling it with companies based simply on their covariances but with no understanding of economic fundamentals.

What core portfolios do is economize on the most important resources that we as investors have: our attention and time. Instead of trying to grasp the entire list of 6,000 or so companies on the U.S. company exchanges and the nearly 45,000 worldwide, we narrow the focus to a handful of companies that, bought at attractive prices, promise to give both downside protection and a steady upside over the medium to long term.

When bought at attractive prices and in sufficient quantities to have a meaningful impact on portfolio performance, such companies also obviate the need for their constant monitoring. Instead, through selective and periodic reading of the mandatory company filings (say, once every quarter), investors maintain focus on the fundamental attributes that drive their ability to deliver steady economic performance.

Such focus on building and maintaining core portfolios also gives investors a simple way to deal with the abundance of noise in the markets: simply ignore the hype and the cacophony. Since the objective is to locate just a few companies with attractive valuations and long-term prospects, investors can simply ignore or easily refute most listed companies. In fact, depending on their objectives, investors can quickly pare down the 6,000 or so companies listed on the NYSE and NASDAQ to just a few hundred. Preliminary refutation can bring the list down to a much lower number, to about 50 or so. From this much shorter list, the task then is to locate about 10 or so companies that meet certain criteria, build a portfolio from them, and then monitor them with the full knowledge of what makes them tick.

Once investors construct such a core portfolio, they then evaluate all other investment opportunities that come along in light of the improvements they might be able to make to the existing group of companies. When you have additional funds to invest, the most productive use of those funds is likely to be investment in companies already in the core portfolio—or in another company with an enticing valuation and in a sector not yet adequately represented. More likely than not, additions to your core portfolio will come from the intermediate list of 50 or so companies derived from your preliminary efforts to refute and disconfirm a much larger list.

Depending on your confidence in the quality of valuation and the discount of price from it, you may be able to allocate between 50 and 80 percent of your total investment to the core portfolio. In special cases where the valuation is particularly attractive in spite of rigorous disconfirmation analysis, a particularly thorough investor may be able to allocate up to 20 percent of the investment to a single company. You can then set aside the remainder for experimentation and opportunistic investments that may come about from periodic panic about the prospects of a sound company or more generally from market-wide disenchantment with particular sectors or companies.

Core portfolios reduce the noise that can overwhelm investors, improving the overall quality of the investment experience. With greater knowledge of a few companies comprising the portfolio comes confidence in the ability to monitor them and, therefore, less anxiety about sudden changes in their fortunes. Commitments to companies in the core portfolio lower the destructive impulses to speculate and chase performance. Both trading and short-term performance chasing not only increase the transaction costs that inevitably mount up, they also lead to lost opportunities by dissipating energies and trapping capital in nonproductive activities, leaving little or nothing to invest when genuine opportunities come along.

In a way, the core portfolio is to a good investor as a defensive pocket is to a good quarterback. It relieves pressure from the outside and gives you time to find attractive opportunities. The difference is that a well-constructed core portfolio almost never collapses, as defensive pockets are prone to do in the face of aggressive opponents; you have all the time necessary to locate and evaluate additional investment candidates that will further strengthen investment performance.

Certainly, investors need to be open to the possibility that the performance of any one or more companies in the core portfolio may deteriorate over time. Such deterioration is often a long time in the making and is usually visible through periodic, perhaps quarterly, disconfirmation analysis of companies that may be undergoing discontinuous change. With skill and diligence, in other words, it is generally possible for investors to see when a particular company is beginning to go in the wrong direction and take corrective measures, such as redefining the portfolio by eliminating or replacing the corrupted company.

In essence, carefully constructing a core portfolio is the common-sense answer to the obfuscating math of modern portfolio theory. It brings investing back to business analysis and valuation of individual companies. Yet, by recognizing the benefits of grouping, as articulated by Markowitz more than 60 years ago, core portfolios also integrate business analysis with the common-sense notion of spreading your bets, while keeping focus on making good bets.

CHAPTER TWENTY-FOUR

Growth

ADOPTING A CAUTIOUS orientation to building a core portfolio of a few good companies raises some obvious questions: What about growth? Wouldn't the focus on defensive valuation and caution remove from consideration those growth companies that have the potential to provide extraordinary returns?

Yes and no. Operationalizing and applying the principle of negation, as we have done, encourages investors to accept the opportunity cost of possibly missing out on fast-growing companies. In trying to avoid the Type I error of potentially choosing a poor investment, cautious investors end up with a good number of Type II errors of not investing in what turns out to be a good investment. But a cautious orientation and calibrated patience also help preserve capital for bold allocations when clearly discernible opportunities do come along. Growth investing highlights this dilemma.

The Hazards of Growth Investing

Investors have good reasons to avoid fast-growing companies. They usually trade at high prices relative to cautious valuations and are, therefore, easily refutable using the quantitative criteria we have developed in this book. Prices incorporate high expectations of future growth, with implied growth rates much in excess of historical growth rates; sometimes, high prices prevail in spite of the lack of much operating history. Eager investors justify lofty prices by extrapolating recent high growth rates well into the distant future, sometimes even conjuring up a future far removed from reality.

Earnings yields are usually very low and dividends mostly nonexistent for fast-growing companies, as they typically do not generate enough free cash flow to justify shareholder-friendly actions. Instead, as they pursue an expanding set of opportunities, growth companies raise much-needed capital either by taking on debt or by issuing more equity, which dilutes the ownership of existing shareholders.

Rapidly rising prices make growth companies highly visible and fodder for endless speculation in the media, thereby providing them the marketing exposure that other stocks don't usually get. The hype around such names then creates demand and attracts a mix of traders, gamblers, speculators, and the masses of retail investors, all afraid of missing what seems like a spectacular opportunity.

Moreover, defensive valuation plays only a small role, or none at all, in the pricing of high-flying growth stocks. The high prices at which they usually trade cannot be justified using any combination of reasonable assumptions in the discount model. All this makes growth stocks tantalizing and a source of much excitement. Untethered to economic value as they might be, growth stocks can continue rising to new heights, only to come crashing down when the spell breaks. Their performance depends almost entirely on collective imaginings about the future.

Mixed in with the speculative stocks, however, are the stocks of genuine growth companies with sound business models and competent leadership; but it is not easy to distinguish one from the other. There is little by way of short cuts that can help sort true growth stocks from the ones that only appear to be so. A great deal of uncertainty often surrounds the investment potential of fast-growing companies, and it is seldom obvious whether they will continue on their rapid growth trajectory or come to a screeching halt.

It is little surprise, then, that growth stocks tend to attract adrenaline-seeking traders and momentum investors who buy to gain from the rising prices; they are also quick to sell when prices seem to be turning the other way. As such, not only do growth stocks tend to become disconnected from any underlying economic reality of the companies in question, they are usually much more volatile than other stocks.

This kind of excitement is often too much for cautious investors. They are, for the most part, neither interested in nor psychologically equipped to ride the emotional roller coaster that speculators may find appealing. Typically, they are disinclined to allow the performance of their core portfolio to depend on the impossible task of correctly anticipating when the herd will turn one way or the other. The constant fear of imminent price collapse more than negates any joy they may derive from a temporary ascent to a new high.

There are many reasons why high-flying stocks come crashing down. If the expected rapid growth does not materialize or the company falters for any of the many reasons, price is prone to plummet. A general economic slowdown, a darkening of the social mood, a reduction in demand for the company's products, missteps by management, or any number of other factors internal or external to the firm can easily create investor disenchantment and, as a result, mass exodus.

So, growth companies and stocks pose a dilemma for cautious investors. They offer the chance to make outsized profits but at potentially significant hazards to otherwise well-constructed core portfolios. How, then, can you build growth into your investment program?

Solving the Growth Puzzle

In this section, I discuss two broad ways of inserting growth into a defense-oriented approach to building core portfolios. Safe growth continues to emphasize caution and disconfirmation, but with an openness to opportunities that arise periodically from temporary mispricing in the markets. For instance, buying undervalued growth companies and buying good companies during market panics can both add a growth boost to performance.

Second, risky growth involves relaxing caution somewhat, relying instead on deep qualitative analysis to understand the motivation and ability of managers to capture business opportunities. Cautious investors can pursue risky growth from a defensive perch either by investigating the turnaround of good companies that previously got in trouble or by scrutinizing select companies that are leaders in emerging new sectors of the economy.

Safe Growth: Value Mispricing

Given the danger that what seems to be a growth stock may actually be a highly speculative bet, a cautious attitude remains indispensable for growth investing.

Yet, caution can lead to growth for the simple reason that purchasing at a price sufficiently below robust estimates of intrinsic value brings with it the potential of upside.

Consider a stock trading at $20 per share when conservative estimates suggest an intrinsic valuation of about $50, and we cannot refute the investment thesis on the usual criteria. We can expect that the price will rise over time as the market weighs the differential and corrects the mispricing. This way of obtaining growth is perhaps the closest to the spirit of disconfirmation with its emphasis on safety.

This approach provides only temporary growth, however, as the catching up of price to approximate value removes the opportunity for further gain. As such, mispriced companies that have a history of steady growth provide the next obvious upside for the portfolio. A temporary setback in delivering expected performance can sometimes push prices down to unreasonable levels and provide good opportunities for growth when company performance gets back on track.

Consider again a stock trading at $20 when conservative valuation puts it in the range of $50, and historical trend shows intrinsic valuation growing at an annual rate of, say, 12 percent. The intrinsic valuation of such a company could grow to about $100 in six years and therefore provide growth to the portfolio. That is, the undercurrents of business growth provide continuing opportunities for steadily rising prices even after the markets eventually correct the initial mispricing.

Clearly, the risk for investors is that historical growth rates may not materialize, that the seeming mispricing is actually an indication of a fundamental structural change. Hence, such investment decisions need to follow the thorough process of disconfirmation using extensive qualitative data. A cautious evaluation would limit consideration to those companies where the fundamentals of good value remain in place. The mispricing of such steadily growing companies can provide substantial opportunities for growth in the core portfolios.

Safe Growth: Panic Mispricing

Closely related to investing in temporarily mispriced but solid companies is the purchase of healthy and steadily growing companies during a market-wide panic. Virtually every broad sell-off creates opportunities to investigate a short list of strong companies, as their prices fall for reasons not specific to them; one reason could be general disenchantment with the stock market or with a particular sector. The expectation that prices will drop puts selling pressure on the stock, which then triggers additional selling as traders and speculators try to avoid short-term loss and capitalize on the momentum of falling prices.

Remember that the intrinsic valuation of a company is driven by its long-term prospects and, specifically, by the expected permanence and growth of future cash flows. As such, strong companies have their valuation tied to deeply entrenched market positions, sound financial condition, and competent leadership, which together reflect the ability to continue generating healthy cash flows.

To the extent that the economic fundamentals of a company remain strong and in place, its intrinsic valuation should remain stable even though stock prices rise or fall in response to the emotions of the moment or systemic failures.

Periodic disruption or distortion endogenous to the markets may create opportunities, in other words, to invest in sound companies at attractive prices. The key to being able to do so is the ability to see that in spite of widespread fear and broad sell-off, economic fundamentals remain strong. A defensive orientation and the disconfirmation approach remain indispensable, therefore, in retaining the focus on such fundamentals and in selectively focusing on companies that can add growth to a portfolio.

Risky Growth: Turnaround and Transformation

While the mispricing of fundamentally sound companies can provide opportunities for growth, good companies do sometimes get in trouble and their prices fall to reflect worsening fundamentals. Yet, depending on the reasons for their past troubles and depending on the quality of the managers leading the turnaround or transformation, some such companies may offer good opportunities for adding growth to a core portfolio. When successful, transformation reinvigorates companies, and their renewed growth shows up in fast-rising economics.

Of course, not all companies are good candidates for successful turnaround, and very few are worth the trouble. Circumstances internal and external to the company can be so overwhelming that managers simply are not up to the task. As a result, for companies in the doldrums, investors face considerable uncertainties about their future prospects. For companies such as Blockbuster and American Italian Pasta Company, and any number of other companies that have gotten in trouble, a downward spiral eventually led to bankruptcy.

It is important for investors to be highly selective, therefore, and to understand very specifically the basis on which the managers may return a company to its previous heights. Companies with strong brands or market position are, therefore, good candidates for a turnaround. For instance, Apple and J. Crew were successful turnarounds based on the strength of the products developed and the brand repositioning that management accomplished, respectively. Unless such reasons for trouble are credible and the positive story compelling, however, it is best to stay away from companies that get in trouble because of poor management or because they are in industries undergoing secular decline.

Because of the complexity of turning around or transforming a company in trouble, defensively oriented investors must limit their search to companies that are deeply entrenched in stable or growing markets and have a strong competitive position even if that position has been weakened for a time. The fundamentals to look for in turnaround situations are the same as those in all core investments.

Turnarounds usually accompany a change in the top management and a sharply articulated commitment to reinvigorate the core businesses of the company. Investors need to closely monitor what the managers say and follow their progress over at least a year to clearly see if they agree with the game plan and to ensure that their renewal efforts are indeed getting traction. Large companies have complex operating structures and byzantine politics; successfully reinvigorating the business is usually a multiyear process and takes considerable leadership skills. The people recruited to lead such efforts are critically important.

Naturally, monitoring and investing in turnaround situations require considerable analytical and conceptual skills. Quantitative skills are less helpful in such cases, as the historical record is not a good indicator of things to come. More helpful are qualitative analysis skills: the ability to evaluate the coherence of the turnaround plan and to assess the people who are to deliver on it. Given that such analysis requires considerable skill, investors should be realistic about their motivations and the preparation needed to engage with such situations.

When done well, however, turnaround analysis can provide rare opportunities for strong long-term growth in core portfolios. Strong companies with decades of operating history have undergone transformations that lifted them from years of anemic performance to sustained periods of strong growth.

Companies such as General Electric (Jack Welch), International Business Machines (Louis Gerstner), and Apple (Steve Jobs) are some of the largest names that have gone through a significant positive change. In each case, the company had stagnated for a period of years, because of which a change in management started a process of rebuilding that reinstalled it as a highly profitable leader in its industry. Rare though they are, such opportunities can provide a significant boost for investors who have the skills and patience to methodically uncover the relevant data and follow companies undergoing a renewal.

Risky Growth: Emerging Leaders

Perhaps the most exciting and most challenging way to seek growth is through new companies in emerging niches or in entirely new industries. When most people think about growth investing, they have in mind the fast-growing small companies of yesteryear that have come to dominate the economic landscape today. In fact, all dominant companies in our midst now were once very small. Companies such as Walmart, Home Depot, and many others were once fast-growing small companies.

Walmart, for instance, had revenues of about $44.3 million in 1970, its first year as a publicly traded company. It grew exceedingly fast over the next several years and reported revenues in excess of $1.2 billion by 1979 fiscal year end. During the same period, the market value of the company's equity increased more than 12-fold from $44.8 million to just under $540 million. Similarly, Home Depot reported revenues of $22.3 million in 1980; by the end of fiscal 1990, revenues had grown to $3.8 billion, and the market value of common equity had climbed to $5.1 billion. Examples are numerous, with such stalwarts today as Microsoft, Intel, Starbucks, Amazon, and others that continue to grow, albeit at a much slower pace.

These examples tell only one side of the story, however. They ignore the fact that for every small company that later became a giant, many others fell by the wayside. The successes of a few must be seen in light of an equal or greater number of companies that did not deliver on the promise of growth that was evident in the pace of their first few years.

Perhaps the greatest mistake people make when seeking growth is paying attention not to economics, but to fast-rising stock prices. There were many instances of this during the heyday of the late 1990s, when the lay public got sucked into the hype of companies that had anything to do with the Internet. Among the many examples of faux growth is e.Digital, a Canadian producer of the earliest portable digital voice-recording devices. The company began in 1988 as 340520 B.C. Ltd., changed its name twice before listing in 1993, and then traded between $2 and $4 per share for many years. Its share price then began a rapid decline down to about 6 cents in early 1999, at which time shareholders approved the name change to e.Digital. Then, perhaps caught up in the hype of the era, the share price of the company made its rapid ascent, rising to almost $16 per share in early 2000 and then, on January 24, to an intraday high of $24.50 per share—only to plummet back to under a dollar by late 2001. As of February 2016, the company was trading at under 4 cents a share.

Throughout its rise and fall, e.Digital never reported operating profits. Yet, investors stampeded to purchase shares when prices started rising fast, only to see their investment destroyed when the spell broke. There were many companies like e.Digital during the Internet bubble, before and after. The fact that such companies don't have a sustainable business does not seem to matter for those chasing fast-rising stock prices.

The real problem for defense-oriented investors does not arise from chasing fast-rising stocks with no sustainable business model. The problem in fact arises from misjudging and paying too much for genuine growth by exaggerating future prospects.

Consider Cisco Systems, for instance, which went public in 1989 with annual revenues of $28 million. By 1999, annual revenues grew to $12 billion, and then 50 percent more to $18 billion in 2000. Fast growth created demand for the stock, and the company's market value shot up to $467 billion, about 26 times revenue for the year.

Clearly, Cisco was a genuine growth company, but investors were paying more than a hefty premium to own a piece of it. A short time later, the technology-fueled bull market collapsed, and the company's share prices dropped sharply.

Cisco was not the only company to have taken growth investors on an unfortunate ride. During the same period, those investing in other dominant companies, such as Walmart, Home Depot, Microsoft, and Intel, experienced a similar fate. They paid too much for good companies. Interestingly, as of February 2016, the market value of equity for Cisco was about $127 billion on revenue of just over $49 billion. That is, the company was selling for well under three times annual revenue.

As such, investors do get in trouble even when the companies in which they invest are excellent operators and dominant in their respective spheres of activity. Paying too much in the hopes of growing the portfolio can actually backfire when high prices come tumbling down, destroying the painstaking gains made elsewhere.

For every investor who is able to catch a rising star and exit before its collapse, there are many more who get in at the top and then stay too long, only to see their investments plummet or disappear altogether. That is a natural, and even expected, consequence of carelessly pursuing risky growth. Both turnaround situations and fast-growing companies bring with them hopes of outsized gains, yet only a few deliver.

The question remains, therefore, whether we can sort productive growth opportunities, such as Home Depot and Walmart in their early years, from imagined growth opportunities, such as the same two companies in the late 1990s, or from the likes of Enron. The short answer is that a well-calibrated skepticism is essential for making that determination. But this remains a key issue for investors. Given the focus in this book on developing a cautious mindset, I will have to leave growth investing to another project, perhaps a treatise in its own right.

In short, growth investing relies greatly on qualitative analysis, on judgments about the sources of value creation and the quality of the leadership in charge of executing a well-articulated strategy. Turnarounds and fast growth demand highly competent management, and the leadership of such companies need especially careful evaluation.

Along with a sound strategy and looking for strong leadership in a company, a cautious temperament and a grounding in economic realities remain important for successfully investing in growth companies. Investors routinely get in trouble when they pay too much for strong and well-managed companies, optimistic that a growing company will continue its breakneck pace indefinitely. Sure, depending on the situation, growth opportunities may justify relaxing one's assumptions about uncertainty and growth in the discount flow model. But those assumptions still need to be reasonable given that real companies in the real world can only do so much. Unwisely chosen growth companies can create illusions of profits but are liable to produce significant losses.

Yet, experienced and cautious investors can accomplish growth by applying the portfolio logic of mathematical expectations to a small group of well-chosen companies, each selected using refutation analysis and the thesis for each being unable to be disconfirmed despite serious attempts to do so. By inserting companies with a marginally higher probability of loss but with a much higher potential for upside than those of others in their portfolios, investors can significantly improve their long-term expected returns.

Consider, for instance, an equal-weighted portfolio of five companies as in table 23.1, where each company has a 10 percent probability of 20 percent loss, a 40 percent probability of zero return, and a 50 percent probability of a +20 percent gain. If we further assume that the economic performance of the companies is largely independent from those of the others, the mathematical expectation for the portfolio as a whole computes to 40 percent.

Next, suppose that you replace one of the five companies with another, whose asymmetric returns are as follows: a higher, 30 percent, probability of a 20 percent loss; a 40 percent probability of no return; and a 50 percent probability of a much higher, +100 percent, gain. In this scenario, the mathematical expectation for returns to the portfolio as a whole rises almost two times to 76 percent. That is, investors who have the ability to find growth companies with asymmetric returns, as in the second case here, can substantially increase the profit potential of their portfolios with only a marginally larger increase in the probability of loss.

Identifying genuine growth opportunities can be very profitable for investors—provided, of course, they use disconfirmation analysis and portfolio logic to turn the mathematical odds strongly in their favor. In this context, investors may be able to boost their portfolios quite significantly by identifying companies that have strong potential to continue to grow consistently over time.

CHAPTER TWENTY-FIVE

The Buffett Portfolio

ONE WORTHY ILLUSTRATION of a core portfolio is that of Berkshire Hathaway—built and managed by Warren Buffett. In the illustration that follows, I provide a brief analysis of the stock holdings data that Buffett presents in the company's annual reports.

Buffett has been unusually candid in these well-read letters; he discloses not only the number of shares and market value of these holdings at the end of each fiscal year but also the cost basis for all major stock holdings. He does not report the minor positions in the annual report, however, revealing only the most significant ones. Those interested can access more extensive disclosures in 13F filings, but these do not go far enough back for us to be able to understand the portfolio long term.

While Buffett puts Berkshire Hathaway's capital to work in many different ways, I limit this brief analysis to the stock portfolio. Not covered in this analysis are other investment operations, such as in convertibles, bonds, and private company transactions.

From the public record and periodic announcements, it is evident that Berkshire Hathaway has been active in the market for corporate control, frequently buying whole companies, both private and public. As Buffett has stated, however, his approach to investment analysis remains about the same whether a company is private or public. The main difference between the two is that the purchase of private companies does not engage the public equity markets, whereas the purchase of publicly traded companies requires a degree of sophistication about market operations. In the latter case, Berkshire sometimes acquires a portion of the outstanding common shares and, occasionally, convertible preferred shares or bonds. Sometimes, as in the case of Burlington Northern Santa Fe (BNSF), Lubrizol, and Precision Castparts, Berkshire Hathaway has increased its initial minority equity stake to buy up whole companies.

Portfolio Overview

In a September 13F filing made public in November 2011, Berkshire disclosed that it had purchased about 57.4 million shares of International Business Machines (IBM) for a total commitment of just over $10 billion. As such, IBM was one of 33 stocks held by the company at the time and accounted for about 17 percent of the $59 billion stock portfolio. The average position at the end of the quarter was just under $1.8 billion per stock.

Table 25.1 shows the context in which Buffett purchased the IBM stock. As of the end of the quarter in June 2011, Berkshire Hathaway had $52 billion invested in equities of 27 companies; yet, just 5 companies accounted for nearly 76 percent, or almost $40 billion, of the total; the top 10 companies comprised about 95 percent, or nearly $50 billion, of the total stock portfolio.

In essence, the stock portfolio was highly concentrated in just a few companies. Portfolio performance was dependent on the performance

TABLE 25.1

		% Portfolio	
Company	Ticker	June 2011	Industry
Coca-Cola	KO	25.77%	Nonalcoholic beverages
Wells Fargo	WFC	18.93%	Money center bank
American Express	AXP	15.01%	Credit and travel services
Procter & Gamble	PG	9.35%	Personal products
Kraft Foods	KFT	6.71%	Packaged foods
Johnson & Johnson	JNJ	5.16%	Healthcare
ConocoPhillips	COP	4.19%	Integrated oil
Walmart	WMT	3.97%	Discount retail
U.S. Bancorp	USB	3.37%	Regional bank
Moody's	MCO	2.09%	Credit ratings and services
Top 10 as % total portfolio		94.56%	
Top 5 as % total portfolio		75.78%	
Total portfolio ($bn)		$52.22	

of the largest investments; errors in judgment when selecting these companies would be very costly. The key to building such a concentrated portfolio is to avoid unforced errors by sparing no effort in due diligence.

Note also that while the top 10 positions were all in large American companies, they were also in different sectors of the economy, ranging from nonalcoholic beverages to credit rating services.

Table 25.2 illustrates that as of the September 2015 13F filing, the holding periods for four of the top five companies in Berkshire Hathaway's stock portfolio were roughly 27 years (Coca-Cola), 25 years (Wells Fargo), 24 years (Procter & Gamble), and 21 years (American Express). Note that Procter & Gamble came into the portfolio after it acquired Gillette in 2005. Gillette, in turn, had been in the common stock portfolio since 1991, at which time Berkshire Hathaway converted its $600 million preferred share holdings to common shares. The company had purchased its preferred shares in 1989. The average holding period for the top 10 companies was well over a decade. Clearly, the top of the portfolio turned over very little. The second largest holding, Kraft Heinz, accounted for about 18 percent of the portfolio and came into Berkshire by way of the 2015 takeover by Heinz of long-time holding, Kraft, which Berkshire had bought in 2007.

The initial outlay in each of the four holdings shown in table 25.2 was significant as well. When Berkshire bought Coca-Cola in 1988, it committed $592 million for more than 14 million shares. This represented about 20 percent of the $3 billion stock portfolio at the time. Similarly, when Berkshire converted its Gillette preferred shares into common stock in 1991, its $600 million commitment represented 6.67 percent of the $9 billion stock portfolio.

The initial outlay in Wells Fargo in 1991 was $289 million, or more than 5 percent of the portfolio at the time. American Express began

TABLE 25.2

		Holding Period		Initial Outlay	
Company	Ticker	Since	Years	$ Million	% Port*
Coca-Cola	KO	1988	27	592	20%
Wells Fargo	WFC	1990	25	289	5%
American Express	AXP	1994	21	724	6%
Procter & Gamble/ Gillette	PG	1991	24	600	15%

*As percent of stock portfolio in the year of initial outlay

showing up in the top 10 in 1994, with an initial outlay of $723 million, or about 5 percent of the stock portfolio at the time. Even though smaller than those for Coca-Cola and Gillette, both these initial outlays were also significant commitments. Similarly, the initial investment in Kraft was a 2007 purchase of more than 123 million shares for about $4.2 billion, accounting for 5.41 percent of the Berkshire portfolio at the time.

It was in this historical context that Berkshire Hathaway made its large investment in IBM, making it the second largest holding in the updated stock portfolio. Clearly, IBM was a big bet.

As shown in table 25.3, Berkshire's stock portfolio remained highly concentrated immediately after the IBM commitment. The top five companies at the time accounted for more than 74 percent, and the top 10 companies accounted for 93 percent of the portfolio. Coca-Cola, Wells Fargo, American Express, and Procter & Gamble all maintained a strong presence in the changed portfolio. Moreover, since no software-and-services company had previously in the portfolio, the IBM purchase also represented a sensible but controlled spreading of bets.

From 1981 through 2014, Berkshire allocated an average of 91 percent of its stock portfolio to just under 10 companies. From 1991 through 1994, 10 or fewer companies received the entire allocation. It appears, therefore, that Berkshire accomplished controlled

TABLE 25.3

		% Portfolio	
Company	Ticker	September 2011	June 2011
Coca-Cola	KO	22.88%	25.77%
IBM	IBM	16.98%	*
Wells Fargo	WFC	14.76%	18.93%
American Express	AXP	11.53%	15.01%
Procter & Gamble	PG	8.21%	9.35%
Kraft Foods	KFT	5.10%	6.71%
Johnson & Johnson	JNJ	4.04%	5.16%
ConocoPhillips	COP	3.43%	3.97%
Walmart	WMT	3.12%	4.19%
US Bancorp	USB	2.75%	3.37%
Moody's	MCO	1.47%	2.09%
Top 10 as % total portfolio		92.81%	94.56%
Top 5 as % total portfolio		74.36%	75.78%
Total portfolio ($bn)		$59.05	$52.22

diversification intuitively and most likely without consideration of standard deviations and variance–covariance matrices. From public comments made by Buffett, a rough valuation based on the quality of a business and its leadership is usually the main driver of selections for and significant changes to the portfolio.[1]

Investing in just a few companies at a time and holding on to positions for at least a few years seems to be the hallmark of how Buffett participates in the stock market. As evident in table 25.4, this pattern of selective investment across a range of business sectors and the low turnover of major positions reflects a measured approach and well-researched choices. In fact, the four major positions—Coca-Cola, Wells Fargo, American Express, and IBM, since 2011—continue to dominate the stock portfolio, accounting for almost 50 percent of the holdings, as reported in the November 2015 13F report.

Evaluating IBM

Given Berkshire Hathaway's significant commitment to IBM, let's try to refute the thesis that IBM was an attractive investment opportunity at the time of inclusion in Berkshire's stock portfolio.

In the annual report that followed the purchase, Buffett disclosed 63,905,931 shares of IBM at a cost basis of $10.586 billion, or approximately $170 per share. In the previous fiscal year ending December 2010, IBM had reported diluted earnings of $12.06 per share, and the three-year average earnings were $10.32 per share. As such, the earnings yields for one and three years were 7.09 percent (EY1) and 6.07 percent (EY3), respectively.

In order to estimate the discount rate, let's consider yields on the company's long-term bonds. In November 2011, IBM issued a 10-year bond (CUSIP 459200HA2) with a fixed coupon of 2.90 percent. Assuming that there was no significant speculation on these bonds, we take the discount rate as about three times this yield, rounding it up to 9 percent. These values then reveal that for EY1, the annualized long-term implied growth (g1) was 1.78 percent; for EY3, the implied growth rate (g3) was 2.76 percent.

Historically, IBM had grown diluted earnings at an annualized rate of 11.43 percent since 2001 and at an annualized rate of 17.18 percent since 2006. As such, the implied growth was considerably below the

TABLE 25.4

Company	Ticker	2010	2011	2012	2013	2014	Industry
Coca-Cola	KO	21.38%	18.18%	16.54%	14.06%	14.38%	Nonalcoholic beverages
IBM	IBM	*	15.26%	14.88%	10.87%	10.51%	Software and business services
Wells Fargo	WFC	18.08%	14.32%	17.79%	18.68%	22.56%	Money center bank
American Express	AXP	10.58%	9.29%	9.94%	11.71%	12.01%	Credit and travel services
Procter & Gamble/Gillette	PG	7.57%	6.27%	4.06%	3.64%	3.99%	Personal products
Kraft Foods	KFT	4.98%	3.84%	*	*	*	Packaged foods
Munich Re	N/A	4.75%	3.20%	4.11%	3.76%	3.42%	Reinsurance
Johnson & Johnson	JNJ	4.53%	2.68%	*	*	*	Diversified
Walmart	WMT	3.42%	3.03%	4.27%	3.80%	4.95%	Grocery, general merchandise
ExxonMobil	XOM	*	*	*	3.54%	*	Integrated oil
U.S. Bancorp	USB	3.42%	2.74%	2.84%	3.30%	3.71%	Regional bank
ConocoPhillips	COP	3.22%	2.75%	1.60%	*	*	Independent energy
POSCO	PKX	2.77%	1.69%	1.48%	*	*	Basic materials
Sanofi Aventis	SNY	2.69%	2.47%	2.78%	2.00%	1.73%	Pharmaceutical
Goldman Sachs	GS	*	*	*	1.97%	2.16%	Investment bank
Moody's	MCO	*	*	1.63%	1.65%	2.01%	Rating agency
Tesco	TSCO	2.61%	2.37%	2.59%	1.42%	*	Grocery, general merchandise
DirecTV	DTV	*	*	1%	1.31%	1.82%	Satellite service
DaVita Healthcare Partners	DVA	*	*	*	*	1.19%	Healthcare
Deere & Company	DE	*	*	*	*	1.16%	Industrial goods/farm equipment
BYD Co Ltd	N/A	1.92%	*	*	*	*	Automobile (China)
Phillips 66	PSX	*	*	1.25%	1.36%	*	Independent energy
USG Corporation	USG	*	*	*	*	1.03%	Construction materials
Top 10 as % total portfolio		82%	79%	80%	75%	80%	
Top 5 as % total portfolio		63%	63%	63%	59%	64%	
Total portfolio ($bn)		$62	$77	$88	$118	$117	
Number of companies reported in annual report		14	14	15	15	15	
Percent of stock portfolio in the above companies		92%	88%	87%	83%	87%	

Source: Computed from data reported in Berkshire Hathaway's annual reports

rate of earnings growth that the company had delivered in recent years. Hence, at the purchase price of $170 per share, the market was pricing IBM with the expectation of future growth much lower than what it had delivered in the recent past. That is, the market was pessimistic about the future prospects for a company that had in recent years been delivering strong growth.

A closer look shows that even though IBM grew per-share earnings at a good clip, its revenue growth was anemic. The company's top line grew from under $89 billion in 2001 to just under $100 billion as of the end of fiscal 2010, making for a compounded annual growth rate of 1.69 percent. During the same period, the company's total net income grew at an annualized rate of 7.5 percent, and the book value remained essentially flat. The slow top-line growth during the preceding 10 years had occurred in spite of the fact that the company had been on an acquisitions spree, having spent more than $26 billion purchasing property and assets all around the world.

Further reading shows that IBM had been undergoing a major transformation since 1993, when Louis Gerstner was brought in to reinvigorate the then faltering company. He made massive changes and initiated a significant shift in its mix of businesses, which was continued by Samuel Palmisano who followed him as CEO.[2] For several years before Buffett's investment, even as the company grew the top line rather slowly, it was expanding margins by changing the mix away from low-margin hardware to higher-margin software and services. The difference in top-line and bottom-line growth rates was, therefore, driven by structural changes to accommodate a new strategy.

IBM also showed high growth on a per-share basis because it bought back over $66 billion worth of its common stock during the 2001–2010 period, thus reducing share count by almost 29 percent. In addition, the company paid just under $18 billion in cash dividends during those years. It likely made these shareholder-friendly actions because of high profitability (strong margins) and significant free cash flows. In spite of these rationalizations, slow top-line growth remains a concern, and we must try to better understand its implications for equity investors.

Additional analysis shows that the company's three-year earnings yield at about 6.07 percent was comfortably higher than the yields then prevailing on the 10-year treasury or corporate bonds. The operating earnings yields and free cash flow yields were also respectable. IBM had a long history of paying cash dividends on common stock.

The dividend yield prevailing about the time of purchase was just about 1.45 percent, with dividends per share at the time growing at a 10-year average annual rate of more than 18 percent. At $170 per share, therefore, we could not at that time refute the investment thesis for IBM based on implied growth rate or yield tests.

Stability tests show that IBM had delivered stable performance over the preceding decade. Margins were strong and growing, and inventory turns were stable with a slight uptick over several years. Furthermore, although the total debt-to-equity ratio at the end of fiscal 2010 was high at 1.24, it was so because of the high leverage (about 7 to 1) the company maintained in its financing business. About two-thirds of the total debt was attributable to the financing business. Leverage on non-finance businesses appeared to be reasonable. The net interest coverage ratio was about 45. In addition, the balance sheet showed almost $30 billion in cash plus short/long investments. Careful investors would make sure that there were no significant liabilities hidden from view in the thicket of the company's filings and that its assets were of high quality.

Given both quantitative analysis and a quick reading of the company literature, we are unable to refute the IBM investment thesis based on implied growth, yield, stability, or strength tests.

Slow growth in the top line still remains a concern, however, and requires digging into the company literature to evaluate competitive positioning and future prospects. A first-cut qualitative evaluation shows that IBM was a strong company with a good recent history, a marquee brand, and a competent yet shareholder-friendly leadership team. It was a premium, high-margin player in a robust and growing global market for enterprise software and business process consulting. Even so, the larger business climate was moving quickly with changes in technology and well-resourced by aggressive competitors; a strong international presence also made IBM vulnerable to geopolitical upheavals. For serious investors looking to make a commitment to IBM as an investment thesis, a thorough qualitative understanding of these larger forces remained indispensable.

The compensation policies of the company seemed appropriate as well. Top executive compensation depended on deliverables through the annual incentive plan and on performance equity awards. Salary accounted for 9 percent for the CEO and 14 percent for the senior vice-presidents. Funding of the annual incentive program, which affected about 4,800 executives in 2009 and 2010, was based on performance as measured by net income (60 percent), revenue growth (20 percent), and cash flow (20 percent). Equity grants to executives depended on rolling three-year earnings per share (80 percent) and cash flow (20 percent). Further evaluation of the compensation structure reveals that the chairman and CEO, Sam Palmisano, was by far the highest-paid executive and rewarded largely with variable pay.

The company's emphasis on profitability, top-line growth, and cash flows seems reasonable, although heavy emphasis on accrual earnings and then on earnings per share raises some concern about incentives for aggressive accounting and possibly an aggressive share repurchase program. Even so, the compensation structure for the top executives seemed appropriate overall and did not provide grounds for disconfirming the investment thesis.

A review of the pension plans revealed underfunding, but within reason in relation to the company's annual free cash flows. Annual operating lease commitments were significant in relation to annual interest expense, but adjusted fixed expenses were still comfortably much lower than operating income and cash flows. Again, small doubts but nothing fatal as of yet.

While it's unclear what Buffett may have seen when evaluating the company, it appears that IBM had good fundamentals and was a strong company well-positioned in growing businesses. It is likely that, at $170 per share, Buffett was unable to disconfirm the positive narrative about the company: IBM appeared to be leading the charge into the secular trends of globalization and technological innovation.

Notwithstanding a few wrinkles revealed in the evaluation, both quantitative and qualitative analyses are unable to cast serious doubt on the thesis that IBM was an attractive investment at the then purchase price of $170 per share. Soon after Buffett took a stake in IBM (between June 30, 2011, and September 30, 2011), however, the company announced the retirement of Samuel Palmisano, who had led the company since 2002 and had been instrumental in developing the company's new strategy. Leadership changes created some uncertainty for investors; the new CEO, Ginni Rometty, had an impressive background as a long-tenured IBM executive, and she beat out two other candidates for the job.

Update on the IBM Thesis

As I review my analysis in July 2015, IBM has continued to transform from a historically hardware-focused company to one increasingly emphasizing software and business services. Shedding more hardware businesses and sluggish growth in important international markets, along with currency headwinds, has undermined its top line performance in the past several years. In addition, the company has faced public relations challenges in abandoning a highly publicized earnings target set by previous CEO Sam Palmisano. Facing intense competition from a very entrepreneurial Amazon (providing web services), a resurgent Microsoft, and other aggressive big technology companies, Rometty has evolved strategic priorities, refocusing the company on data, the cloud, security, mobile, and infrastructure. The move away from hardware has continued, but the transformation does not seem to have progressed at a fast enough pace for investors, and the company's market valuation has suffered because of that.

As of July 2015, the company was trading at about $160 per share. So, let's re-evaluate it in light of its recent operating and financial performance.

As is evident from tables 25.5, 25.6, and 25.7, the company's top line has shrunk significantly in the last five years, in large part from shedding hardware businesses, but also from anemic growth in other parts of the company. Both net income and operating cash flows have followed suit. Even so, the company has continued to purchase its own shares, reducing the count by just under 15 percent, from 1.16 billion in February 2012 to 988 million in February 2015, while significantly

TABLE 25.5
Results of Operations

	REV	Net Inc	OCF
2014	92,793	12,022	16,868
2013	99,751	16,483	17,485
2012	104,507	16,604	19,586
2011	106,916	15,855	19,847
2010	99,871	14,833	19,549

Note: All data in $mm; REV = total revenues, Net Inc = total net income, OCF = operating cash flows

TABLE 25.6
Share Dilution and Dividends

	CSHO	DIL	Dividends Per Share ($)
2014	991	2.0%	4.2
2013	1,054	4.6%	3.7
2012	1,117	3.4%	3.3
2011	1,163	4.3%	2.9
2010	1,228	4.8%	2.5

Note: CSHO = shares outstanding, DIL = share dilution, DPS = Dividends Per Share

TABLE 25.7
Financial Performance

	ROA	ROE	ROC
2014	10.2%	101.3%	25.6%
2013	13.1%	72.3%	29.6%
2012	13.9%	88.0%	38.7%
2011	13.6%	78.7%	36.9%
2010	13.1%	64.4%	33.0%

Note: ROA = return on assets, ROE = return on equity, ROC = return on capital

decreasing dilution. Partly as a result, in spite of the shrinking top line, it has consistently increased dividends per share. So, while decreasing net income has resulted in a lower return on capital, share repurchases have allowed the company to substantially increase return on equity.

Tables 25.8, through 25.11 show the results of the tests discussed in chapters 14 and 15. The share price of $160 in July 2015 implied a future long-term earnings growth rate of about 0.62 percent. This implied growth was in line with its recent (five-year) growth in earnings per share but substantially lower than growth rates in revenue per share and cash flow per share. That is, at $160 per share, the market was expecting that the company would hardly grow earnings per share in the long run, that the strategic initiatives the company had in place would not lead to much growth into the long future. Perhaps recent operating performance has influenced this assessment, substantially discounting the ability of the current management team to execute and deliver on their growth initiatives.

TABLE 25.8

Implied Growth Rate Test

Implied growth rate = 0.62%

	Growth Rate
Revenues	4.3%
Net earnings	0.8%
Operating cash flow	2.4%
Free cash flow	2.2%

Note: Growth Rate = per share historical growth rate

TABLE 25.9

Yield Test

10-year treasury bond yield	2.22%
10-year corporate bond yield	3.50%
Earnings yield	7.44%
Operating cash flow yield	10.44%
Free cash flow yield	8.12%
Dividend yield	2.64%

TABLE 25.10

Strength Test

	LTD/E	LTD/FCF3	Cov
2014	2.96	2.48	17.81
2013	1.44	2.19	19.18
2012	1.28	1.55	20.72
2011	1.14	1.42	19.71
2010	0.95	1.38	20.20

Note: LTD/E = long-term debt/equity, LTD/FCF3 = long-term debt/3-yr average free cash Flow, Cov = coverage ratio

TABLE 25.11

Stability Test

	GM	OpM	OCFM
2014	55.4%	19.8%	18.2%
2013	53.9%	19.4%	17.5%
2012	53.1%	20.3%	18.7%
2011	52.0%	19.6%	18.6%
2010	51.5%	18.8%	19.6%

Note: GM = gross margin, OpM = operating margin, OCFM = operating cash flow margin. Also note that acquisitions and divestments make IBM financials difficult to pin down, so these ratios are approximate.

The yield test shows that, compared with the yield on the company's long-term bond and compared with 10-year treasuries, the shares of the company are yielding a substantial premium. The dividend yield is 58 percent higher than the yield available on treasuries and is three-quarters of the yield on the company's own bonds. That is, we cannot refute the investment thesis for IBM based on implied growth or yield tests.

Also evident in tables 25.8 through 25.11 is that the company's debt-to-equity ratio has increased substantially. We see a rapid increase in debt, largely to repurchase shares, but this was a shareholder-friendly move as it increased the ownership value of each remaining share. However, the greater amount of debt increases the company's vulnerability if interest rates happen to go up quickly, in which case it may have to drastically slow down the rate of its share repurchases. Even so, the coverage ratio is a very healthy 18, and the company generates sufficient free cash flows to be able to pay off its entire debt in less than two and half years; it is not in any imminent danger of getting in trouble with creditors. Therefore, we cannot refute the investment thesis for IBM based on the results of the strength test.

Finally, over the last several years, IBM has been expanding its gross margins and holding steady on historically higher levels of operating margins and operating cash flow margins. Although these are approximate numbers, because the continuous streams of acquisitions and divestments make the financials hard to pin down, the general trend toward improved margins is clear. Declining revenues create some doubt, but given the company's stated objective of moving away from hardware, these are understandable. We cannot refute the investment thesis on the basis of stability.

Although the company faces challenges in terms of top-line growth, the quick analysis we've performed here indicates that we cannot refute the thesis for IBM as an investment candidate at the prevailing price of $160 per share. How it actually performs in the medium to long term depends on how productive and successful its strategic initiatives turn out to be. Long-term investors in the company must evaluate the quality of its value propositions and operating model in each key business area. Quantitative tests do not provide grounds for rejecting the thesis of investing in the company; qualitative factors, such as the business model and its leadership and execution, remain key to IBM's future success.

In sum, the historical record and current composition of Buffett's stock portfolio illustrates the usefulness of constructing core portfolios of a few carefully selected companies whose investment theses cannot be refuted in spite of diligent efforts to do so; particular focus must remain on an analysis of the leadership team and the business model of each company that is a candidate for the core portfolio.

Conclusion

Noise Control

IN THE WORLD of investment research, there's so much information to process and interpret that anybody can easily drown in it. Numerous mandatory filings, marketing materials, third-party reports and commentaries, and the unending streams of opinions that public companies invite all have the capacity to overwhelm the senses. The challenge for investors is to cut through the noise obfuscating the nuggets of data that may be critical to developing a keen understanding of an investment thesis. Sometimes, there are no nuggets of data at all, only a vast jumble of plausible but confusing claims and counterclaims.

The overabundance of information is not the only problem, however; acute problems arise from our emotional and psychological vulnerabilities. Emotions, part of our biological heritage, help us to organize the information around us and guide our perceptions by shifting attention from some facts to others. In this sense, while emotions are integral to how we make sense of the world around us, they also can have the effect of distorting even the simplest information.

Investors can easily dilute their efforts by chasing any number of seemingly plausible but really bad ideas or by becoming mired in meaningless detail. In spite of their best efforts, they can also misinterpret signals and stray deeper into the information jungle with no way out. It is frighteningly easy, in other words, for even experienced investors to get lost in the noise and make any number of unforced errors.

So, what can we do to sort through and make meaning from the vast troves of information, when emotional and psychological factors can so impede true understanding? How do we get to the nub of the problem in a world full of sights and sounds that confuse and distract, persistent sales pitches that fuel hopes and fears, and more? How, in short, do we invest sanely in the insane world of investing and do so with such a defective computing apparatus as that bestowed on us by eons of biological evolution?

Impossible though investing seems, there are things that we as investors can do to improve our odds of success. Paramount for investing successfully, as I have argued in this book, is a cautious temperament and a well-grounded approach that helps stabilize emotions, encourages focus on relevant facts, and facilitates careful analysis. Central to this approach is posing the investor as a sense-maker in an incredibly complex world of fact and fiction, with the distinction between the two not always clear. Let's review the keys to our approach.

The first step in becoming a wise investor is to define investing as a problem of choice as opposed to defining it as a problem of chance. Putting choice at the center of investing tempers the propensity to gamble and to take unnecessary chances in the hope that luck might shine our way. Even though the markets are unpredictable and prices can shift randomly in the short run, gambling in investing is a fool's errand, as it invites reckless behavior that dissipates both energy and capital. Instead, investors must endeavor to deliberately deploy capital in sound businesses and do so on economically favorable terms such that the preservation of capital remains paramount as an objective.

The second step in learning to invest wisely is to understand that good choices do not always mean good results. Because the strongest emotions of the moment drive prices in the short run, good analysis does not guarantee success, nor does poor analysis (or no analysis at all) guarantee failure in the near term. The chaos of the markets obfuscates the connections that may exist between thoughtful analysis and investment performance—making some mistakenly conclude that analysis is pointless.

What thoughtful analysis does is improve the odds of good performance over time. It structures our thinking and helps us to make selections based on sound economic fundamentals; it enables us to put events and news in perspective and avoid overreacting to every bit of new information that comes along. Not having a good analysis in which to anchor investment choices is, in fact, the undoing of many who dabble in the markets. Unprepared investors are highly vulnerable to being whiplashed by unpredictable price swings, entering the markets with optimism and hope, but then quickly abandoning their positions when the mood darkens and prices suddenly plummet. The absence of analysis almost inevitably leads to wrong choices. Hence, thoughtful and thorough analysis is of utmost important for investing wisely.

The third step in becoming a wise investor is to understand that, in many ways, investing is a "head game," in the sense that it requires considerable judgments about where to invest and when and when to stay put and how to fold. It also requires being able to see deceptions and self-deceptions that could trap invested capital. Of course, analytical skills are critical to making such judgments; but success in investing comes from stabilizing the mind so that we may be able to grasp the essence of things and differentiate true opportunity from the many illusions out there. Doing so requires that investors invest first in self-reflection—in gaining knowledge about how our own minds work, how we think, how we process information, and how our moods and emotions influence the choices we make.

That is, success in investing requires that we cultivate a capacity for self-awareness and self-reflection, for metacognition—thinking about thinking—and for understanding how we know what we know so that we may be able to deliberately regulate our own learning process.

The importance of this kind of self-awareness cannot be overstated. We are usually under the sway of a great many influences of which we are only dimly aware. The larger environment of hope and fear powerfully affects how we evaluate opportunities and, absent self-awareness, can easily lead us into stunningly poor choices. Rising markets create optimism, for instance, and encourage hopeful valuations; falling markets create pessimism, which usually results in fearful valuations. For most of us, this dynamic induces the wrong kinds of reactive behavior, where we buy high on hope and sell low on fear. Self-aware investors, on the other hand, are likely to integrate analytical skill with mindfulness to be better prepared to selectively deploy their precious capital in clearly understood and promising investment opportunities.

The fourth step for investing wisely is to develop an analytical strategy for correctly channeling our emotions and controlling our biases. In particular, we have discussed at length the potentially harmful role of confirmation bias, or our deep-seated inclination to seek data that agree with our prior beliefs and to interpret those data such that they support our preconceptions. As an antidote to confirmation bias, we have formalized the principle of negation and proposed that investing is a negative art. That is, we have sought to improve the quality of our choices by being skeptical about our own hunches, carefully shaping them into testable investment theses, and trying to systematically disconfirm them using both quantitative and qualitative analysis.

Instead of simply acting on a hunch or trying to prove why our investment thesis has merit, our approach is to doubt the validity of the thesis and to develop formal methods with which to try to disconfirm it. This analytical strategy has the dual advantage of controlling our many biases while also helping us manage the overabundance of information that invades our senses. In actively seeking information that may invalidate our thesis, we at once control our urge to confirm and limit the range of information we need in order to conduct good investment analysis.

The principle of negation and the framework for refutation and disconfirmation provide investors the conceptual apparatus with which to home in on signals that are directly relevant for developing and testing a well-specified investment thesis. Together, they help us cut our way through the noise so that we may be able to make good investment choices. The cautious approach to investment analysis is particularly important because of our view that measures of objective risk are misleading and that investors should rely instead on subjectively evaluating the many uncertainties that surround an investment thesis. Such subjective evaluations can easily succumb to our many biases, however, so investors need to sequentially and gradually update the thesis in light of new information. Throughout the process of testing and updating the thesis based on new learning, investors must retain a skeptical orientation that seeks to refute and disconfirm.

Of course, the purpose of this formal approach is to develop good habits, to ingrain caution and defense in our way of thinking. Once internalized, these habits will in themselves act as filters such that poor ideas are quickly seen for what they are, and we can our focus analytical efforts on thoroughly investigating the potential of the few new ideas that pass through those filters.

Finally, constructing a robust portfolio is integral to investing wisely. No matter how thorough the analysis of companies and securities, every investment thesis will suffer from unknowns and unknowables, as well as factors that can neither be controlled nor anticipated by even the best of analysts. Irreducible uncertainties remain no matter what, and new uncertainties emerge as the world changes.

Investors can mitigate the adverse effects of such irreducible uncertainties by constructing diversified portfolios. Grouping carefully selected stocks into a well-conceived portfolio is, therefore, the final step in investing wisely. Portfolio-level thinking remains important for investing well. As Markowitz noted back in the 1950s, and many others such as Edgar Lawrence Smith had recognized long before, investors should think of their investment program not in terms of individual securities but in terms of all the assets they own. The investment portfolio is a unit, and investors should evaluate individual selections in the context of the other assets they already own. Grouping companies that are uncorrelated or only partially correlated on economic fundamentals can markedly reduce the potential adverse effects of irreducible uncertainties and unknown risks.

But this does not mean that investors should ignore the particulars and wealth-creating machinery of each company in their portfolio. They must not lose the trees for the forest. Trying to at once grasp the particulars of too many companies is likely to make information overload a problem and undermine the ability to construct a robust portfolio. Avoiding this problem is paramount; investors must retain focus on deeply understanding each individual company in the portfolio. The final key to investing wisely is, therefore, to form portfolios with only a handful of core holdings, each carefully selected using a well-constructed investment thesis that has survived serious attempts at refutation and disconfirmation.

Analysis and Intuition

Note that while diligence and analysis are both important, wise investors also allow their sixth sense, or intuition, to play an important role in security selection and portfolio formation.

Overemphasizing hard analysis creates the danger of becoming mired in unnecessary detail and getting lost in the data. The process of making good investment choices requires more than simply the analysis of hard facts; it also requires discernment, or a keen sense of the larger and deeper meanings that the data are capable of illustrating. It requires silence of the mind, quiet listening, and taking your time, allowing the various aspects of your understanding to settle in so that you can think holistically about the situation at hand.

For investors contemplating committing significant capital to a particular investment, perhaps the greatest enemy is a sense of urgency, and the best friend is a lack of pressure to make decisions quickly. Time allows the cerebral cortex to kick in and avoid the destruction that reptilian reactions can impose on us; time allows us to calm our internal urges so that critical information can come into focus, so that we may see the interconnections and get true insight. Acting slowly, giving intuition the space to piece together true understanding, is crucial for investing wisely.

Slowing down the decision-making process also allows investors to ask such meta-analytic questions like what is truly happening with this company? What is the company really trying to accomplish? What larger trends appear to be emerging, and how might they affect the company's operating performance over time? How is the company leveraging, or suffering from, evolving technologies and consumption patterns? What are the headwinds? What are the tailwinds?

Answers to such questions, even incomplete ones, encourage investors to look beyond the data and outside particular analytical objectives to get a sense of the bigger picture, and to perhaps better understand the consequences of the choices they are about to make. Incorporating the larger context into our thinking and weaving a cautious narrative is critically important.

Another important component of making good choices is for investors to be aware of and to resist the rigidity that can sometimes set in when using decision frameworks. The principle of negation and the disconfirmation framework we have developed in this book are just that: a framework. And a framework is a tool, not a solution. It is a means for thoroughly evaluating an investment thesis; it not an end unto itself.

Sure, the disconfirmation framework is grounded in more than 2,000 years of progressively insightful thought about human reasoning. Yet, as investors, we are still left to sort out the much harder aspect of maintaining mental flexibility without becoming unhinged from the facts at hand. We need to ask the right questions, develop insights to set up proper investment theses, and subject our theses to the rigors of disconfirmation, but with an eye toward the larger goal of making good choices.

Investors should strive, therefore, to consider the refutation and disconfirmation framework as resilient but malleable, and subject to modification. Not only should we see the data in terms of the framework, we should also put the framework itself to the test. This dialectic between the framework and the data, the back and forth between the two, is the essential way for us to make sense of the world with a truly open mind.

To the extent that the framework is helpful and leads to good choices, it makes sense to continue refining it to one's personal style. When it begins to lead us into dark alleys and dead ends, it's time to rethink or even abandon it altogether. Ultimately, investors must exercise thoughtful choice at every turn.

Investor Temperament

We should note that refutation and disconfirmation, although encouraging analysis and emphasizing caution, are really about reinforcing, or acquiring and cultivating, the correct temperament for investing cautiously and wisely with a medium- to long-term investment horizon.

Independence of thought, diligence, emotional stability, caution, and patience are the hallmarks of a good temperament for investing wisely. Absent these traits, it is difficult to apply the approach to investing that we have discussed in this book. Without these, any manner of mishaps or perturbation in the larger environment can distract investors from the mental discipline required for sustained success; it can induce blind imitation or reckless gambling—and quickly undo years of painstaking work that may have gone into building one or more core portfolios. Hence, cultivating the correct temperament is essential for learning to be a wise investor.

Certainly, the traits that make up a complete value investor are a tall order for most of us humans. Given our many emotional and psychological vulnerabilities, we all fall short one way or the other most of the time, especially when engaged in as complex an endeavor as investing. Yet, the ideal temperament and its supporting traits are something to strive for, not only so we may become better investors but so that we may continue striving to become better people who make good choices.

Notes

Preface

1. See Buffett (1984), a now-famous speech made at the Columbia University School of Business in honor of the fiftieth anniversary of the publication of *Security Analysis* by Benjamin Graham and David Dodd.

2. See, for instance, Price and Kelly (2004).

3. The social and psychological underpinnings of economic behavior were very much part of early theorizing in economics, but they were gradually ignored and largely eliminated following the development, starting in the late nineteenth century, of what is loosely called neoclassical economics. This shift was propelled in part by what is called the marginal revolution and in part by an increasing desire among some economists to develop economics in the manner of natural sciences such as physics (see note 4 below), and it required strong assumptions about economic actors. Yet, formulating economics around strong simplifying assumptions was not without detractors even among early institutional economists such as Thorstein Veblen, and the dissent has continued in our times through such well-known figures as Amos Tversky, Daniel Kahneman, Robert Shiller, and Richard Thaler.

4. There is a long history of economists wanting to study the economy as physicists examine the physical world (see Sornette, 2014), and that may be why the mathematical tools common in physics often find their way into economics as well. For physicists interested in the physical world, mathematics is the language of choice because it helps uncover and faithfully represent the symmetry and economy presumed in their subject matter (see Wilczek, 2015). Mathematics is the language with which to figure out the laws of nature, those persistent regularities that exist but remain inaccessible to our five senses. To economists taking inspiration from physicists, if the markets are

ordered (or "efficient"), there must be symmetry and economy in their deep underlying structure, and these too may be amenable to discovery through the application of mathematical tools. Given how deep rooted the notion of efficiency remains in finance research and education, this link to physics is plausible. If so, this might be a misdirection of good tools that work in one domain (physics) to another domain (economics) which is laden with fundamentally different kinds of causality problems—those that arise not directly from the physical universe but that are endemic to human agency.

5. My friend Larry Zacharias tells me that Adolf Berle, of the Berle-and-Means duo who wrote the 1932 classic on corporate governance, *The Modern Corporation and Private Property*, argued as far back as 1952 that shareholders were little more than gamblers and, therefore, their interests ought to be subordinated to those of employees and customers.

Prologue

1. See Markowitz (1952) and Markowitz (1999). The second paper is a retrospective on modern portfolio theory.

2. Arthur Stone Dewing's encyclopedic *The Financial Policy of Corporations* (with editions published between 1919 and 1953) was the dominant text used in formal education to teach corporate finance. It is highly likely that Benjamin Graham was aware of this text as being taught at Columbia University where he wrote *Security Analysis*, and it is plausible that he was strongly influenced by Dewing's formal treatment of corporate securities in which the general public had become increasingly interested. Graham's innovation appears to have been to connect the body of knowledge compiled by Dewing to the behavior of investors in the financial markets.

3. In a small but powerful book, about 100 pages long, Smith had long before (1924) shown that a broadly diversified portfolio of stocks handily beat high-quality bonds provided the investment time horizon was sufficiently long.

4. In his dissertation, Markowitz specifically referred to chapter 9 (on mathematical expectations) of a text popular at the time, *Introduction to Mathematical Probability* by Uspensky, published in 1937.

5. See Bayes and Price (1763). The essay was read to the Royal Society of London by Richard Price but only after he had updated the raw manuscript he had found among Bayes's papers. (Bayes had died in 1761.)

6. Interestingly, Markowitz wrote the foreword to a recent book by Jimmie Savage's son, Sam Savage, *The Flaw of Averages: Why We Underestimate Risk in the Face of Uncertainty*, published in 2009.

7. See Savage (1954).

8. Interestingly, such an issue was on the minds of Jack Treynor and Fischer Black in their 1973 paper on using security analysis for improving portfolio selection. Alas, they did not go far enough and returned within the paper itself to formulating mathematical solutions.

9. A few years later, in 1962, Friedman was to write an immensely popular book, *Capitalism and Freedom*. The book encapsulated his belief that political freedom was inseparable from economic freedom. Free markets play an important role in this ideology, and market efficiency is an important part of that argument. Perhaps, Markowitz had Friedman's blessings to make the fundamental assumption of market efficiency when proposing his model for portfolio selection that became the basis for modern portfolio theory. Market efficiency was an important piece of the portfolio optimization puzzle.

10. Uspensky did cover subjective probability in chapter 4 of his text on Bayes' theorem. Yet, consistent with the low esteem in which statisticians of the period held Bayes, he devoted only that one chapter to it and ended it with "criticism of underlying assumptions."

11. Bob Nakosteen reminds me that, although subjective judgments are all too common in real life, the math required for applying Bayes's rule to subjective probability and updating those probabilities is incredibly cumbersome and complex—especially when compared with the relatively much easier math that Markowitz ended up using. As a graduate student who had found and defined a topic for his thesis and obtained the blessing of his advisers, therefore, Markowitz had strong incentives to pursue the path of least resistance. He could have come back to subjectivity later on, but he never did. The rest is history.

12. An excellent social history of modern finance can be found in MacKenzie (2006). MacKenzie shows that a handful of researchers with strong professional interconnections were at the heart of the new financial revolution. He shows that the initial wave of mathematicians, comprising such researchers as Harry Markowitz, William Sharpe, John Lintner, and Eugene Fama, was followed by another wave of hyper-mathematicians, such as J. Michael Harrison and David M. Kreps, in the 1980s and 1990s. The momentum of discoveries and the path dependency thus created made investment education irretrievably mathematical and drove those who were inclined to think about investing in terms of subjective business analysis out of finance departments.

13. Recognizing the limitations of normal distribution in defining risk, researchers have considered other tools, such as fat tails, skewed distributions, power laws, and, lately, jump models, in which stock prices are expected to "jump" as they quite frequently do. Yet, the focus remains on mathematical risk where the particulars of underlying economic activity remain opaque.

14. Perhaps influenced by Savage, Markowitz had in fact counseled that risk be assessed using statistical analysis as well as judgments based on security

analysis. But he focused on the former and never showed how to incorporate subjective assessments of risk into his model; those academics and researchers who followed him essentially ignored the importance of carefully making judgments about business risks.

15. The fifth and last edition of Arthur Stone Dewing's two-volume encyclopedic *The Financial Policy of Corporations* (1953) was published one year after Markowitz's first paper and two years before his dissertation. Graham published *The Intelligent Investor*, a less technical version of *Security Analysis*, in 1949.

16. This is the thesis developed at length by Donald MacKenzie (2006), who builds on Barry Barnes's work to argue that the mathematical models that came to dominate finance were not simply a reflection of the markets but actually shaped them through the practices of traders who adopted those models.

17. As Donald MacKenzie shows, the initial reaction of practitioners and academics to mathematical finance was decidedly hostile but was easily shrugged off by the mathematicians who were clearly in the ascendancy at most top-ranked business schools.

18. Ben Branch reminds me that objections to the idea of a fully rational economic agent have been longstanding. Already by the late 1890s, economists such as Thorstein Veblen and those aligned with the Austrian school were questioning the assumption that historical, social, and institutional contexts did not figure prominently in economic choices. See Branch (2008).

19. See Mandelbrot and Hudson (2004).

20. See Taleb (2007).

21. See Kuhn, *The Structure of Scientific Revolutions*, 24.

22. For a discussion of Kuhn's view that social factors affect scientific endeavors to a very large degree, see Barnes (1982). This view is strongly expressed by Lee (2009), who claims that the dominance of neoclassical economics in academia (and of efficient market hypothesis in investment education) came about in part because of ideological bullying (see pp. 42, 68, and 165).

23. Work in this regard is already building up substantially. See MacKenzie (2006), Ho (2009), and Van der Zwan (2014).

24. See Black (1986).

25. Some of the greatest breakthroughs in physics came when concepts such as gravity and time, which had long been assumed to be constants, were recast as variables. Similarly, acknowledging that market efficiency is a variable opens up investing to be recast as an opportunistic search for specific inefficiencies. Then the question can be asked: How do you look for efficiencies, and which kinds do you look for? Hence this book.

26. In fact, there is considerable work on finance developing in disciplines such as sociology and anthropology. In addition to MacKenzie (2006) are

Smith (1990), an excellent work on auctions; Smith (2001), consisting of interviews with investment professionals; and Ho (2009), an ethnography of Wall Street. In effect, the study of finance is no longer the sole domain of mathematicians.

27. There is nothing wrong with mathematics per se when investing. In fact, in the second half of this book, I will use a mathematical model of sorts and identify the key elements of that model to aid investors in evaluation of companies. The difference is that while the models of the mathematicians are abstract and built on unrealistic assumption, my model is grounded in the fact that investors are real people trying to comprehend a difficult subject and it focuses the attention of investors on the particulars of the investment thesis under evaluation.

28. See Pfleiderer (2014).

29. See Lowenstein (1994).

30. See MacKenzie (2006).

31. Again, see Pfleiderer (2014).

Introduction

1. A series of papers by professors Brad Barber and Terrance Odean lead to this conclusion. See, for instance, Barber and Odean (2000).

2. Just before sending this book to press for the first book draft, I came upon a *New York Times Magazine* article on this point. In the article, Nate Silver argued that defense does indeed win championships. He showed that, in 40 of the 92 Super Bowls in which the best ranked defensive and offensive teams played, the defensive teams won the Super Bowl nearly 80 percent of the time—including three games in which both competitors were strong defensive teams. See Silver (2013). In the most recent Super Bowl (2016), where the Denver Broncos and the Carolina Panthers were the first and second-ranked defensive teams, the Broncos won by shutting out the talented offense of the Panthers. Interestingly, even the offense in football relies a great deal on the ability of the offensive line to protect (defend) the quarterback or open channels for the running back. And, of course, good defense in football is always very aggressive, as it tries to prevent completion of plays. In this sense, defense always wins!

3. See Lefèvre (1923).

4. See Graham and Dodd (1934). See also Graham (1949).

5. See Fisher (1958).

6. See Soros (1987).

7. See Buffett and Cunningham (2008).

8. See Malkiel (2012).

9. The correct term for this is mathematical expectations, which require estimating weighted probabilities of gains and losses. Both gamblers and investors desire positive mathematical expectations, but they differ greatly in what they consider to be good odds and how they structure their expectations.

10. It is important to note that venture capitalists fall somewhere between gamblers and investors. Like gamblers, they seek very high payoff opportunities and know that the odds of success of any one of their well-selected investments are rather low. Yet, like investors, they are obsessed with trying to understand the factors shaping the underlying odds. The difference is that, unlike investors in the stock market, venture capitalists try to shape the odds by their own due diligence and involvement in decision making in the companies in which they invest. Moreover, they manage the odds by taking a disciplined approach to portfolio logic and the mathematical expectations inherent in that logic. In this sense, venture capitalists are both gamblers *and* investors.

1. Opinions and Beliefs

1. For a very good review article on this topic, see Nickerson (1998). I have learned a great deal, and borrowed liberally, from this article.

2. I have drawn these and several other examples in this chapter from Nickerson (1998), an excellent article that very competently reviews the extant thinking on confirmation bias.

3. See, for example, Croskerry (2003).

4. See, for example, Hastie (1993).

5. See Coval, Hirshleifer, and Teoh (2005). Professor Hirshleifer has built an extensive body of work on herding and other imperfections in the financial markets. Several of his papers are very good reads.

6. See Park, Konana, Gu, Kumar, and Raghunathan (2010).

7. See Mackay (1841). The quote is from the preface of Mackay's book.

8. For an entertaining and highly instructive but very short book on financial manias, see Galbraith (1994). In a similar vein, see also Chancellor (1999).

2. Correlation of Errors

1. The Chicago Board Options Exchange (CBOE) Volatility Index (VIX) is a measure of the expected volatility over the next 30-day period. As such, it measures how much the market expects stocks to fluctuate, or the uncertainty that traders face.

2. See Norris (2008).

3. Serbians consider the original Battle of Kosovo a highly significant event in their history. Many good writings are available on this subject; for our purposes here, a very good read is Zirojevic (2000). The author contends that facts about the battle remain elusive but that the legend of Kosovo was established at a very early date, with religion at its center and Prince Lazar as its main character. The author also reports of an early eighteenth century annihilation of converts to Islam as a direct consequence of the legend and its implication that divisions among the peoples and fears of traitors in their midst were the main reasons for defeat at the Battle of Kosovo. Ironically, such fears can become self-fulfilling prophecies.

4. I thank Dana Johnson for her many insightful comments, based on first-hand experience as a peace activist in Serbia, on Serbian nationalism and the ethnic conflict in the former Yugoslavia.

5. See Verdery (1999), pp. 18, 98.

6. See Bokanowski, T., Fiorini, L. G., and Lewkowicz, S. (2009).

7. For a complex but fascinating discussion of how human action influences an economy, see Minsky (1986).

3. The Dark Arts

1. Those interested can access a vast body of work on the sophists, including the well-known Guthrie, W. K. C. (1971).

2. For a recent modern treatment of rhetoric, see Farnsworth, W. (2011).

3. For example, see the description of the graduate-level required course, "Rhetorical Theory," at the University of Massachusetts Amherst: http://www.umass.edu/english/comprhetrequirements#rhettheory.

4. Purveyors of the Dark Arts

1. These ideas were later captured by Sigmund Freud in *Civilization and Its Discontents* (1930).

2. See Le Bon (1897). All quotes are from the digital copy obtained from the Electronic Text Center at the University of Virginia. The publisher of the digital book is Macmillan, New York.

3. See Bendersky (2007).

4. See Bernays (1928). All quotes are from the third printing (1930).

5. A full complement of Rushkoff's very interesting work is available on his website: rushkoff.com.

5. Victims of the Dark Arts

1. See Loewenstein (1996). The author has built an impressive body of work on the role of emotion and psychology in economic decisions.

2. See Anderson (2007).

3. See Federal Trade Commission (2009). See also Consumer Fraud Research Group (2006).

4. Again, see Loewenstein (1996).

6. Logic—Data—Doubt

1. This quote comes from book 1 of Aristotle's *On Sophistical Refutations.*

2. Specifically, Aristotle identified six tricks of language (ambiguity, amphiboly, combination, division, accent, and form of expression) and seven nonlinguistic fallacies (accident, improper use, ignorance of refutation, false reverse causality, circular logic, false causality, and jumble of questions).

3. See Bacon's *Novum Organon.* All quotes are from the 1863 English translation by Spedding, Ellis, and Heath.

4. See Popper (1963). "Conjectures and Refutations" was first given as a lecture in 1953 at Cambridge University in Cambridge, England, and then published in 1957 as "Philosophy of Science: A Personal Report" in *British Philosophy in the Mid-Century*, C. A. Mace, (ed.), London: Allen and Unwin.

7. Investing as a Negative Art

1. See Graham and Dodd (1934), chapter 6, pp..

2. French sociologist Émile Durkheim once wrote that social phenomena such as values and cultural norms arise from interactions among multitudes of individuals in society. Moreover, he argued, they are more than simply a product of social behavior: values and norms are social facts with coercive power over the individual. In essence, Durkheim defined sociology as an empirical science because, once measured, social facts could be manipulated using standard tools of statistics to uncover regularities or social laws.

3. Perhaps the most relevant historical example of this is Hegel's dialectic inquiry, which utilizes the principle of negation to reveal internal contradictions within a system. For a comprehensive treatise on doubt, see Hecht (2003).

8. Shaping the Investment Thesis

1. See Schuster (1964). This is just one of many illusory geometric figures, such as Necker's cube, Schroeder's stairs, and Mach's book, which illustrate challenges of perception.

2. Much of this discussion is inspired by William James (1890), who continues to inform modern scientists by his many incredible insights.

3. I draw here largely on Bernard Baars's very accessible and fascinating book, *In the Theater of Consciousness: The Workspace of the Mind.*

4. I owe this section to Douglas Hofstadter. For more, see his 1995 masterpiece, *Fluid Concepts and Creative Analogies: Computer Models of the Fundamental Mechanisms of Thought.* Rumor has it that it was the first book sold by Amazon.com.

5. See Baars (1997).

6. See Kent (2015).

7. See Lewis (2011). In 2015, a movie version of *The Big Short* was released.

8. The data for median earnings in the United States are available from the Bureau of Labor Statistics: http://www.bls.gov/cps/tables.htm.

10. The Art of Looking

1. See Hirshleifer and Teoh (2003). The two seminal papers on herd behavior among investors are Banerjee (1992) and Bikhchandani, Hirshleifer, and Welch (1992). This literature suggests that herding is "rational" because it often makes sense for people to follow others or, technically, to value their own private information about a stock less than information available elsewhere.

2. See Malkiel (2012).

3. See Park, Konana, Gu, Kumar, and Raghunathan (2010).

11. Price and Value

1. See Williams (1938)

2. The three conceptions are sociological, linguistic, and economic. See Graeber (2001).

3. See Smith (1776), chapter IV, p. 37.

4. See Hayek (1975) and Black (1986).

5. See Soros (1987).

6. This argument is well travelled in academic literature, especially among those who see prices not as incorporating all information but, being clearly

visible, as creating incentives for different kinds of economic behavior. As such, the causal relationship between price and value is complex. High or rising prices, for instance, can sometimes invite speculators whose buying action pushes prices even higher; low or falling prices can sometimes create selling pressure and push prices lower.

7. The fact that prices are endogenous to the actions of traders means that price data are very different from—and much more complex to model than—data in disciplines such as physics or astronomy. See Sornette (2014).

8. Much of behavioral finance makes this point. For early papers on this, see Shiller (1981) on the relationship between prices and subsequent dividends and also Bondt and Thaler (1985) on the overreaction hypothesis.

9. Along with Soros's book, *The Alchemy of Finance* (1987), see also "The General Theory of Reflexivity," one of a series of lectures available from the Open Society Foundations: https://www.opensocietyfoundations.org/multimedia/george-soros-open-society-financial-crisis-and-way-ahead#general-theory-of-reflexivity.

10. See, for example, Sornette (2014), pp. 14–16.

11. For a detailed theoretical and empirical review of this line of argument, see Shleifer's 2000 review of behavioral finance.

12. On this, see also Friedrich Hayek's Nobel Prize acceptance speech from 1974, available at http://www.nobelprize.org/nobel_prizes/economic-sciences/laureates/1974/hayek-lecture.html.

12. How to Value a Business

1. Estimates of worth depend much on the context of the impending transaction. For instance, the valuation of an asset would be different if the context were one of liquidation versus the breakup, spin-off, or control through ownership. Here, I limit the discussion to two common techniques for the valuation of publicly traded companies for investors engaging in arms-length market transactions.

2. I have obtained or derived all financial information in this book from the Compustat database, which I accessed through Wharton Research Data Services (WRDS), available through subscription from the Wharton School at the University of Pennsylvania. These are public data, however, and investors can compile them from mandatory filings or free websites such as wikinvest.com. Although the WRDS database is reliable for research, I cannot guarantee the accuracy of the numbers used in analyses. Please consider the computations in this text illustrative only, not as a basis for making actual investing decisions.

3. Free cash flow (FCF) = operating cash flow (OCF) – capital expenditures (CapEx). FCF increases if the company cuts CapEx. This reduction in CapEx may be legitimate, but it can also be a way to miscast FCF.

13. Risk and Uncertainty

1. See Knight (1921).

2. Another important concept is that of ambiguity, where the same facts inspire many different, conflicting interpretations, or no clear interpretation at all. In ambiguous situations, investors don't know what to make of a particular event or piece of information. Such ambiguity is common in investing, but I will fold it here into the broader concept of uncertainty. Suffice it to say, investors must work through ambiguous situations until their minds slowly settle on plausible interpretations supported by logic, data, and doubt.

3. There appears to be no credible theory that guides empirical choices regarding the time window for computing β or the index against which to measure it. Researchers also know that β itself is unstable and changes over time.

4. See Mandelbrot and Hudson (2004).

5. See Friedrich Hayek's Nobel Prize acceptance speech from 1974, available at http://www.nobelprize.org/nobel_prizes/economic-sciences/laureates/1974/hayek-lecture.html.

6. For an early synthesis of technical ideas related to subjective risk, see Savage (1954). See also Jeffrey (2004).

7. Here I refer to the Bayes rule, of course, about systematically updating beliefs, a logic for reasoning in a world where objectivity and precision are unattainable. For a history of the Bayes rule, see McGrayne (2011).

14. The Simple Math of Valuation

1. According to Graham's purported formula, intrinsic value 1 (V1) = earnings per share (EPS)· (8.5 + 2 × expected EPS growth rate).

2. In October 2013, Icahn sent an open letter to Apple CEO Tim Cook, urging the company to buy back up to $150 billion of its own shares. See Russolillo (2013).

3. Einhorn actually sued Apple, demanding that it issue preferred stock with a 4 percent dividend. See Ablan and Gupta (2013).

4. This approach of reverse engineering to derive assumptions embedded in price is owed to Williams (1938).

5. An alternative formulation for implied growth rate can be derived using the price-to-book (PB) and return-on-equity (ROE) ratios: $g = (PB \cdot r - ROE)/(PB + ROE)$. Once again, it's necessary to assume the discount rate for estimating the growth rate implied in prevailing prices.

6. For a full discussion of the capital asset pricing model (CAPM), see any standard investment text, or see Fama and French (2004).

15. Yield—Stability—Strength

1. Benjamin Graham inspired the choice of these three factors when he noted that "The investor should demand . . . a satisfactory ratio of earnings to price, a sufficiently strong financial position, and the prospect that [the company's] earnings will at least be maintained over the years" (1949: 103).

16. Depth Analysis

1. For a full list of SEC forms, see http://www.sec.gov/info/edgar/forms/edgform.pdf or http://www.sec.gov/about/forms/secformsalpha.htm.

2. To put this in context, the number of people on Walmart's payroll is higher than the number of state and local government workers in the state of California (1.85 million at the end of 2010).

17. Dive for Strength

1. A technical discussion entitled "Leases—Joint Project of the FASB and the IASB," is available on the FASB website: http://www.fasb.org/jsp/FASB/FASBContent_C/ProjectUpdatePage&cid=900000011123#decisions.

2. See Rapoport, M. (2015) for a related article.

3. See Davies, Sakoui, and Tett (2008), http://www.ft.com/intl/cms/s/0/8c80ff6e-901a-11dd-9890-0000779fd18c.html#axzz40BQTPSCM.

4. See Robinson (2008).

5. See Neate (2009), http://www.telegraph.co.uk/finance/newsbysector/banksandfinance/5769361/400bn-SIV-market-sold-off-in-two-years.html.

6. See Galbraith (1994).

7. See Valukas (2010).

18. Define Good Business

1. For a discussion and some related empirical evidence, see Sharma, Branch, Chawla, and Qiu (2013).

19. Watch the Game

1. As of the final revision of this text in February 2016, the market capitalization of the company was $9.6 billion.

2. Note that, in spite of razor-thin margins (1.3 percent versus 3.6 percent for WMT), Kroger still delivers strong return on equity (26.4 percent versus 21.9 percent for WMT). That, however, is largely through much higher leverage (5.5 versus 2.4 for WMT) and higher asset turnover (3.6 versus 2.3 for WMT), using five-year averages.

19. Watch the Game

1. As of the final revision of this text in February 2016, the market capitalization of the company was $9.6 billion.

2. Note that, in spite of razor-thin margins (1.3 percent versus 3.6 percent for WMT), Kroger still delivers strong return on equity (26.4 percent versus 21.9 percent for WMT). That, however, is largely through much higher leverage (5.5 versus 2.4 for WMT) and higher asset turnover (3.6 versus 2.3 for WMT), using five-year averages.

20. Meet the Managers

1. Dispersion of ownership of American corporations was noted long ago by Berle and Means (1932), and it characterized most large corporations throughout the twentieth century. In recent years, however, scholars have noted the rise of large institutional ("Universal") investors who own meaningful proportion of shares of a wide range of companies across the economic landscape (see Hawley & Williams, 2000, 2007). There is also a resurgence recently of activist investors who provide active oversight of managers and some measure of control over what they do. Even so, managers of most publicly traded companies continue to enjoy sufficient executive authority to have a great deal of discretion over how they allocate resources under their control.

2. Repurchasing shares appears to be a tradition largely in American and some European companies. Chinese (e.g., China Petroleum and Chemical Corp., SNP; PetroChina Co. Ltd., PTR), Indian (e.g., Infosys Ltd., INFY; Tata Motors Ltd., TTM), and Brazilian companies (e.g., Petrobras, PBR) do not seem to have a tradition of buying back their own shares.

3. See Browning (2015).

4. For fiscal year ended January 2015, this ratio was 0.46 percent. About 25.5 percent of total NEO compensation went to the CEO.

5. For fiscal year ended January 2015, this ratio was 7.78 percent. The CEO salary was 6.19 percent of his total compensation.

21. Diversification

1. Technically, two events are independent when p(B) = p(B|A) and p(A) = p(A|B). That is, events A and B are independent when the conditional probability of one given the other is unchanged from the probability of it happening on its own.

2. The full formulations for portfolio risk with two stocks, A and B, is $\sigma_P^2 = w_A^2 \sigma_A^2 + w_B^2 \sigma_B^2 + 2w_A w_B \sigma_A \sigma_B \rho_{AB}$, where σ_P^2 is portfolio variance, σ_A^2 and σ_B^2 are variances of the two stocks, and σ_A and σ_B are standard deviations of their returns; w_A and w_B are weights, such that $w_A + w_B = 1$; and ρ_{AB} is the correlation coefficient between the returns of A and B. By this definition, portfolio risk depends on the variances of the two stocks and the covariance between them. Covariance is of particular interest because as the number of stocks in the portfolio increases, the number of covariance terms increases much faster, and the equation (risk) becomes dominated by the covariance terms. By this definition, the more independent the stocks in the portfolio, the lower the risk. This definition, then, became the basis of the argument that one can reduce portfolio variance ("risk") simply by having uncorrelated stocks, irrespective of how they were priced in relation to underlying economic worth—and for that, one must assume that efficient markets were correctly pricing the stocks.

3. Note that, theoretically, the covariance needs to be between the expected future returns of the two stocks. In practice, however, data for future expected returns are rarely credible and, for the long future, not available at all. As such, past returns are typically used to compute variances and covariances.

4. Nassim Taleb made the same point at a recent seminar at the University of Massachusetts.

22. Another Way to Portfolio

1. See Evans and Archer (1968). The authors end the paper stating that, "The results also raise doubts concerning the economic justification of increasing portfolio sizes beyond 10 or so securities" (p. 767). For more recent evidence, see Santos (2015). See also Zhou (2014). This remains a controversial issue, however, as modern portfolio theorists argue for a much larger number of stocks in the portfolio for acceptable risk reduction. See, for example, Statman (1987).

25. The Buffett Portfolio

1. See Buffett and Cunningham (2008).

2. See Gerstner (2002).

Bibliography

Ablan, J., and P. Gupta. 2013. "Einhorn Sues Apple, Marks Biggest Investor Challenge in Years." *Reuters*, February 7. http://www.reuters.com/article/2013/02/08/us-apple-greenlight-idUSBRE9160MI20130208.

Anderson, K. B. 2007. *Consumer Fraud in the United States: The Second FTC Survey. Staff Report of the Bureaus of Economics and Consumer Protection.* Federal Trade Commission.

Aristotle. 2012. *On Sophistical Refutations*, trans. W.A. Pickard. Adelaide, Australia: University of Adelaide (ebooks@adelaide). https://ebooks.adelaide.edu.au/a/aristotle/sophistical/.

Baars, B. 1997. *In the Theater of Consciousness: The Workspace of the Mind.* New York: Oxford University Press.

Bacon, F. 1863. [1620]. *The New Organon or True Directions Concerning the Interpretation of Nature*, trans. J. Spedding, R. L. Ellis, and D. D. Heath. London: Longmans.

Banerjee, A. V. 1992. "A Simple Model of Herd Behavior." *The Quarterly Journal of Economics* 107: 797–817.

Barber, B. M., and T. Odean. 2000. "Trading Is Hazardous to Your Wealth: The Common Stock Investment Performance of Individual Investors." *The Journal of Finance* 55:773–806.

Barnes, B. 1982. *TS Kuhn and Social Science.* New York: Columbia University Press.

Bayes, M., and M. Price. 1763. "An Essay Towards Solving a Problem in the Doctrine of Chances. By the late Rev. Mr. Bayes, F. R. S. communicated by Mr. Price, in a letter to John Canton, A. M. F. R. S." *Philosophical Transactions* 53: 370–418.

Bendersky, J. W. 2007. "'Panic'": The Impact of Le Bon's Crowd Psychology on US Military Thought." *Journal of the History of the Behavioral Sciences* 43: 257–283.

Berle, A., and Means, G. 1932. *The modern corporate and private property.* New York: Macmillan.

Bernays, E. L. 1928. *Propaganda.* New York: Liveright.

Bikhchandani, S., D. Hirshleifer, and I. Welch. 1992. "A Theory of Fads, Fashion, Custom, and Cultural Change as Informational Cascades." *Journal of Political Economy* 100: 992–1026.

Black, F. 1986. "Noise." *Journal of Finance* 41: 529–543.

Bokanowski, T., L. G. Fiorini, and S. Lewkowicz, eds. 2009. *On Freud's "Mourning and Melancholia."* London: Karnac.

Bondt, W. F., and R. Thaler. 1985. "Does the Stock Market Overreact?" *The Journal of Finance* 40: 793–805.

Branch, B. 2008. "Institutional Economics and Behavioral Finance." Working paper. Isenberg School of Management, University of Massachusetts Amherst.

Browning, E. S. 2015. "Is the Surge in Stock Buybacks Good or Evil?" *The Wall Street Journal*, November 22. http://www.wsj.com/articles/is-the-surge-in-stock-buybacks-good-or-evil-1448188684.

Buffett, W. E. 1984. "The Superinvestors of Graham-and-Doddsville." *Hermes: The Columbia Business School Magazine* 17: 4–15.

Buffett, W. E., and L. A. Cunningham. 2008. *The Essays of Warren Buffett: Lessons for Corporate America.* New York: Cunningham.

Chancellor, E. 1999. *Devil Take the Hindmost: A History of Financial Speculation.* New York: Farrar, Straus, Giroux.

Consumer Fraud Research Group. 2006. *Investor Fraud Study Final Report.* Washington, DC: NASD Investor Education Foundation.

Coval, J., D. Hirshleifer, and S. H. Teoh. 2005. "Self-Deception and Deception in Capital Markets." In C. Gerschlager, ed., *Deception in Markets: An Economic Analysis*, 113–130. Basingstoke, UK: Palgrave Macmillan.

Croskerry, P. 2003. "The Importance of Cognitive Errors in Diagnosis and Strategies to Minimize Them." *Academic Medicine* 78:775.

Davies, P. J. 2008. "Sigma collapse ends shadow bank project." FT October 2. http://www.ft.com/intl/cms/s/0/8c80ff6e-901a-11dd-9890-0000779fd18c.html#axzz40BQTPSCM. 4. See Robinson (2008).

Dewing, A. S. 1953. *The Financial Policy of Corporations*, 5th ed. New York: Ronald.

Evans, J. L., and S. H. Archer. 1968. Diversification and the reduction of dispersion: an empirical analysis. *The Journal of Finance* 23(5): 761–767.

Fama, E. F., and K. R. French. 2004. "The Capital Asset Pricing Model: Theory and Evidence." *Journal of Economic Perspectives* 18, 25–46.

Farnsworth, W. 2010. *Farnsworth's Classical English Rhetoric.* Boston: David R. Godine.

Federal Trade Commission. 2009. *A Staff Report on the Federal Trade Commission's Fraud Forum.* Washington, DC: Federal Trade Commission.

Fisher, P. A. 1958. *Common Stocks and Uncommon Profits.* New York: Harper.

Freud, S. 1930. *Civilization and Its Discontents.* London: Hogarth.

Friedman, M. 1962. *Capitalism and Freedom.* Chicago: University of Chicago Press.

Galbraith, J. K. 1994. *A Short History of Financial Euphoria.* New York: Whittle/Viking.

Gerstner, L. V. 2002. *Who Says Elephants Can't Dance? Inside IBM's Historic Turnaround.* New York: Harper Business.

Graeber, D. 2001. *Toward an Anthropological Theory of Value: The False Coin of Our Own Dreams.* Basingstoke, UK: Palgrave Macmillan.

Graham, B. 1949. *The Intelligent Investor: A Book of Practical Counsel.* New York: Harper.

Graham, B., and D. L. Dodd. 1934. *Security Analysis.* San Francisco: Whittlesey House.

Guthrie, W. K. C. 1971. *A History of Greek Philosophy.* Vol. 3: *The Fifth-Century Enlightenment—Part 1: The Sophists.* Cambridge, UK: Cambridge University Press.

Hastie, R. 1993. *Inside the Juror: The Psychology of Juror Decision Making.* Cambridge, UK: Cambridge University Press.

Hawley, J. P., and A. T. Williams. (2000). *The rise of fiduciary capitalism: How institutional investors can make corporate America more democratic.* Philadelphia: University of Pennsylvania Press.

——. 2007. Universal owners: Challenges and opportunities. *Corporate Governance: An International Review* 15: 415–420.

Hayek, F. A. 1975. "The Pretence of Knowledge." *The Swedish Journal of Economic* 77: 433–442.

Hecht, J. M., (2003). *Doubt: A History: The Great Doubters and Their Legacy of Innovation, from Socrates and Jesus to Thomas Jefferson and Emily Dickinson.* San Francisco: HarperSanFrancisco.

Hirshleifer, D., and S. H. Teoh. 2003. "Herd Behaviour and Cascading in Capital Markets: A Review and Synthesis." *European Financial Management* 9: 25–66.

Ho, K. 2009. *Liquidated: An Ethnography of Wall Street.* Durham, NC: Duke University Press.

Hofstadter, D. R. 1995. *Fluid Concepts and Creative Analogies: Computer Models of the Fundamental Mechanisms of Thought.* New York: Basic.

James, W. 1890. *The Principles of Psychology.* New York: Henry Holt.

Jeffrey, R. C. 2004. *Subjective Probability: The Real Thing.* Cambridge, UK: Cambridge University Press.

Kent, S. 2015. "OPEC's Faith in Oil Demand Rise Rests on Shaky Ground." *The Wall Street Journal,* December 3. http://www.wsj.com/articles/opecs-faith-in-oil-demand-rise-rests-on-shaky-ground-1449120603.

Knight, F. H. 1921. *Risk, Uncertainty and Profit.* Boston: Houghton Mifflin.

Kuhn, T. S. 1962. *The Structure of Scientific Revolutions.* Chicago: University of Chicago Press.

Le Bon, G. 1897. *The Crowd: A Study of the Popular Mind.* New York: Macmillan.

Lee, F. 2009. *A History of Heterodox Economics: Challenging the mainstream in the twentieth century.* New York: Routledge.

Lefèvre, E. 1923. *Reminiscences of a Stock Operator.* New York: Doran.

Lewis, M. 2011. *The Big Short: Inside the Doomsday Machine.* New York: Norton.

Lintner, J. 1965a. "The Valuation of Risk Assets and the Selection of Risky Investments in Stock Portfolios and Capital Budgets". *The Review of Economics and Statistics* 47: 13–37.

——. 1965b. "Security Prices, Risk, and Maximal Gains from Diversification." *The Journal of Finance* 20: 587–615.

Loewenstein, G. 1996. "Out of Control: Visceral Influences on Behavior." *Organizational Behavior and Human Decision Processes* 65: 272–292.

Lowenstein, L. 1994. "Efficient Market Theory: Let the Punishment Fit the Crime." *Washington and Lee Law Review* 51: 925.

Mackay, C. 1841. *Memoirs of Extraordinary Popular Delusions and the Madness of Crowds.* New York: Harmony.

MacKenzie, D. 2006. *An Engine, Not a Camera: How Financial Models Shape Markets.* Cambridge, MA: MIT Press.

Malkiel, B. G. 2012. *A Random Walk down Wall Street: The Time-Tested Strategy for Successful Investing.* New York: Norton.

Mandelbrot, B. B., and R. L. Hudson. 2004. *The (Mis)Behavior of Markets: A Fractal View of Risk, Ruin, and Reward.* New York: Basic Books.

Markowitz, H. M. 1952. "Portfolio Selection." *The Journal of Finance* 7: 77–91.

——. 1999. "The Early History of Portfolio Theory: 1600–1960." *Financial Analysts Journal* 55: 5–16.

McGrayne, S. B. 2011. *The Theory That Would Not Die: How Bayes' Rule Cracked the Enigma Code, Hunted Down Russian Submarines, and Emerged Triumphant from Two Centuries of Controversy.* New Haven, CT: Yale University Press.

Meijers, A., ed. 2001. *Explaining Beliefs: Lynne Rudder Baker and Her Critics.* Stanford: CSLI.

Minsky, H. P. 1986. *Stabilizing an Unstable Economy.* New Haven, CT: Yale University Press.

Neate, R. 2009. "$400bn SIV market sold off in two years." The Telegraph, July 7. http://www.telegraph.co.uk/finance/newsbysector/banksandfinance/5769361/400bn-SIV-market-sold-off-in-two-years.html.

Nickerson, R. S. 1998. "Confirmation Bias: A Ubiquitous Phenomenon in Many Guises." *Review of General Psychology* 2: 175–220.

Nofsinger, J. R. 2005. "Social Mood and Financial Economics." *The Journal of Behavioral Finance* 6: 144–160.

Norris, F. 2008. "United Panic." *The New York Times*, October 24. http://economix.blogs.nytimes.com/2008/10/24/united-panic/.

Park, J. H., P. Konana, B. Gu, A. Kumar, and R. Raghunathan. 2010. *Confirmation Bias, Overconfidence, and Investment Performance: Evidence from Stock Message Boards.* McCombs Research Paper Series No. IROM-07-10.

Pfleiderer, P. 2014. "Chameleons: The Misuse of Theoretical Models in Finance and Economics." *Revista de Economía Institucional* 16: 23–60.

Popper, K. R. 1963. *Conjectures and Refutations: The Growth of Scientific Knowledge.* London: Routledge.

Price, J., and E. Kelly. 2004. "Warren Buffett: Investment Genius or Statistical Anomaly?" In *Intelligent finance: A convergence of mathematical finance with technical and fundamental analysis. Proceedings of the first international workshop on intelligent finance, University of Ballarat, Australia*, ed. H. Pan, D. Sornette, and K. Kortanek. http://svc160.wic022v.server-web.com/articles/news/conference/iwif.pdf.

Rapoport, M. 2015. "Lease-Accounting Overhaul Gets Green Light, Could Swell Balance Sheets by $2 Trillion." *The Wall Street Journal*, November 11. http://www.wsj.com/articles/fasb-votes-to-proceed-with-lease-accounting-overhaul-1447278233.

Robinson, G. 2008. "Sigma Collapse Marks End of SIV Era." *FT Alphaville*, October 2. http://ftalphaville.ft.com/blog/2008/10/02/16576/sigma-collapse-marks-end-of-siv-era/.

Russolillo, S. 2013. "Carl Icahn's Letter to Apple CEO Tim Cook." *The Wall Street Journal*, October 24. http://blogs.wsj.com/moneybeat/2013/10/24/carl-icahns-letter-to-apple-ceo-tim-cook/.

Santos, A. A. 2015. "Beating the Market with Small Portfolios: Evidence from Brazil." *EconomiA* 16: 22–31.

Savage, L. J. 1954. *The Foundations of Statistics.* New York: Wiley.

Savage, S. L. 2009. *The Flaw of Averages: Why We Underestimate Risk in the Face of Uncertainty.* New York: Wiley.

Schuster, D. H. 1964. "A New Ambiguous Figure: A Three-Stick Clevis." *The American Journal of Psychology* 77: 673.

Sharma, A., B. Branch, C. Chawla, and L. Qiu. 2013. "Explaining Market-to-Book: The Relative Impact of Firm Performance, Growth, and Risk." *Business Quest.* http://www.westga.edu/~bquest/2013/research2013.htm.

Sharpe, W. F. 1963. "A Simplified Model for Portfolio Analysis." *Management Science* 9: 277–293.

——. 1964. "Capital Asset Prices: A Theory of Market Equilibrium under Conditions of Risk." *The Journal of Finance* 19: 425–442.

Shiller, R. J. 1981. "Do Stock Prices Move Too Much to be Justified by Subsequent Changes in Dividends?" *The American Economic Review* 71: 421–436.

Shleifer, A. 2000. *Inefficient Markets: An Introduction to Behavioral Finance.* Oxford, UK: Oxford University Press.

Silver, N. 2013. "Nate Silver Picks the Super Bowl!" *The New York Times Magazine*, January 30. http://www.nytimes.com/2013/02/03/magazine/nate-silver-super-bowl.html.

Smith, Adam. *An Inquiry Into the Nature And Causes of the Wealth of Nations.* London: J. Maynard [etc.], 1811.

Smith, C. W. 1990. *Auctions: The Social Construction of Value.* Berkeley: University of California Press.

——. 2001. *Success and Survival on Wall Street: Understanding the Mind of the Market.* Lanham, MD: Rowman & Littlefield.

Smith, E. L. 1924. *Common Stocks as Long Term Investments.* New York: Macmillan.

Sornette, D. 2014. "Physics and Financial Economics (1776–2014): Puzzles, Ising and Agent-Based Models." *Reports on Progress in Physics* 77, 062001.

Soros, G. 1987. *The Alchemy of Finance: Reading the Mind of the Market.* New York: Simon & Schuster.

Statman, M. 1987. "How Many Stocks Make a Diversified Portfolio?" *Journal of Financial and Quantitative Analysis* 22: 353–363.

Taleb, N. 2007. *The Black Swan: The Impact of the Highly Improbable.* New York: Random House.

Treynor, J. L., & F. Black. 1973. "How to Use Security Analysis to Improve Portfolio Selection." *Journal of Business* 46: 66–86.

Uspensky, J. V. 1937. *Introduction to Mathematical Probability.* New York: McGraw-Hill.

Valukas, A. R. 2010. Lehman Brothers Holdings Inc. Chapter 11 proceedings examiner's report. US Bankruptcy Court Southern District of New York, Jenner and Block LLP.

Van der Zwan, N. 2014. "Making Sense of Financialization." *Socio-Economic Review* 12: 99–129.

Verdery, K. 1999. *The Political Lives of Dead Bodies: Reburial and Postsocialist Change.* New York: Columbia University Press.

Wilczek, F. 2015. *A Beautiful Question: Finding Nature's Deep Design.* New York: Penguin.

Williams, J. B. 1938. *The Theory of Investment Value.* Cambridge, MA: Harvard University Press.

Zhou, Y. 2014. "Number of Stocks in Portfolio and Risk Reduction." Master's thesis, University of California, Los Angeles.

Zirojevic, O. 2000. "Kosovo in the Collective Memory." In *The Road to War in Serbia: Trauma and Catharsis*, ed. N. Popov, 189–211. Budapest, Hungary: Central European University Press.

Index